EFFECTIVE PRESENTATION

Personal Communicativeness

UNIT I

W. A. Mambert

Executive Director

National Communication and Education Association

D1597941

Wiley Professional Development Programs

Advisory Editor

Steven C. Wheelwright

Harvard Business School

John Wiley & Sons Inc.

New York • London • Sydney • Toronto

Library of Congress Catalogue Card Number: 75-39750

ISBN 0-471-01627-6

Printed in the United States of America

10 9 8 7 6 5 4 3 2 1

Introduction

1 WHO CAN USE THIS SELF-TEACHING GUIDE

There are so many people in today's world who must make effective presentations that it probably would be easier to compile a list of those who don't need to. Begin with students who are in the process of learning their specialties and may, for some reason, not be able to or want to take a formal class. Include persons in the business and professional world who make presentations on a variety of subjects to different types of audiences. Salesmen, engineers, scientists, researchers, teachers, managers, supervisors are but a few of the many possible categories of people who will find very specific use for this program. And, of course, for anyone just starting in his profession or wanting to move ahead, effective presentation is a must.

2 THE LEARNING OBJECTIVE OF THIS PROGRAM

The objective of this program is to provide its user with a basic awareness of the steps necessary for making an effective oral presentation. After completing this course of study, the learner should have the following attitudes and skills:

- *An increased awareness of and perspective on the nature of a presentation as an act of human communication—which is the best foundation for developing effective techniques and using specific skills.*
- *A knowledge of the specific principles and techniques which must inhere in any oral presentation if it is to be effective.*
- *An increased capability to use and apply the principles and techniques learned.*
- *The capability to measure one's own degree of professionalism and effectiveness.*
- *A sound foundation for continued building of personal presentation and other communicative skills.*

3 HOW THIS PROGRAM IS ORGANIZED AND HOW IT SHOULD BE USED

Many books are merely read once and then stored on a shelf for occasional reference or simply to gather dust. Most books, too, are essentially one-way conversations from author to reader; that is, the reader has little or no opportunity to converse with the author. Not so with this program on both of these counts.

First, this program is designed to live and grow with you as you use it, in a very real and personalized way. If you use it as it is intended to be used, you will rightly be able to consider yourself a "coauthor" of the final product that will result. For the course will be something quite different after you have used it as a learning tool than it was when you first opened it. You will see why and how this is possible as you progress through its learning segments and use the learning devices incorporated into it.

Second, and also the main reason that it will "live" for and with you, this course is not intended as a one-way, author-to-reader transmission of information. It is very specially designed as a two-way dialogue between the author and you, its reader and user, much in the same way that the teaching/learning process in an actual classroom is a dialogue between teacher and student. During this two-way teaching/learning process, certain material of necessity will be transmitted to you. But we cannot stress too strongly what should be the other half of this process. You also will be asked to contribute to the dialogue, to respond to what you read and experience, to provide the necessary feedback to make it a two-way process. Nor is this merely a suggestion. It is an injunction to you, if you want to get the most possible benefit from this program.

Question: State three ways in which you think a reader might be able to converse with an author.

1. _____

2. _____

3. _____

Answer: You see, it is quite possible for a reader to have a dialogue with an author, and we want to get you into the habit of conversing with us in this manner as early as possible. And, of course, invariably answer you back. For example:

Three ways in which a reader and author might converse are:
- The author can ask questions.
- The reader can answer them.
- The author can respond with an answer for the reader to check his against.

4 INCREMENTAL LEARNING

It is well established that the learning and remembering processes are greatly enhanced when information is presented and absorbed by its recipient in relatively small segments, interspersed with periods of rest, thinking, or other activity. This is one of the reasons that live classes are spread over periods of weeks or months. It is therefore important that you treat and use this program in a similar way. Think of it as a course you are taking and individual class sessions you are attending.

Plan now to space your "attendance" in these one-person classes over a period of time that is comfortable for you. Do not try to take the whole course in a single reading session, but don't needlessly protract the total time either. One of the advantages of this course is that it is a highly individualized form of teaching/learning, and that each user will be able to progress at his or her own speed without competing with other members of a class or group.

5 THE LEARNING UNITS AND SEGMENTS

As we've just stressed, your use of this program should be a two-way conversation. True, there are certain limitations to such conversation imposed by the printed page, but there also are many more possibilities for such dialogue than most authors and readers use. We believe that we've taken maximum advantage of these possibilities, and that you will find many of them exciting and stimulating.

When we talk about idea structure later on, you will see the importance of "parallel structure" as an idea presentation device. We have used this device in the construction and organization of this program and the subdivisions of its subject matter, to give some consistent pattern and regularity to the material you encounter. It is easier to grasp ideas presented in regular patterns.

There are thirty-one Learning Segments, representing about the same amount of study and practice you would get in a semester-length college course. These segments are contained in ten major Learning Units, which we'll tell you more about in Segment 1, which gives an overview of the course. Each Learning Segment is constructed in the following identical pattern:

- SEGMENT TITLE

- THE PREMISE: *A brief statement of the underlying reason for this segment.*

- SEGMENT OBJECTIVE: *A good instructor (which we hope we are) will tell his student at the very beginning of each Learning Segment exactly where he hopes to lead him or her in the learning process, what he or she should have, possess, or be able to do at the end of the segment. Therefore, each segment begins with a statement of its learning objective.*

- TEXT: *We obviously cannot escape telling you certain things—our side of the teaching/learning dialogue. Thus, each segment has textual portions which you should read and think about carefully.*

- YOUR PARTICIPATION AND RESPONSE: *A pen or pencil is an absolute necessity in the use of this program. Each segment provides numerous and varied opportunities for your interaction. As is done in a classroom, sometimes we'll ask you to summarize or paraphrase what you are learning as you go. Sometimes we'll ask you provocative questions before we present material. Other times, we'll ask you summary-type questions. We'll also frequently ask you to test yourself or do an exercise. You'll even get a chance to give a presentation and draw a chalkboard illustration which we'll check for you to see how well you've done. In short, we're seeking your maximum participation and response, because we know how important what we are trying to convey to you is in your process of self-actualizing.*

- SUMMARY EXERCISE: *These will vary in format, but basically this is a kind of wrap-up activity similar to an exercise a classroom teacher might give on the assumption that anyone who has covered the material ought to be able to put what he has learned together and do it.*

- SCORABLE TEST: *This is the self-measurement step for each segment. It is an objective-type test with each question having a % value which will give you a good idea of how well you're progressing through the course.*

6 A FEW SUGGESTIONS

1. Since regularity reinforces learning, may we suggest that you set yourself a regular schedule and study in the same place each time.

2. Plan on spending about an hour per segment with some kind of break or diversion between sessions.

3. You can, of course, learn at your own speed, but a segment a day would be an ideal arrangement, giving you a little "settling time" between each, and yet allowing you to complete the whole course in about a month.

4. Do each segment completely before progressing to the next. Don't read ahead, since the course is designed for you to progress step by step.

5. The exercises and dialogues are designed as an integral part of this program. Although at times you may feel that you can skip some and simply go on reading, we strongly suggest that you do each in its turn to the best of your ability.

So, without further ado, you're ready to begin Segment 1. Good luck!

LEARNING 1 SEGMENT

Mastering The Thought Pattern Of This Course

PREMISE: That logical structure and pattern are major keys to the transfer of ideas from the mind of one person to the mind of another. Your knowing this will be important to both you and your audience when you plan and make your oral presentations. That is, when an idea is isolated and grasped in its entirety, as a whole idea, and its main parts or subdivisions are known in advance, its transfer is greatly facilitated. This course is a presentation in its own right. Therefore, the soundest approach in this, the first Learning Segment, is to provide a mental grasp of the whole thought sequence pattern of the course.

SEGMENT OBJECTIVE: That you develop the necessary grasp of the big picture of this course and the main pattern of subdivision of the ideas within that big picture.

Question A: Before reading any further, list below, in logical sequence, what you think are the necessary steps and ingredients for making an effective oral presentation. In other words, on the basis of your own thinking and knowledge, list how you would outline this course if you were preparing it.

1. _____   6. _____

2. _____   7. _____

3. _____   8. _____

4. _____   9. _____

5. _____   10. _____

Answer to Question A: This, of course, is our devious way of giving you the thought pattern of this course and making you do a little thinking about it. The thought pattern is quite simple. There are certain things that anyone who wants to make a really effective presentation ought to know or do. Call these the steps in making an effective presentation, if you like. For convenience, within the context of this course, we'll also call these steps Learning Units. Each step, or Learning Unit, represents a composite of specific things that you ought to know or be able to do in order to make an effective presentation. These specifics we call Learning Segments. So, below is the entire outline of the Learning Units and the Learning Segments that logically fall within them, thus giving you the outline of the whole course.

5

Unit One: Personal Communicativeness

This is the proper beginning point for anyone who wants to take a really purposeful and strategic approach to his or her communicating efforts. There must be a good, solid, realistic look at self—an evaluation of the resources at hand, so to speak. Besides this segment, the three segments in this unit are:

Segment 2: Acquiring a Communicator's Perspective
Segment 3: Acquiring the Qualities of Personal Communicativeness
Segment 4: Understanding Communication and Audiences in General

Unit Two: Structure and Thesis

A knowledge of the principles of logic and reasoning, as well as the development of a rationale, are absolute essentials. The three segments in this unit are:

Segment 5: Understanding the Need for Idea Structure
Segment 6: Understanding the Genesis of Structure
Segment 7: Understanding Thesis

Unit Three: The Kinds of Structure

When it comes to putting idea presentations together, most people are stuck with a very sparse knowledge of one or two kinds of structure. Your versatility and flexibility in handling and transferring ideas will be a direct product of your knowing the kinds of idea structure available to you. The four segments in this unit are:

Segment 8: Understanding the Deductive and Inductive Processes
Segment 9: Understanding Causal Structure
Segment 10: Understanding the Order of State, Condition, Quality, and Degree
Segment 11: Understanding Two-Sided and Other Structure Combinations

Unit Four: The Functional Approach

Here again, the average person is sorely lacking in his understanding of functional, objective-oriented approaches to practical communication. Without a grasp of the basic principles of functional communicating, it will be very difficult for you to make a presentation that actually accomplishes something measurable. There is only one segment in this unit. It is:

Segment 12: Understanding the Functional Approach and Formulating a Presentation Objective

Unit Five: Idea Support and Reinforcement

Here again, the restrictions on the novice idea presenter stem from a lack of sufficient knowledge of the tools available to him, as well as from a lack of capability to distinguish between ideas and their parts, from a lack of knowledge of the techniques of evidence and persuasion, and a lack of knowledge of how to handle detail. The four segments in this unit are:

Segment 13: Understanding Idea Support
Segment 14: Understanding Physical/Sensory Communication
Segment 15: Understanding Psychological and Emotional Reinforcement
Segment 16: Analyzing the Specific Audience/Situation

Unit Six: Outlining and Data Gathering

You can't build a house without a framework, and you can't make a good presentation without an outline. Consequently, once you have a presentation framework, you must know the best kinds of material to build into that framework and the best way to do that building. As with any skilled craft, there are also some mechanical shortcuts. The two segments in this unit are:

Segment 17: Making a Workable Outline
Segment 18: Gathering Data and Taking Notes

Unit Seven: Idea Integrity

Any good presentation exhibits unity and homogeneity, which is to say it exhibits idea integrity. There are certain very specific devices and techniques for imparting this important quality. The three segments in this unit are:

Segment 19: Preparing an Effective Introduction
Segment 20: Giving the Presentation Internal Cohesiveness
Segment 21: Preparing an Effective Conclusion

Unit Eight: Visual and Other Aids

Again, amateurs and novices often have an inverted view of the function of aids, graphics, and similar material and hence don't use them as effectively as they could use them. The two segments in this unit are:

Segment 22: Understanding Aids
Segment 23: Using Do-It-Yourself Visual Aids

Unit Nine: Preparing to Face the Audience

This is your moment of truth, and it ought to be planned strategically, just like anything else in a purposeful approach to idea handling and communication. The five segments in this unit are:

Segment 24: Preparing Notes for Delivery
Segment 25: Rehearsing the Presentation
Segment 26: Understanding Stage Fright
Segment 27: Understanding Self-Motivation
Segment 28: Improving Voice and Speech

Unit Ten: At the Podium

When you finally do get to a podium, platform, or rostrum from which to deliver your presentation to a live audience, there are things that you ought to know if you are to make your interchange with that audience as effective as possible. The three segments in this unit are:

Segment 29: Developing Correct Podium Behavior
Segment 30: Getting and Maintaining Audience Attention
Segment 31: Analyzing Audience Feedback

NOTE . . .
If your answers to Question A approximated the Learning Unit titles, we'd be pretty safe in saying that you're off to a running start. If not, don't worry. That's what we're here for, and the pieces will fall into place for you as you progress.

1 THE THESIS OF THIS COURSE

There is a thread that runs through all the segments. This thread is our main thesis:

To be effective, any idea presentation must be a series of deliberate and strategically calculated acts and must contain or embody certain specific elements.

That is, if you take the trouble to examine the anatomy of any successful idea presentation, and you know what you're looking for, your analysis will reveal that certain steps and elements were present. Conversely, examination of the ineffective presentation will reveal that certain things were missing. It's that simple.

Answer to Question B: As stated, it is: **To be effective, any idea presentation must be a series of deliberate and strategically calculated acts and must contain or embody certain specific elements.**

2 MANY WAYS OF STATING AND DESCRIBING

There are of course many ways of stating and describing the elements of effective presentation. And, you can break them down and categorize them in different ways. Doubtless, headings other than ours could be used to describe the ideas we'll be dealing with here. But what you call them isn't important. It's having and using them that is essential. Each represents in reality a composite quality. The whole process begins with your personal realization and possession of certain mental qualities and insights, a kind of communicator's perspective. That is, your own mental characteristics are the essential foundation on which all else is built and from which your working technique should evolve. If you begin here, *the process of developing a good presentation approach and technique will evolve very naturally, will become an extension of you and what you are as a person.* And that process will evolve so smoothly and naturally and logically that, almost indistinguishably, you will one day or moment realize that we are talking about technique, hardly aware that a transition from talking about you has taken place.

Summary Exercise: Now let's manipulate the ideas we've just dealt with a little and do a bit of forecasting as well. Following is a list of twelve ideas, or steps, based on what you have just read. They may not be stated exactly as you read them, because it is important to the idea handler to be able to recognize similar ideas under different names, as well as to be able to restate those ideas.

- **Presentation result**
- **Deliver the presentation**
- **Compare the outcome with the objective**
- **Feedback for next presentation**
- **Outline the presentation**
- **Analyze the specific audience situation**
- **Select the right amount and kind of detail**

- Prepare delivery notes
- Compose the presentation
- Acquire a communicator's perspective
- Understand audiences in general
- Develop a presentation objective

As we'll also discuss in considerable detail later on, the talent of stating your ideas and thinking graphically is a very useful capability to the would-be idea presenter. The flowchart, or flow diagram, is often a very useful tool in doing this. As you'll see later on, there may even be times when you'll want to flowchart your own presentation. For the moment, let's use this approach as a device to help you measure your grasp and retention of the ideas covered in this segment. This exercise will also give you an opportunity to extrapolate the basic thinking a bit.

Below is a blank flowchart. The twelve ideas in the above list are not necessarily in any proper sequence. Your task: Place the ideas in proper sequence in the chart so that they represent a logical idea flow. For comparison, you'll find our answer after the scorable quiz. But don't look ahead until you've tested your own thinking.

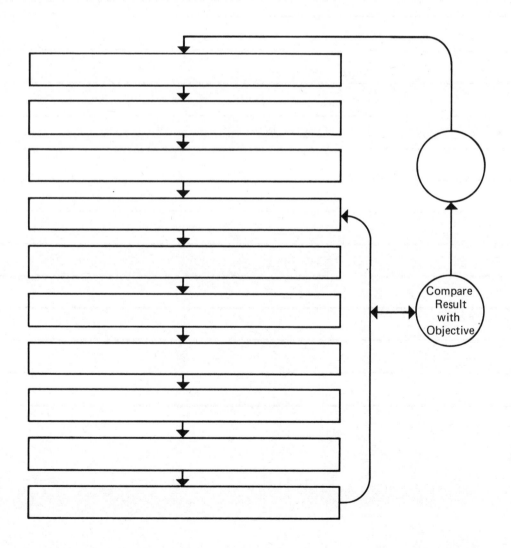

Scorable Quiz: List, in any sequence, the ten major Learning Units of this course.

1. _____
   _____

2. _____
   _____

3. _____
   _____

4. _____
   _____

5. _____
   _____

6. _____
   _____

7. _____
   _____

8. _____
   _____

9. _____
   _____

10. _____
    _____

Answers to Summary Exercise: Here is your flowchart filled in. As we said, we've purposely introduced some ideas that represent extended thinking based on what you've read: for example, the idea of comparing your presentation result with your presentation objective which is a very key concept in what hopefully you'll shortly be calling functional presentation.

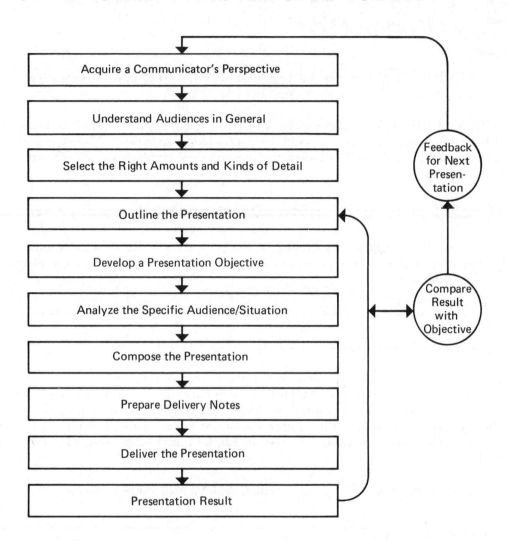

Answers to Scorable Quiz (Each correct answer = 10%): personal communicativeness, the basic concepts of structure and thesis, the kinds of structure, the functional approach, idea support and reinforcement, outlining and data gathering, idea integrity, visual and other aids, preparing to face an audience, at the podium.

Acquiring A Communicator's Perspective

LEARNING 2 SEGMENT

PREMISE: That a purposeful presenter of ideas must have a basic objectivity and a capability to shift point of view.

SEGMENT OBJECTIVE: That you personally engage in the most elemental and essential first step toward building an effective presentation approach. This step is the acquisition of the capability to observe the presentation situation and its elements realistically and objectively.

Question A: Let's start right off by looking at the presentation situation more analytically, objectively, and strategically. Every presentation situation has at least three major elements. List what you think they are:

1. _____   3. _____

2. _____

Question B: It often helps to view verbal descriptions graphically. So, let's try to diagram what has just been described; that is, the capability to step back and to focus one's point of view on various elements of the presentation situation. Below is a roughed out diagram and a list of terms for labeling its various elements. Fill in each numbered circle, arrow, and box to complete the diagram as a graphic representation. The answer can be found in the following text, but don't look ahead.

THE ELEMENT DESCRIPTIONS

THE DIAGRAM AND YOUR ANSWER

Step back to view whole

Self

Focus on audience

Contents

Focus on self

Audience

Focus on contents

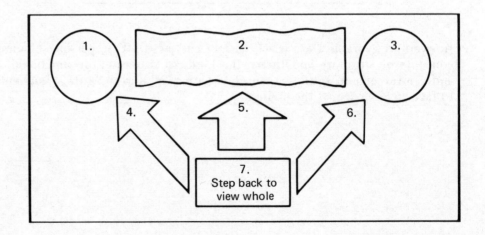

Question C: What would you say is the main difference between the kind of idea presenter we're going to be talking about in this course and the average untrained or nonprofessional person who makes a presentation?

_____

_____

_____

1 THE TRUE BEGINNING POINT

Somewhere in his career almost every successful idea presenter has arrived at a set of values, insights, and attitudes within his own mind and being that can best be described as a communicator's perspective. It is not likely that many call it by this name, if they articulate it at all. But if they are successful and effective, they have in fact arrived at a personal vantage point that the average layman or novice communicator does not have. They have acquired a working (not just a theoretical) capability to:

1. _Back off from the presentation situation sufficiently to see the whole situation and also to shift point of view from one aspect of that situation to another._
2. _Focus analytically on self as a major element in the communicative interchange._
3. _Focus on the other person (the audience member) in a similar analytical and strategic way._
4. _Focus on the many and varied aspects of the contents of the situation, with the strategic intent of manipulating, structuring, and controlling those contents in order to accomplish a specific objective._

Obviously, we can't talk about all of these things at once. In fact, this whole course will develop out of these shiftings of point of view.

Answer to Question A: There are many things that may happen in any idea presentation situation. But there are always at least three major elements: (1) you, (2) your audience, (3) the contents of the situation (which will ultimately include your presentation or message).

Answer to Question B: Easy, wasn't it? We'll be using this diagraming technique throughout this course as one of our devices for conversing with you.

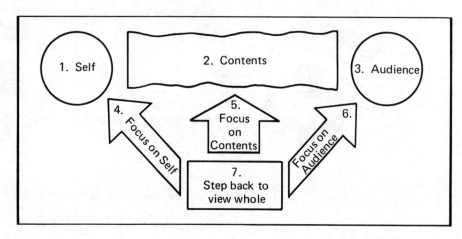

13

Answer to Question C: The main difference between the skilled and amateur idea presenter lies in the strategic (or, if you will, the problem-solving, objective, analytical) approach that the skilled presenter takes.

2 A MOMENTARY INTENSIFICATION

This is probably the best way to describe it: A presentation is merely a momentary intensification of a continuing, cumulative process that began long before the presenting period and will continue long after it. If you are to do the job right, you must view it this way. You yourself represent—intellectually, psychologically, and emotionally—the result of a cumulative process. For many years you have been building a self-image, prejudices, attitudinal patterns, preoccupations, and many other motives and drives, in addition to such fundamental needs as your cravings or drives for recognition, survival, romance, acquisition and similar basic human movie forces. In short, you are a personality of composite and complex social, emotional, egocentric, moral, and ethical patterns. Your audience similarly brings to the presentation situation many feelings, thoughts, and motive forces, which are directly parallel to similar needs and forces in you, who could, for example, evoke his fear or hostility by something as simple as knowing more about anything than he does. There are scores of such possibilities, ranging from simple jealousy to complex guilt. Can you know the entire psychological makeup of your audience? Of course not. But you can be aware of the possibilities that do exist when such complex entities as human beings are flung together for a few moments out of their individual developmental and behavioral living patterns. To expect them to make some kind of mysterious connection of mind, personality, and perhaps spirit just because information is flowing is literally asking for a miracle. At least one of the correspondents must have some insight into the real foundations of the human communication process. For example, what is the nature of the idea presentation act, what is the chain of events involved in an attempt to communicate an idea, how are the involved parties constructed emotionally, and so on.

With this in mind, let's expand on the illustration you completed a moment ago. The following diagram illustrates pretty well what we're talking about in this segment.

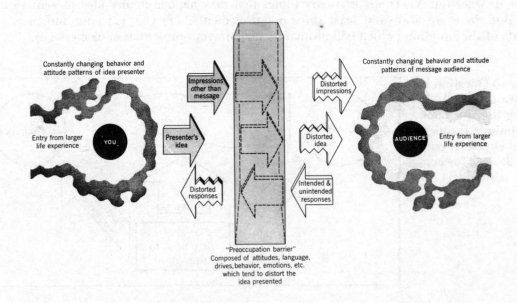

3 A CONTINUING, TWO-WAY PROCESS

One of the most important things to remain constantly aware of is that the act of making a presentation is not a one-way, or static process. Viewed more closely, it can be seen as a two-way, flowing interchange not only of intended ideas, but of unintended thoughts, emotions, and impressions. It is quite important to remember that it is continuous, that it is not limited to a specific time-frame, presentation or otherwise. Pertinent information, impressions, attitudes, prejudices, and emotions constantly flow between or among the correspondents before, during, and after the formally-stated presentation period. It is also important to remember that many of these effects are unintended. Your aim is to engage in as little unintended behavior and attitudinal action as possible. Further, it must be remembered that human beings are conditioned to conceal their true reactions. They rarely reveal themselves to people close to them, let alone to a stranger attempting to influence them. Only when they are assured that it is safe to do so will they hazard a revelation of what they really intend or want. For example, the audience member who raises his hand to ask a question might want to know the answer, or (and the chances of this are often greater) in asking a question he might really be saying, "I know something too," "I need recognition," "I think you are wrong," or many other things. Regardless of what such an inquirer means by his reaction or question, you must be aware of the possibilities and remain as psychologically empathic to him as possible if you wish to retain him as an attentive, interested participant.

At this point, let's just concentrate on what you ought to see at that first shifting of point of view in terms of the whole situation. Remember, too, we're no longer talking about the casual view that the nonprofessional or nonstrategic person normally takes, but rather the very purposeful, analytical observation a strategist would take. In this sense, what should you, as a would-be communicator, see as you take that initial step back? You might symbolically represent your audience member as a target that appears to have been pressed out of shape, representative of the fact that no person is a perfectly symmetrical being in terms of his thoughts, emotions, feelings, response patterns, and so on. In reality, we all represent patterns within patterns, and all these patterns overlap and interact.

In addition to the message that you're trying to get across and the great variety of impressions, unintended actions and reactions, emotions, and feelings there may be language barriers and differences in education and social background, entering into the situation out of both your and your audience's larger life experiences. For example, what if one person is a college graduate and the other uneducated? One an alien, the other a native? One a Northerner, the other a Southerner? One a customer, the other a seller? The possibilities are almost unlimited. Words themselves have different meaning for different people. Language must be known both intellectually and emotionally. What cannot a Frenchman convey with the absence of words—a simple shrug of the shoulders? One must understand much about the language itself. There are problems of locale, environment, and social conditioning. Even commonplace words and phrases mean different things to different people, depending on where or when they are used, who says them or hears them, and the manner, voice, or reputation of the speaker. For example, the word "conservative" might indicate approval, disapproval or soundness. "Liberal" can mean radical, foolhardy, or generous. Even words such as "big," "small," or "wise" can convey derision, respect, dislike, honor, or dishonor.

There are similar language barriers in the business-technological world. "Controller," "storage," "total system," "information retrieval," "program," "input," "processor," and hundreds of others have such problems connected with them. Add to these problems such factors as the ego defense mechanisms present in every human being, stereotyped ideas, pride in belonging to an organization, even hunger, thirst, and fatigue—or even the weather or time of day—and one suddenly becomes aware that true communication is indeed a miracle.

Notice, too, that you, the idea presenter, are represented by the same kind of pattern as is your audience. Your role as presenter doesn't alter your basic psychological makeup, your motivations, your emotions, conditioned behavior, and the like. And, of course, both ends of the situation are open, thus graphically representing the fact that your so-called presentation is indeed only a momentary intensification of life processes that began long before it and will continue long after it.

4 THE PREOCCUPATION BARRIER
Put all such influences and factors together, and they form a kind of screen or barrier of preoccupations that tends to distort and filter almost everything that passes between you and your audience. Many professional presenters actually call this effect the "preoccupation barrier."

Anyone who has objectively observed an audience is aware of this barrier: People seem to be listening when they are not, when in reality their minds are almost constantly preoccupied with a score of conscious and instinctive interests, needs, feelings, fears, anxieties, and memories. Their eyes may be looking at you, but are the minds behind them looking? By their very nature they do not want to look or listen. It is alien to their whole emotional structure. They unconsciously view each life situation with self at the center and all other factors, influences, and people composing an egocentric universe.

A momentary idea presentation cannot change human nature. You must gain and keep their attention by becoming in effect a planet in their existing universe if you want your ideas to have effect. Everything that you do and say must revolve in relation to the system's center.

This, of course, involves your going against your own nature and psychological needs to some degree. But it is what you must be able to do if you want to communicate in a purposeful way. Unless you can relate your ideas to what your audience already is feeling, thinking, wants, needs, hates, loves, and fears, you'll have a difficult time in getting them across. You may talk to an audience and they may "hear." But communication probably won't take place, not the kind of communication we're talking about in this course.

5 WHAT CAN YOU DO?
In all of this, there's no intent to discourage you with a picture of hopeless complexity. But we'd be seriously remiss if we didn't begin with the necessity of facing the realities of the human communicative interchange. It is a human process. As such, it is indeed complex, unpredictable, changing and plastic, and those who understand this basic nature make the best communicators. The simple fact is that today too many business people and technologists do often forget that they are engaged in this human process. Their attitude is essentially one of detachment from reality. They dispense information as a commodity and communicate into vacuums. They actually ignore the fact that they are dealing with people and that all communicating

must be done on the level of personal understanding, not on a mass basis. In short, they lose the human touch and with it their presentations.

What can you do about all this? Therein lies the tale of this course. But, specifically, for the moment, you're much ahead of the game simply by beginning with the kind of awareness of the nature of what's going on that we've spoken of here. Then, on the basis of this awareness, you can build some good technique that will help you to increase the number of times you succeed at making effective presentations. Nobody, of course, "wins 'em all," but it is possible to win more of them by making all your presentations deliberately planned situations in which you deliberately attempt to maintain a control over what's happening.

Summary Exercise: Answer each of the following questions briefly.

1. What should you see upon first stepping outside of the interchange between yourself and your audience?

   _____

   _____

2. What should be your basic aim in terms of your own behavior, attitudes, feelings, and thinking during a presentation?

   _____

   _____

3. What do we call that composite of influences in a presentation situation that tends to distort and filter the ideas and impressions flowing between you and your audience?

   _____

   _____

4. What was the objective of this segment?

   _____

   _____

(You'll find the answers after the Scorable Quiz. Don't look ahead, though.)

Scorable Quiz: Fill in the missing word or words.

1. The true beginning point in the preparation of any functional presentation is at the

   _____ .

2. A "communicator's perspective" requires that one have the capability to shift

   _____ .

3. Ultimately, at least a part of the contents of a situation will become your

   _____ .

4. A presentation is really only a momentary _____ of a larger life process.

5. We call that collection of attitudes, language barriers, preconceived ideas and unintentional impressions always present in a communication situation the _____

   barrier.

6. Any presentation always will be a _____ -way process.

7. Your aim is to engage in as little_____ behavior as possible.

8. There are always at least three major elements in a presentation situation: They are

   (a)_____ , (b) _____ , and (c)_____

   of the situation.

Answers to Summary Exercise:

1. The whole interchange, including yourself, the audience, and the conditions.
2. As much deliberate action and control as possible as opposed to happenstance.
3. The preoccupation barrier.
4. That you personally engage in the most elemental and essential first step toward building an effective presentation approach. This is the acquisition of the capability to observe the presentation situation and its elements realistically and objectively.

Answers to Scorable Quiz (Each correct answer = 10%): (1) end (2) point of view (3) presentation (4) intensification (5) preoccupation (6) two (7) unintended (8a) you (8b) your audience (8c) the contents.

Acquiring The Qualities
Of Personal Communicativeness

PREMISES: (1) That people have identifiable qualities of personal communicativeness beyond their capability to look and see what is happening at the total level. (2) That these qualities ideally ought to be "native" to the would-be idea presenter, but they can be acquired.

SEGMENT OBJECTIVES: (1) That you become more aware of yourself as a major element in any presentation. (2) That you know what the main qualities of personal communicativeness are. (3) That you begin now to acquire, build, or refine these qualities in yourself.

Question A: Picture yourself just having made a presentation before a live audience. The people are standing around talking about your presentation. You have the opportunity to overhear what they are saying. List below as many things as you can think of that you would like to hear them saying about you and/or your presentation.

1. _____
2. _____
3. _____
4. _____
5. _____

6. _____
7. _____
8. _____
9. _____
10. _____

1 THE FIRST FOCUS

There is a simple fact of life. Most people know it. Too many ignore it. The truly serious communicator cannot ignore it and get very far as a communicative person. It is this:

The only sound first step in any form of personal improvement or development is self-confrontation and self-examination.

We could trot out quotes from the great thinkers of past and present to substantiate this venerable maxim, but we won't. Suffice it to say that this is especially true in the communicative arts. For here indeed, what you are can speak so loudly that what you say or do cannot be heard or seen. Now, we do not have any intention of making this course a sensitivity and awareness session. But, remember, we are speaking of real-

19

istic, strategic communication. And any strategist who enters the fray without a realistic knowledge of his own resources must be classified at the very least as foolhardy. We repeat: you are a major element in any presentation you make, just as major as your audience or your message. Thus, you must subject yourself to the same sort of objective analysis and strategic control that you are seeking for them.

In short, your first shifting of point of view after stepping back to view your presentation situation must be a focus on yourself as an element in that situation.

Answers to Question A: It would, of course, be assuming a lot to expect your average audience to play the role of objective evaluator of your presentation. Most of your audiences will be reacting in a different, more subjective way. But the qualities that should be looked for would be along the lines of the following:

1. Objectivity
2. A capability to compartmentalize and concentrate
3. A functional frame of mind
4. A strategic frame of mind
5. Flexibility
6. Structured thinking
7. An ability to handle detail
8. Sensitivity and awareness
9. Wit and humor
10. Courage and motivation
11. Personal style
12. Practicality and realism

2 THERE ARE OBSERVABLE QUALITIES

Most people know that what we've just listed are generally desirable qualities. We've all looked at the successfully communicative person from time to time, perhaps admired him or her, perhaps asked, "How does he do it?" "What does he have that makes him communicative?" "Oh," you'll hear someone say, "he's just got it." "He has charisma." "He's got that certain something." And off we go, content that we've adequately analyzed the anatomy of personal communicativeness. This may do for the layman. But it won't suffice for the person who himself is seeking to be communicative. It won't do for the person who wants to deal with his own need to communicate as a problem to be solved. He must have something more specific to go on, something that can be observed and acquired. He wants to know if there actually are some things, some resources, that can be acquired or improved that will dispose him also toward greater personal communicativeness.

Our whole point here is that there are such qualities. That is, if you actually will take the trouble to dissect that certain something. There are, in fact, certain mental sets, qualities of mind, insights and outlooks, attitudes and characteristics, that do favorably dispose an individual toward use of actual communicative skills and techniques. If, by virtue of who you already are and where you're coming from, you already have some of these qualities, you're lucky. For you have a better beginning place from which to do such things as analyze audience/situations, develop presentation objectives, structure and outline your presentations, and deal effectively at the rational, sensory, and emotional levels.

If, on the other hand, you've personally developed in an environment and atmosphere that has not fostered these predispositions, you'll have a little harder time adapting to the skills and techniques. For another simple fact of life is:

The deeper into one's personality and character the roots of skill and technique go, the better and more effective the use of those skills and techniques will be.

Let's take a moment and illustrate this important premise in graphic form. If we were in a classroom, we would have been doing this while making the above commentary. We'll also be able to see how this premise ties into what we just listed in Segment 1 in terms of the outline of this course, as well as into the skills and techniques needed for effective presentation. Picture the whole process as a "tree" if you will. The roots are those predispositions we're talking about here. The branches and foliage are the skills we've listed as the major learning units and learning segments. We hope you don't find our tree analogy too elemental. We've used it often in the live classroom and have found that it really helps in getting an important premise across. Now, let's take a quick look at what we mean by some of these things. We'll try not to belabor the obvious.

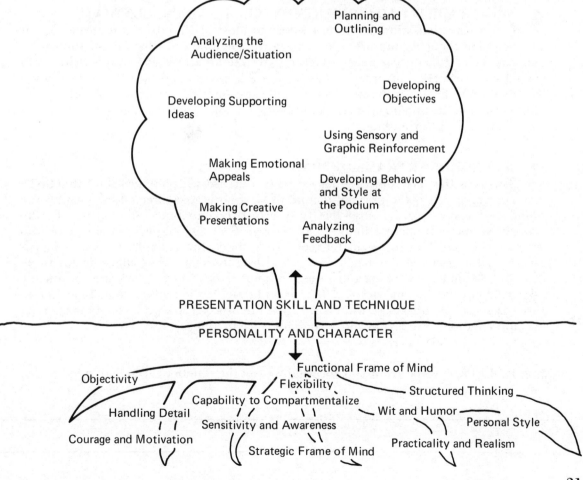

21

3 OBJECTIVITY

Much desired and sought by many, attained in any true sense by few, objectivity is undoubtedly your most important base as a strategic communicator. All human beings have a built-in tendency to interpret and react one-sidedly to ideas and happenings around them. The more you combat this instinct in yourself, the greater becomes your capability to reach other people. Another way of saying what really happens when you effectively communicate with a person is that you have shown him how what you have to say relates to how he thinks and feels. You'll have great difficulty in doing this if you cannot at least allow within yourself that something can be validly experienced in terms other than your own, in relationship to something or someone other than your own self.

Equally important, so long as you experience and interpret only in your own terms, it will be quite difficult for you to have an accurate and realistic picture of what's really going on in any interchange between yourself and another person. You will be like someone standing inside a house attempting to see and describe what's on the outside. You'll always be operating with only a partial view.

Third, so long as you remain subject to your own emotional reactions and preconceived ideas, they will constantly interfere with your strategy and skill. You will be like a person trying to fire a gun while trembling with fear or rage. How accurate can such an aim be?

4 THE CAPABILITY TO COMPARTMENTALIZE AND CONCENTRATE

Compartmentalization is a term familiar to most psychologists. It means to shut out undesired thoughts and often has a negative connotation. But we use it in a positive sense here. It is the capability to place a given set of affairs, ideas, or activities into mental compartments, in order to bring one's full powers and faculties to bear upon the situation at hand. In terms of our tree illustration, this is the basic mental set that predisposes one to isolating ideas, establishing workable objectives, and a "show must go on" attitude at the podium.

5 A FUNCTIONAL FRAME OF MIND

This is at the very root of what we hope you also will soon be calling functional communication. It is the pragmatic point of view. It is goal-directed thinking. We've found over many years of observing truly effective communicators that people who actually accomplish and get things done through their communication are those who are routinely function-oriented thinkers. They think, for example, in terms of goals rather than in terms of the machinations that lead to them. They almost instinctively seek to add things up, to measure the results of their efforts. They are continually asking themselves to what account they have turned certain amounts of time and effort. Such people obviously would be highly predisposed toward trying to make their idea presentations actually do and accomplish specific things.

Question B: List here some synonyms for what we call the functional frame of mind.

1. _____ 3. _____

2. _____ 4. _____

Answer to Question B: Some synonyms for functional frame of mind are: goal-directed thinking, the pragmatic view, objective–oriented thinking, result–oriented thinking.

6 A STRATEGIC FRAME OF MIND

We've already introduced this idea. Good strategists—people with naturally calculating minds, make the best communicators. These are people who instinctively operate from the "high ground," from positions of strength instead of weakness; who leave themselves "routes of strategic withdrawal"; who don't try to hold untenable positions; and so forth. They operate offensively instead of defensively. They consider alternatives and contingencies before instead of after they've occurred. They instinctively know that good strategy underlies effective use of tactics. There's no doubt that this kind of person arrives at a presentation situation much better equipped to plan and execute his attempt to communicate.

Question C: List here some synonyms for the idea of sensitivity and awareness.

1. _____ 3. _____

2. _____ 4. _____

7 SENSITIVITY AND AWARENESS

We could write another book about this one. The more aware and sensitive a person is to his environment, the more capable of communicating he becomes. The circumstances under which an idea and an audience may be found or put vary and usually have a profound effect upon any attempt to communicate that idea. Anything from the time of day, to the weather, the air people breathe, the chairs they sit in, the looks on your and their faces, their body movements, the color of the room, or the lighting, affects your idea presentation. Even empty space speaks a language to those who have ears to hear and eyes to see.

Under this heading we could list such qualities as empathy, subtlety, tact, finesse, caring, loving, appetite, curiosity, and maturity, to mention a few. The key is to become more aware of and sensitive to everything, to sharpen every perceptive sense. To look and see. To listen and hear.

Answers to Question C: empathy, tact, finesse, "tuned-in" and "turned on," caring, receptiveness, perceptiveness.

8 FLEXIBILITY

Perhaps an expansion of the ideas of sensitivity and awareness (you'll find that many of the things we're describing here do overlap) is another observable characteristic of the person who is consistently communicative. He is a multidimensional thinker. He is basically uninhibited; he doesn't let his hangups keep him from going over into other people's worlds. The simple fact is that inhibited people don't make very good communicators. They're not very creative. We're not suggesting that you must strip yourself naked before an audience or give up some cherished belief (although you may have to set it aside momentarily if you really want to reach someone). You must, however, be capable of genuinely releasing yourself from your own sense of orthodoxy as a given situation demands in order to communicate. The alternative may be to give up the hope of communicating. You may have to shout when you don't feel like it, use a swear word, not feel guilt or embarrassment, stand on your head, or feel the way a person you're talking to feels. The basic question always will be: Just how badly do you want to communicate with that person? Only you will ever be able to answer that question.

9 STRUCTURED THINKING
Tie this to the ideas of compartmentalization and strategy, if you like. But the capability to seek and find order and relationships in ideas, to distinguish between ideas and their parts, between main thoughts and subordinate thoughts, is the root of the capability to effectively isolate, divide, and deal with the ideas you want to handle and communicate.

10 ABILITY TO HANDLE DETAIL
When it comes time to handle the evidence and persuasion that support your presentation idea, this capability will represent an important "tool in your kit." We'll wind up calling it idea support (and look at it in a variety of ways). But make no mistake about it, having the big picture is rarely enough in professional, purposeful communicating. You must also have the skills that enable you to build into your presentation the right amounts, kinds, and variety of detail. And if you're already a person who handles detail well, you're halfway home, as they say.

11 WIT AND HUMOR
We find so many people taking themselves too seriously these days that this seems worth mentioning too. A good sense of humor is vital to the communicator who must work day by day with people, their thoughts, their feelings, their prejudices, and their attempts to cope with life. But more important, it is an innate wit that will often help to keep you sane, sensible, and realistic in a world so often out of touch with reality, so often crazily reeling, full of inequities, false issues, inconsistencies, and paradoxes. It will keep your morale and motivation up and your frustrations down. But, too, the keenness of a person's sense of humor is often an excellent measurement of his true insight into the human problem, which is what you're really dealing with when you "don the mantle" of the professional communicator.

12 PERSONAL STYLE
We're all just numbers in a big data bank these days, they say. In a score of ways, the system tells us that it's a sin to have a unique and stand-out personality. Bunk! People with truly unique personalities give the best presentations.

13 COURAGE AND MOTIVATION
You can have all the awareness, objectivity, purpose, and strategy that it is possible to have. Yet, without personal motivation and the courage to take a stand and carry through, these other things are relatively useless. They merely represent potentiality without force, energy, or movement. In fact, the word motivation means to have force and movement. The greater your motivation, the greater the force and movement toward your presentation objectives. The person who wants something so badly that he'll not take no for an answer—so thoroughly that he'll attack any obstacle in his way—is far ahead of the person who must be goaded into action and is afraid

to "lay his body on the line." No one, of course can give another person motivation and courage. Those qualities must come from within oneself.

14 PRACTICALITY

Rules take up where brains leave off, and vice versa. There is no particular virtue in orthodoxy. People bound by needless adherence to so-called rules and regulations are constantly being hindered in their attempts to communicate. Establish in your own mind the difference between such matters as policy, administrative law, regulations, sacred cows, bureaucracy, and the like. Learn the real difference between right and wrong; do not let artifical guilt imposed by someone else's moral codes needlessly inhibit you in trying to reach other people. Establish your own morality, take responsibility for your own actions and go! "Who unto himself is law, needs no law." There is one rule it is often wise to abide by, however, for society can make it quite uncomfortable for those who break it. This is the rule of "don't let society catch you messing around with its sacred cows."

Summary Exercise: You'll need a very common household item for this exercise; namely, a mirror—table size will do, but full-length is better. Remember, this course won't work for you if you don't follow it. We can picture you at this moment; reading along, perhaps comfortably situated—perhaps even at this point saying to yourself that this segment has been just another one of those self-improvement formulas. We hope not. Because we have a couple of decades of experiences that say what you've just read is important foundational material. Who wants to get up and look for a mirror, anyway? Please! Just take the whole book into the bathroom for a moment if you feel lazy.

You also may feel a bit awkward doing the following exercise, but do it anyway. It's the equivalent of what all professional communicators do, and the best we can do for you via the printed page. All professionals are quite accustomed to practicing before mirrors or viewing themselves on TV monitors. Now do the following:

1. Study yourself carefully in the mirror. First, this is what your audience is going to see when you stand before them to make a presentation.

2. Now, in the space provided below, and as honestly and objectively as you can, ask yourself if you personally possess the qualities we've just enumerated, which we've relisted as both a summary of the segment and a checklist for you. Place a checkmark in the yes or no column, to indicate whether or not you think you have them.

THE QUALITIES OF PERSONAL COMMUNICATIVENESS	YES	NO
1. Objectivity		
2. Capability to compartmentalize and concentrate		
3. A functional frame of mind		
4. A strategic frame of mind		
5. Sensitivity and awareness		
6. Flexibility		

7. Structured thinking		
8. Ability to handle detail		
9. Wit and humor		
10. Personal style		
11. Courage and motivation		
12. Practicality		

Scorable Quiz: Indicate whether each item is true (T) or false (F), or fill in the missing words.

1. The process of human communication is so complex that there really aren't any identifiable characteristics of personal communicativeness. ____

2. Some people seem to come naturally by their predispositions toward personal communicativeness. ____

3. Your first point of focus after stepping back to view the whole situation ought to be on the audience. ____

4. The deeper into one's character the roots of skill and technique go, the better and more effective those skills and techniques become. ____

5. Compartmentalization, the shutting out of undesired thoughts or feelings, is undesirable, because it makes a presentation less "real." ____

6. A manipulative type of person makes a very poor communicator. ____

7. Structured thinking makes for too rigid an approach for the kind of communicating we talk about in this course. ____

8. Presentations in business are no place for wit and humor. ____

9. The ability to handle detail is not necessary, but the capability to structure ideas is. ____

10. If, when you observe yourself in a mirror and conclude that you possess most of the qualities of personal communication, you probably need a _____.

Answers to Summary Exercise: If all of your answers are "yes," you've probably gotten hold of one of those "magic mirrors on the wall." Don't tell anyone you have it! Just one more simple thing. Recall the list that we asked you to make in Question A? Turn back to it for a moment and compare the checklist you've just made with the checklist you made there. Check to see:

1. How closely the two lists match.

2. How objective and analytical you were at the beginning of this segment as compared to now, after our discussion of the scientifically observable qualities we've enumerated.

3. And finally, we believe that you'll know what to do from here on about your own qualities of personal communicativeness.

Answers to Scorable Quiz: 1. F, 2. T, 3. F, 4. T, 5. F, 6. F, 7. F, 8. F, 9. F, 10. New mirror.

Understanding Communication And Audiences In General

PREMISE: That all human communication situations have certain aspects and dimensions in common, and that understanding these things is the basis for any meaningful analysis of any specific audience/situation—an oral presentation, for example.

SEGMENT OBJECTIVE: That you have a conscious awareness of the underlying "constants" in any specific interchange that you have with other persons, and that you take these into account as a general basis in any presentation situation.

Question A: Specific people and the specific circumstances under which you encounter them vary greatly. Yet, because you always will be dealing with human beings, there are several important things that will remain the same in every situation. Can you think of what some of these things are? List them below, and as you work with this segment, check your answers against our main headings in this segment.

1. _____   4. _____

2. _____   5. _____

3. _____   6. _____

1 DON'T OVER-ISOLATE

Many novice presenters tend to overisolate specific interchanges between themselves and other people. As a result, they frequently bungle their attempts to communicate in a number of ways, ranging from using the wrong words or language to treating people as if they were born yesterday, or otherwise emotionally or intellectually offending them. One way to avoid such pitfalls is to consciously remind yourself that every written or spoken interchange is part of something much larger than itself. As already stated, it is at best only a momentary intensification of continuing, cumulative life processes that began long before it and will continue long after it.

The question naturally arises, "How can one know all of the things in another person's life that can affect an interchange with him?" This is obviously impossible. But there are some things that you can do that will help you immeasurably. You can at least be aware that such things do exist, and you can constantly strive to know as many of them as possible about the people with whom you communicate. In actuality, you already know much more than you might realize. Even when you think you are encountering a person for the first time, through either the printed or spoken word, you have "met" him before in some way or another. If you stop and think about it for a moment, you'll quickly realize that you already know a great deal about each other simply by virtue of the fact that you are both people. You both live in the same society. You both have been exposed to many of the same ideas, impressions, experiences, and so on.

But, perhaps even more significantly, you'll know that there are a great many things that you do not know about this person. In any case, simply knowing that this particular interchange—no matter how well you know each other—is only a momentary convergence of two much larger life processes will place you in a much stronger, more desirable, and more strategic position.

NOTE . . .
Remember: Answers to Question A are main headings 2 through 6.

Question B: How many people are there in any presentation? _____
(If this seems like a foolish question, think about it a minute and put a figure in the blank space before reading on.)

2 TWO PEOPLE: NO MORE, NO LESS

You may be speaking or writing to ten or a thousand people at the same time. Yet, you are always communicating with only one person. A proper approach to communication always dictates that you think and deal in terms of individual persons. People in a group may be very much alike in terms of mutual interests, but they think and react individually. There is such a thing as getting a group of people to think or act as a single body. It is a known psychological fact that people gathered together in groups are much more easily influenced than when alone. This is much like the "rotten apple in a barrel" principle. If one person in a group laughs, cries, refuses, agrees, or hates, the others are much more likely to do the same than if they were alone. The classic example of this, of course, is mob action, which is based on the phenomenon that individual behavior intensifies in groups.

But when you analyze what really takes place in such situations, you realize that each individual in the group has been communicated with and led to his decision to act at the individual level. Thus, there are always only two people involved in any attempt to communicate: you and the other person. This is true no matter how many other persons there are.

Why is this reasoning important to you? First, remember why you are "in business" in the first place: to do and accomplish specific things that you can see and measure. In the case of communication, this means accomplishing specific changes in specific people. Your whole aim is to reduce your communicating attempts to the problem-solving level, which includes measurement of your accomplishments. This means that you will be naming specific objectives and trying to accomplish them, and then counting up, as it were, how many of those objectives you have accomplished.

In other words, all practical communication is based upon the principle of working the percentages. And remaining individual-oriented helps you to do this in an effective and measurable way. It also helps you to retain your own confidence and to place your failures to communicate in proper perspective. It does this because you go into any situation knowing from the outset that, because it is a human situation, you can't "win 'em all," but that you are trying to win as many as possible.

Thus, you will be able to see a single change in a single person, out of perhaps a hundred tries, as a success, and that is often a good percentage. Any salesman, for example, will tell you that a single sale out of twenty tries often represents a very good average. Any teacher will tell you that if a single student says, "Now I see," he goes away feeling that he has succeeded, and he has. Learn from the failures. Then reject those failures. "Leave them to heaven," and move on. Professional communicators learn to live and operate by this philosophy early in their careers, or they usually do not remain "in the business." For there are few professions in which failure can be more crushing and discouraging—although there are few, also, in which success is sweeter. Obviously, the more successes the merrier, and the smaller the number of tries, the more critical becomes the necessity to increase the possibility and probability of success through a strategic, problem-solving approach.

Answer to Question B: Only two: you and each audience member.

Question C: When will your audience react objectively to you? _____

3 **THE OTHER PERSON IS ALWAYS EGOCENTRIC**
No matter how he appears or what he says, your safest assumption always will be that the other person is self- or ego-centered. Even if someone is trained to be objective, it still will be safer and wiser to assume that he will interpret you, what you are trying to communicate, and most of the things that occur in the interchange primarily in terms of his own experience, language, understanding, etc. The reason for this is simple. A human being is built this way. No matter how well-trained he is in objective thinking techniques, his subjective nature lies constantly waiting to take over at the slightest provocation, at the first moment that he lets his conscious guard down. Remember, too, that this is just as true of you as of any other human being, and this is why you must constantly and consciously remind yourself to be objective.

4 **THE OTHER PERSON IS ALWAYS EGO-DEFENSIVE**
The average person you meet probably will go a step beyond merely passively interpreting things in his own terms. He is much more likely to become quite active in his reactions and responses, for psychologically, he is ego-defensive as well as ego-centric. Either consciously or unconsciously, he will actively try to counteract anything that he cannot relate to himself, anything that in effect poses a threat to his inner sense of self-worth or importance.

For example, if you make yourself seem superior to him in any way, he will attempt to block the imagined or real superiority, perhaps by not liking you or disagreeing with you, as his own internal justification. Something as simple as your looking like someone else he knows (who perhaps once did him wrong), a stereotype, or a preconceived idea could greatly affect your attempt to communicate with him. Sometimes, merely seeming to know or to have anything more than he (which makes him feel inferior, and thus makes you a threat) will be sufficient for him to throw up a barrier.

Answer to Question C: Probably never.

30

Question D: Is the other person aware of his reactions? _____

5 THE OTHER PERSON IS USUALLY UNAWARE

It also is important to continually remind yourself that a person usually will not be consciously aware of how and why he is reacting, but also that he wouldn't tell you if he knew. Society conditions people to hide their true inner drives and motives. They rarely reveal themselves to people close to them (or to themselves). Only when they are assured—both intellectually and emotionally—that it is safe to do so, will they reveal what they really need, want, feel, or think. Your job as a communicative person, in a nutshell, is to make a person feel as safe as possible in accepting, believing or doing whatever you want him to do.

Obviously, you cannot know all of the things that will set off an individual person. But you can know and base your actions on far more specific information about him than you probably now are using. If nothing else, you can exert every effort to remain as psychologically and emotionally inert to the other person as possible. Even if you do not know he will react, you can at least try to do nothing that will directly cause him to react negatively toward you based on what you know to be generally true. All of this, of course, applies if you honestly want to communicate with him. Isn't it much wiser to let sleeping dogs lie until you are strategically ready to awaken them?

Answer to Question D: Rarely

Question E: Every presentation situation will have a r _____ **content,**

a p _____ **content, and an e** _____ **content.**

6 ALWAYS THREE DIMENSIONS

Men still stand incredulous at things that have been known for centuries. Thus, we still wonder why a perfectly logical, clearly presented, and well-substantiated idea may not be accepted or acted upon by the person hearing or seeing it. The reason for this is that human communication is always three-dimensional. No spoken or written message is ever just words or rational thoughts. Every interchange between you and another person has and takes place at the following three intimately related levels, or dimensions, of being:

1. At the emotional, or psychological, level
2. At the physical, or sensory, level
3. At the rational, logical, or thinking level

Almost without exception, any attempt to communicate is doomed to failure if any of these dimensions is neglected.

Your written or spoken message will continue to have this three-dimensional content whether or not you consciously take it into account. Nothing goes away simply because it is ignored. Nor is any of these dimensions likely to merely remain passive and have no effect if it is ignored. It is far more likely to work actively either for or against you. The strategic alternative for the deliberating, planning communicator, therefore, should be obvious. It is to consciously take all dimensions of the attempt to communicate into account, to seek to control them and actively make them work for instead of against him.

These matters may seem quite fundamental, perhaps even things to be taken for granted. But they should not be. For this knowledge is the basis for the use of practically any communicative device or medium you can name. And you cannot use any medium or device in any truly enlightened and effective way without an understanding of the real underlying reason for using it. For example, knowledge of the existence of and need for rational content in any attempt to communicate is the elemental basis for outlining that attempt and understanding the various ways of doing so. Similarly, knowledge of the existence of and need for physical content is the basis and reason for the use of any form of audiovisual aid, graphics, illustrations, or other sensory communicative device. Finally, an underlying grasp of the existence of and need for emotional content is the basis for the use of what is commonly known as emotion appeal in communicating an idea.

Knowledge of this three-dimensional nature is the bedrock of communicating, so to speak. You can't get much closer to real understanding without these realizations. Of course, in dealing with each of the three dimensions, it is possible and necessary to go into greater detail in terms of specific guidelines, procedure, and technique. Later segments develop these ideas further in terms of expanding this basic knowledge into a usable working foundation for improved idea handling and communication. For the moment, if you can clearly see the fundamental three-dimensional nature of any attempt to communicate, you are exactly where you should be in grasping the message of this course.

Answers to Question E: rational, physical, emotional

Answers to Question A:
1. Don't over-isolate
2. Two people : no more, no less
3. The other person is always egocentric
4. The other person is always ego-defensive
5. The other person usually is unaware
6. Always three dimensions

Summary Exercise: This exercise will help you in fixing the ideas and concepts just covered firmly in your mind. Effective idea presenters also must have some skill in visually stating ideas for their audiences. So this also will give you a little advance practice in the development of visual aids.

The problem is this: assume that the following statements are things you might be saying to an audience and that you want to have a flip chart or slide on a screen before them while you are telling them this. Your task here is to create that visual aid. Do this by drawing an illustration of the following statements:

In every presentation, there are at least three elements: (1) the presenter, (2) the idea or message being communicated, (3) the audience. Further, every presentation situation always has at least three dimensions: (1) The rational, (2) The physical, and (3) the emotional (or psychological).

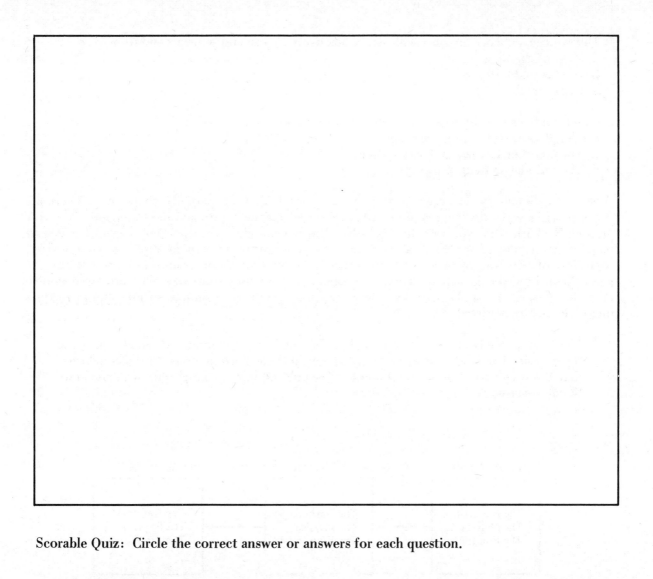

Scorable Quiz: Circle the correct answer or answers for each question.

1. All presentation situations will have the following in common:
   a. A presentation room
   b. Three dimensions of communication
   c. The audience will be reacting egocentrically

2. It can safely be said that all functional presentations should have:
   a. A function
   b. A thesis
   c. An audience

3. Presenters dealing with groups of people realize that they always are "working the percentages." Assuming an audience of twenty people, "objective accomplishment" would mean that you did what you intended to do to, for or with
   a. At least 30% of the audience
   b. Any audience member
   c. Over 50% of the audience

4. The average audience member will react objectively to you and your presentation
   a. Most of the time
   b. If he is told to do so
   c. Pretty rarely

5. You usually can get by in a presentation without taking into account
   a. The physical and sensory aspects
   b. The emotional or psychological aspects
   c. The rational content or aspects

Answers to Summary Exercise: Obviously, this test is at least partially subjective. There are many possible ways that you could combine these six elements into a visual statement. We can't personally check what you've come up with. But we can give you some ideas against which to match what you've done. First, all six elements we've given you should appear in your answer, regardless of how you've rendered them. How you combine them, restate them or visually expand them, however, is almost entirely a product of your own creativity, plus how well you've mentally grasped the study material. Here are three simplified examples of how these six ideas might be visually rendered.

Idea 1 is probably the simplest way that they could be rendered. It simply gives the three basic elements. But even here, the logical thinker would come to the conclusion that the presenter, message, and audience, would all have rational, physical, and emotional dimensions.

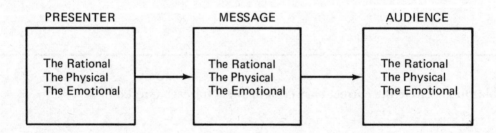

Idea 2 carries the thinking and conclusions a step farther, especially if the textual material has been absorbed, and the illustrator brings a composite of what he has studied to the illustrating task. It allows for the two-way nature of the process as discussed in the text and concludes that if a message from a presenter has a rational, physical, and emotional content, and if the audience has a similar content, then any feedback from that audience to the presenter must also have a similar content or dimension.

Idea 3 gets even more multidimensional, allowing for the feedback factor, as well as taking into account the "preoccupation barrier" idea. We've stuck to the simple flow diagram and box method here, largely in the interests of economy. Try substituting stick figures for some of the elements in these illustrations. Or, if you have artistic talents beyond this, play a little with these ideas, and you'll find that you can come up with some really good visual aids.

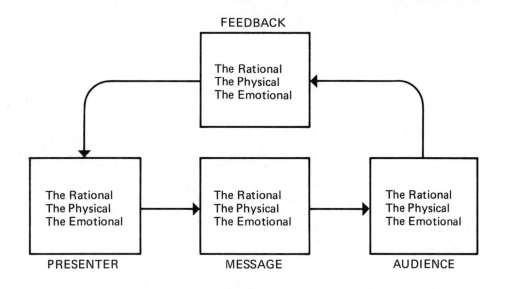

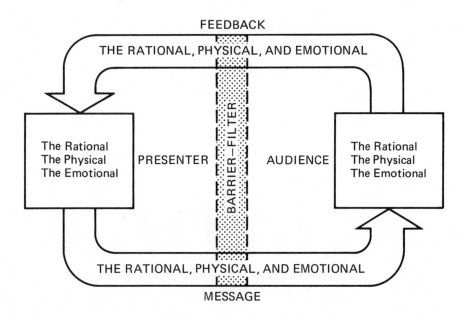

Answers to Scorable Quiz (Value of each answer is in parentheses.): (1) a and b (20%) (2) a, b, and c (30%) (3) b (10%) (4) c (10%) (5) None (30%) (listing a, b, or c is a loss of 10% each.)

ISBN 0-471-01627-6

EFFECTIVE PRESENTATION
Structure And Thesis

UNIT II

W. A. Mambert

Executive Director

National Communication and Education Association

Wiley Professional Development Programs

Advisory Editor

Steven C. Wheelwright

Harvard Business School

John Wiley & Sons Inc.
New York • London • Sydney • Toronto

Library of Congress Catalogue Card Number: 75-39750

ISBN 0-471-01628-4

Printed in the United States of America.

10 9 8 7 6 5 4 3 2 1

Understanding The Need For Idea Structure

PREMISE: That idea structure constitutes the most elemental framework of both idea comprehension and the construction of any idea presentation.

SEGMENT OBJECTIVE: That you have a clear understanding of the need for idea structure, be able to see how it relates and applies to the idea presentation task, and, using this and later segments, be able to apply the principles of idea structure in the actual construction of a presentation.

> *NOTE . . .*
> *There is much to be said about structure as a part of the idea presentation process. This segment merely introduces the subject because this is where it ought to be introduced.*

Question A: List some words or terms that are synonymous with the term idea structure.

_____   _____

_____   _____

_____   _____

Question B: Structure is to the idea presentation as the _____ is to the building.

1 THERE MUST BE A FRAMEWORK

When it comes to dealing with the subject matter of your attempt to communicate, that is, the actual idea(s) that you are handling, you will have great difficulty in exercising any appreciable control over the communication of that idea without some knowledge of the principles of structure. The term is synonymous with such terms as: reasoning, thought sequence, order, logic, logical order, logical pattern, thought pattern, and thesis development.

1

Answers to Question A: You'll find them in the preceding text.

Regardless of what it is called, the important thing is that, in order to be communicated in any meaningful and understandable way, an idea must be set down or put forth in a comprehensible, rational form. Structure is the main key to your own understanding of an idea. It is what gives ideas meaning and relationship. And it is the main vehicle for actually putting your ideas together to form a functional message. The analogy of building a house is quite apropos. It is almost impossible to construct a building without first establishing what the outside parameters of that edifice will be and then building a framework for it. No matter how attractive or perfect any of the parts and details are, without the basic framework upon and within which to place them they remain essentially a disorganized pile of material. Feature, if you can, a carpenter trying to hang a window in thin air. The same applies to idea handling. Until there is a basic structure or framework, all parts of that idea remain disorganized. It is almost impossible to do anything else right. Any idea which you mean to handle in a purposeful, functional way, therefore, must have a basic structure or pattern. The principles and techniques for structuring ideas into meaningful patterns are quite classic and fundamental and can be summarized in the following three steps:

1. *Isolate and identify the specific idea with which you are dealing.*
2. *Determine the inherent, or natural, pattern of that idea.*
3. *Restructure that idea to control its perception by an audience.*

Answer to Question B. Framework.

Question C: What is a thesis statement?

_____

_____

_____

Question D: To effectively comprehend and communicate an idea, one must first

(1) _____ that idea; then determine its inherent or natural

(2) _____ ; then (3) _____ that idea to

control its perception by an audience.

2 ISOLATE AND IDENTIFY THE IDEA

This step is also validly known as establishment of a thesis, or determination of a main or central idea. All purposeful communicative structure must begin at this point. Think of ideas as existing essentially in a random state until you perceive one of them or decide to communicate one of them to another person. You, in effect, must extract or isolate that idea from all other ideas, distinguish it from all those other ideas among which you find it, and yet continue to see its relationship within that larger world of ideas. You must reduce that idea to a manageable level. Thus, what you are seeking is a clear-cut, single statement of exactly what a given idea is and what it is not. Only when you know what the outer borders are will you be ready to begin to construct the internal parts of that idea into a communicable entity, that is, a functional message designed to accomplish a specific aim.

Answer to Question C: You'll find it in the preceding text.

Both you and your audience will remain hopelessly confused as long as the idea stays in its random state. This applies to whatever idea you may wish to deal with. If you were thinking or talking about computers, for example, you would have to reach a point very early in the process where you would be able to state clearly: "Among the many things that computers might be, might be related to, or might be constructed to be, I propose to think of and deal with them as problem-solving tools at this time, in this situation." If you were thinking, talking, or writing about the planting of beans, you would have to say in your mind, and ultimately to the person with whom you were communicating: "I am dealing with the planting of beans, not with onions or carrots or with planting in general, but with beans. I see the relationship of the planting of beans to the planting of carrots, and I allow for it; but today, at this moment, I am dealing only with the planting of beans."

As simple as this step may sound, it represents one of the major stumbling blocks for the average person in his actual handling of specific ideas, in specific situations, to accomplish specific objectives. Perhaps people fail to take this step because it is so obvious and simple. Yet, until an idea can be so isolated and identified, almost anything else done in attempting to handle that idea in your own mind, not to mention trying to communicate it to someone else, amounts to little more than futile machination. For, how can anyone handle anything with any conscious purpose if he does not know what he is handling? No more than he can do anything meaningful if he does not know what he is trying to do.

Answer to Question D: (1) isolate, (2) structure, (3) restructure.

3 SEEK THE IDEA'S INHERENT STRUCTURE

After you have established an idea's larger relationships and parameters, you are ready to deal with it internally in order to identify its parts and their interrelationship. Your next step is to discover that idea's inherent structure. That is, every idea has some structure or pattern, even if that structure is merely the sequence which you perceive it or the spatial relationships of its parts. The significance here is that the natural order in which you find the idea may or may not be the valid or the best functional structure for that idea. There is a very strong tendency in most people simply to accept without question an idea in the form in which it is originally perceived. This is very dangerous to true perception and understanding. For order alone does not impart validity. It thus becomes extremely important to clear thinking to be able to distinguish in one's mind the difference between how an idea is first perceived and (1) what its true form is; and (2) how one restructures that idea to control its perception.

Question E: The best pattern or structure to use in transmitting an idea to someone else invariably will be the same structure or pattern in which you yourself originally perceived that idea. True _____ False _____

Answer to Question E: False. You must always evaluate the matter.

Question F: What is meant by the phrase "form follows function"?

_____

_____

_____

4 FORM FOLLOWS FUNCTION

This is an inviolable maxim for all practical (functional) communication. Whatever form you give an idea in communicating it, that form has validity only in the function it performs. To put this important principle another way: function always precedes structure, medium, and method. This means that you can never make a final decision validly as to what form your idea will take until you know what you want to do with that idea. It also means that you cannot select a medium validly until you know the function. For example, to decide to write a letter, hold a meeting, make a telephone call, write a report, design a brochure, hold a class, and so forth, before deciding upon an objective, is to work backwards. For you cannot possibly know what will best accomplish your objective before you have it. The principle, form follows function, carries throughout the entire handling of the idea, down to the most minute detail.

Every element of every attempt to communicate should have a clear-cut, identifiable relationship to the objective of that attempt. Every visual aid, every word, every sentence, every gesture, every piece of evidence, fact, or detail can be validly included only if it contributes to the objective. To think in terms of structure, media, or device before function is to let the tail wag the dog. It is to be controlled instead of to be in control.

Answer to Question F: You should never make a final decision about the form your idea should take until you know what you want to do with that idea.

5 IN SUMMARY: A MENTAL PATHWAY

Structure is neither more nor less than the development of the original definitive statement of an idea into a full-fledged mental pathway that leads through the reasoning process from one point to another. Recall your first statement of an idea to yourself. You must now make the same statement for the person to whom you are writing or speaking, with the important difference that you control how, where, and when he is told. You may or may not wish to state the idea for him in exactly the same way that you stated it for yourself. This depends on the degree of subtlety required by the situation, the nature of the persuasion involved, the educational or informative nature of the attempt, and so forth. You might merely wish to imply the main idea or to state it outright in unequivocal terms. You might, on the other hand, want merely to reveal pieces of the idea at any given time, gradually leading either to your own revelation of the entire idea or to your audience's drawing its own conclusion.

In short, how, when, and where you unfold your full idea depends upon a great many factors and influences, most of which you will be aware of as a result of your careful analysis. Equally important, this revelation of your idea will be a direct product of your knowledge of the possible structures that are available to you.

As stated, the objective of this segment is merely to introduce the subject of logical structure and to establish the need for it. In succeeding segments, we shall explore the many methods of giving ideas meaningful structures and making the principle, form follows function, a reality.

NOTE ...
What we have just covered here will be expanded in Unit Three.

Summary Exercise: What follows is a random list of ideas. Within this list there is only one set of six ideas which clearly relate to each other. Further, only one of those six ideas is a main idea; the other five are clearly subordinate to it. Your tasks are to (1) identify and isolate that main idea, (2) identify and isolate the five sub-ideas, and (3) list them in outline form.

The random ideas are:

Houses	Classrooms	Slogans
Flies	Firetrucks	Orbital Data
Idea Presentation	Form Follows Function	Space Flight
Computers	Insects	Ants
Feedback	Books	Tools
Colleges	Beetles	Fleas
Mosquitos	Offices	Vehicles
Audiences	Input	Automobiles
	Bees	

Your outline:

I.

    A. _____

    B. _____

    C. _____

    D. _____

    E. _____

Scorable Quiz: Fill in the missing word or words.

1. Two synonyms for the term "idea structure" are _____ and

   _____ .

2. The main idea of a presentation is known as what? _____

   _____ .

3. In the text, we refer to the determination of the presentation's main idea as isolating and

   _____ the primary idea with which you are dealing.

4. When you first perceive an idea, it may have some kind of pattern or structure before you

   even begin to handle it. What do we call this? _____

   _____

5. What do we call the basic principle that any structure you develop for your idea pattern

   must perform a function? _____

   _____

6. The inherent structure of an idea as you find it may be neither its most valid nor the best

   structure for communicating it to someone else. What are you seeking in terms of its structure?

   _____

Answers to Summary Exercise: There is only one set of possibilities here under the conditions set up in the instructions. You would have to really stretch your imagination to come up with anything other than:

   I. Insects

      A. Flies
      B. Mosquitos

            C. Bees
            D. Ants
            E. Fleas

Answers to Scorable Quiz (Value of each answers in parenthesis below):

1. Any two of the following (15% each):

reasoning	logical order
thought sequence	logical pattern
order	thought pattern
logic	thesis development

2. Thesis (10%)
3. Identifying (10%)
4. Form follows function (30%)
5. The best functional structure (20%)

Understanding The Genesis Of Structure

PREMISE: That there is a very natural hierarchy of kinds of structure; that structure is the major key to conveying meaning; and, therefore, that anyone who wants to convey meaning must understand exactly what structure is and how it works.

SEGMENT OBJECTIVE: That you have a clear grasp of what structure is and how its various forms evolve so that you have a foundation for using specific kinds of structure in the planning and outlining of your idea presentations.

Question A: Following is a random list of ideas, some obviously related to each other and others obviously unrelated. Sort this list into three categories so that each contains only those ideas clearly related to each other.

Lessons	Taxes	Dismantle linkage
Remove machine cover	Replacing a cam	Accounts payable
Accounting department	Audiovisuals	Stationery
Journalism	Base screws	Advertising
Expose hinge mechanism	Secretary	Training
Articles	Gear housing	Management
Brainstorming	Billing	Inventory

Category 1:	Category 2:	Category 3:

Answers to Question A: A simple test? Yes. But it's a good beginning practice in the basics of structure. You may have noticed that we've thrown you a couple of slight curves here, for several items could fall into more than one category; e.g., audiovisuals, training, management.* You undoubtedly already know that ideas can be elusive at times. That's why you have to stay in control of them. We didn't ask you to name the categories: we have named them.

Category 1 A good heading would be: "Forms of Communication"	Category 2 A good heading would be: "Office or Administrative Matters"	Category 3 A good heading would be: "Machine Repair Instructions"
Lessons Journalism Articles Brainstorming Audiovisuals* Idea support Training* Advertising	Accounting department Taxes Billing Inventory Secretary Accounts payable Management* Stationery	Remove machine cover Dismantle linkage Expose hinge mechanism Replacing a cam Base screws Gear housing

1 A FORM TO PERFORM A FUNCTION

Many idea presenters do not recognize the true significance of having a good, solid understanding of what idea structure (order, pattern) is and how it works. Nor do many, both professional and novice, give it the weight that it should have in the planning and preparation of a presentation.

You have seen the basic three-dimensional nature of human communication; that is, that there always is a rational, a physical, and a psychological aspect to the perception or communication of an idea or group of ideas. Generally speaking, in the world of unplanned communication, the rational, physical, and emotional aspects and influences involved in attempts to communicate are randomly mixed. They are always present in some way or another, but rarely are they organized for maximum effectiveness.

As already pointed out, the planned presentation, however, is a series of intentional and deliberate acts with a purpose. When you speak of planned presentation, therefore, you move into a different realm. You cross over an imaginary line, as it were. Neither the rational nor the physical nor the emotional dimensions of the idea-handling situation can any longer be allowed to occur in a random, unplanned fashion. So long as they do so, they will tend very strongly to be uncontrollable. Each dimension must become a strategic and tactical device for accomplishing a specific objective, that is, a form to perform a function.

Question B: Of the rational, physical, and emotional dimensions, which should be the first concern in the planning of a purposeful idea presentation?

2 A FORM THAT CAN BE PERCEIVED AND COMPREHENDED

Considerable research in such fields of human communication as writing, presentation, teaching, learning, reading, listening, and so forth, have almost definitely established that rational structure is the primary key to meaning. That is, although all ideas also have a physical and emotional content, there is no way that they can be perceived or reacted to at these levels unless they are first actually comprehended by the human mind. And the key to the human mind's comprehension is pattern, be it simple or complex.

Thus, what we are saying here (and it is difficult to overstate the requirement) is that the first step for the purposeful idea presenter is to give his idea what is required for it to be perceived and comprehended, namely, some form (structure) that the mind can perceive and grasp. Then, the more that idea can be reinforced through other rational, physical, and emotional means, the greater become the chances of its performing an intended function. The answer to Question B, therefore, is as follows:

Answer to Question B: The rational, because it is the main key to clear perception and meaning and to an idea recipient's comprehension of that meaning.

Question C: (This one is for review.) What does the phrase "form follows function" mean?

_____

_____

_____

3 A SINGLE THOUGHT SEQUENCE PATTERN

Generally, because of the way the human mind is constructed and because of its mechanics for perceiving, an audience will perceive and comprehend most efficiently not only when a structure for that perception and comprehension is provided, but also when that structure is simplified as much as possible into a single thought sequence pattern. It is thus important not only that an idea presenter choose a basic thought sequence pattern, but also that he *adhere to the same basic structure throughout his presentation*. Of course, you may use several other forms of idea structure within your thought–sequence pattern but, as will become even clearer as the discussion progresses, the principle of adhering to a single basic pattern relates directly to singular objective development in terms of specific audience response and to most of the other important elements of the presentation.

The main point here is that if you are not aware of the various idea patterns available to you as communicating channels, you obviously are at a disadvantage. You must grope for an effective pattern, perhaps inadvertently stumbling upon one which will partially serve your purpose. More than likely, you will have some kind of pattern since there is a certain degree of order inherent in most ideas. But how can such a random process be a part of or contribute to what is supposed to be a deliberate act except by accident? In a good presentation, very little (and hopefully nothing) happens by accident. It must be remembered that the key to using structure is awareness. Under no circumstances should it dominate, nor should any idea presentation be forced into a mold it doesn't fit. Rather, you should use your knowledge of the various ways of structuring ideas, combined with your knowledge of the other communicating dimensions as a part of your multidimensional function for understanding an audience.

Only you can decide what your best basic thought pattern will be. Your knowledge of the specific subject, audience, and situation will help you in selecting one, but you must have one.

10

Question D: The more complex an idea is, the more complex must be the structure by which it is conveyed. True_____ False_____

The principles of idea structuring are literally as old as the existence of ideas and thinking themselves. That is, ever since there have been ideas, they have fallen into some kind of pattern. It is Aristotle, however, who is credited with making the first attempts to identify and set down in writing the nature of those patterns. He did not invent the patterns; he merely observed them and, as it were, named them. They have never changed and probably never will.

Answer to Question C: Simply that any structure chosen for the presentation of an idea must relate directly to the purpose or objective (function) of the attempt to communicate that idea.

Answer to Question D: False, simplification always is the goal.

NOTE ...
Study the following chart. You will find it helpful as you read through this and the next unit.

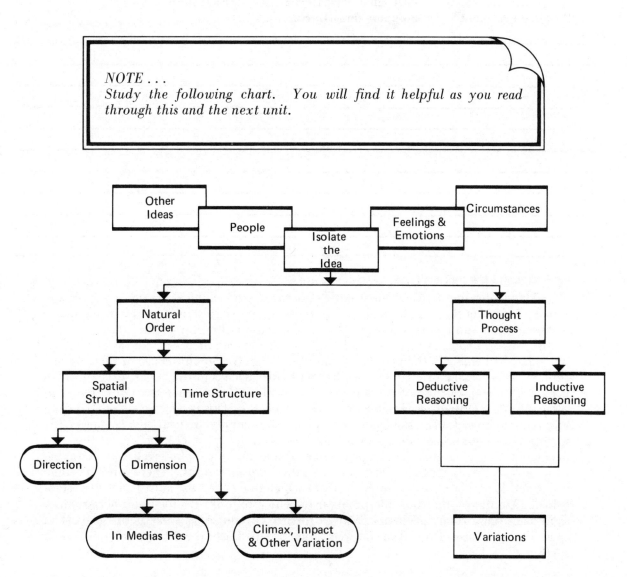

The point of this chart is this: Ideas normally are found or perceived in a relatively random way, although that randomness itself might be construed as some kind of pattern or structure. We can even go a step farther and say that ideas usually are mixed, not only with other ideas but also with feelings (emotions), people, and circumstances. Nor can any attempt to communicate be totally isolated from the larger life process. Yet, in the perception, thinking, and planning of the deliberate communicator, the idea to be dealt with must be extracted, as it were, from its natural surroundings and examined so that both its external and internal structure can be understood. Then, of all of the possible structures in which that idea can be recommunicated, the best and most functional one must be selected.

Question E: Arrange the following items into an outline form that shows spatial relationship:

Second floor	Administration department	Drafting department
Receiving department	Storage room	Blueprint printing department
Assembly department	Packaging department	First floor
Design department	Shipping department	

_____

_____

_____

_____

_____

_____

_____

_____

_____

4 SPATIAL STRUCTURE

This is the simplest and most basic structure by which ideas are perceived or conveyed. Assuming that you have already perceived, you simply tell your audience where things are. As soon as two things exist in space, a relationship occurs. This is above, to the left of, inside of or outside of that. Or it becomes necessary to say that this is not related to that. Certain guidelines impose themselves upon the use of such a structure. It is necessary first to define what part this space is of the larger space in which it exists: to step outside of it, as it were, to establish its parameters. Many times this is easy to do. One often merely says, "This is a car," "This is a factory," or "This is a house," and one clearly establishes such parameters simply by using the language. "It is a split-level suburban house in Chicago" narrows the space even more. It then can become a "white, neatly landscaped, comfortable looking, split-level..." Looking from within this particular space imposes other considerations. There must be some order and logic here, too. The point from which one is looking must be clearly established. Are there other possible points from which to look? Is one point better, more significant, important, necessary, and so forth? Of course, as soon as things exist in space, there is also a direction between them. This is above, within, around, and so forth.

Answer to Question E: Obviously, what we've given you are the elements of what could be the floor plan of a plant or factory of some kind. Depending on how much of your own thinking and logic you put into it, you could come up with a variety of arrangements. A little thinking and logic, however, certainly would tell you that the receiving and shipping departments probably would be on the first floor. On the other hand, Administration, Design, and so forth, could be on either. But, carrying the logical thinking a step further, Drafting and Blueprint printing in all probability would be connected in some way with the Design department. Following is our outline; compare yours.

Simple Spatial Structure

I. First floor
   A. Receiving
   B. Storage
   C. Administration
   D. Shipping

II. Second floor
   A. Design
      1. Drafting
      2. Blueprint printing department
   B. Assembly
   C. Packaging

Question F: Arrange the following in a list of events meaningful time sequence:

- In 1931, a young architect graduated from State Polytechnic Institute.

- Yesterday morning the forty-story Celtic Building collapsed, killing 800 people.

- In 1941, this architect met an unscrupulous politician named Joe Zelch.

_____

_____

_____

Question G: You can use variations of chronological structure for many effects. For example, you can build suspense with it, lead up to a climax by giving ideas in the order of their impression or impact, keep ideas hidden until you're ready to reveal them at just the right moment, and so forth. In outline form, rearrange the following three events chronologically so that they build to their most climactic level.

- Soon picoseconds (1,000,000,000,000ths)
- First milliseconds (1,000ths)
- Ultimately, smaller division of the second became necessary.
- Then microseconds (1,000,000ths)
- Not so long ago, minutes sufficed as a measurement.
- Man once measured the speed of his machines by the hour.

- Now nanoseconds (1,000,000,000ths)
- Soon seconds became the unit of measurement.

_____
_____
_____
_____
_____
_____
_____
_____

5 THE CLOCK AND CALENDAR SOMETIMES DO THE JOB

Time, or chronology, also is a kind of natural order. The clock or calendar actually structures or can be made to structure an idea. For example, reports, instructions, procedures, and similar subjects usually are best perceived and communicated in terms of chains of events, with time forming the pattern or relationships between them. In its basic form, this pattern or structure simply says that this did, can, or will happen; then this; then that.

Almost immediately, however, other structural possibilities will present themselves. Certain events probably will emerge as more significant, necessary, impressive, or meaningful. One thing may cause another, or be the result of something else. One may be more exciting, impressive, climactic, or even occur because of where it takes place, thus incurring a further structural relationship. The idea handler, therefore, is almost immediately presented with several opportunities or necessities for varying chronological structure to emphasize ideas, to keep attention focused on them and in many other ways make an idea clearer or more meaningful, or to give parts of it added impact.

Aristotle called this "in medias res" (in the middle of things), which means simply that when you are dealing with ideas in a time sequence, you not only can start at the beginning or first event, you can start at any place in the past, present, or future as well.

Answer to Question F: You can play with these ideas in several ways. Below, we've chosen to headline the event that occurred just yesterday, and then go back to 1931 and work up through 1941, in effect giving the story behind yesterday's event. You could just as easily start with 1931, then 1941, then the present, which would follow simple chronological order.

  I. Yesterday morning, the forty-story Celtic Building collapsed killing 800 people.
 II. In 1931, a young architect graduated from State Polytechnic Institute.
III. In 1941, this architect met an unscrupulous politician named Joe Zelch.

Answer to Question G: The outline is probably the most effective arrangement. Here, we start in the past and build up to the present, to the climax that the second is now divided into 1,000,000,000,000ths, thus building up to this final impressive idea. Notice, too, that A, B, C, and D under IV clearly lend themselves as second-level subheadings.

  I. Man once measured the speed of his machines by the hour.
 II. Not so long ago, minutes sufficed as a measurement.
III. Soon seconds became the unit of measurement.
IV. Ultimately, smaller division of the second became necessary.

A. First milliseconds (1000ths)
B. Then microseconds (1,000,000ths)
C. Now nanoseconds (1,000,000,000ths)
D. Soon picoseconds (1,000,000,000,000ths)

Question H: (The answer to this one follows immediately. Don't look at it until you've worked it out for yourself.) Let's try working with chronological structure one more time. If you put this one together, there's more than a very good chance that you really do grasp the use of chronological structure as a communicative device. We'll give you a clue here, too. Tenses and parallelism are very important. Here are the events:

- It used developments in Tufflex.
- Tufflex was developed by XYZ Corporation (1954-1956).
- Tufflex was developed by ABC Corporation (1955-1957).
- The Variator took fifteen years to develop.
- Gromnich's work was based on cryogenic discoveries.
- Gromnich's work was based on transistor development.
- Gromnich worked in microcircuitry (1953-1957).
- It will be used as primary power.
- It will be used in power tools.
- It will be used in power appliances.
- It will be used in power hobbies and crafts.
- It will be used in automotive travel guidance and control.
- It will be used in conventional flight guidance and control.
- It will be used in space flight guidance and control.
- It will be a guidance and control device.
- The Variator will have many uses.
- The Variator is highly efficient and durable.
- Its moving elements are made of templon.
- Its housing is constructed of Tufflex.
- It uses microcircuitry.

_____
_____
_____
_____
_____
_____
_____
_____
_____
_____
_____
_____
_____
_____
_____
_____
_____
_____
_____

Answer to Question H: As we said, tense and parallelism are the keys to organization here. It is very easy to group these ideas under the headings of past, present, and future. For example, all ideas with "will be" obviously sort down as future. The three main headings are obviously parallel. Ideas that have a third-level division, e.g., II, A and B and III, A and B, also are quite clearly identifiable and parallel. That is, for example, there is no other place that the two items identified as Gromnich's work could fit, or the guidance and control items, or the Tufflex items, and so forth. As far as the major groupings of past, present, and future are concerned, their order is completely arbitrary. We merely repeated the pattern we introduced in Question F. That is, we began in the present and went to the past, but interspersed the future in between the two because we felt that it had greatest impact this way.

A Relatively Complex Variation of Time Structure

I. The Variator is highly efficient and durable. (Present)
  A. It uses microcircuitry.
  B. Its housing is constructed of Tufflex.
  C. Its moving elements are made of templon.

II. The Variator will have many uses. (Future)
  A. It will be a guidance and control device.
    1. It will be used in space flight guidance and control.
    2. It will be used in conventional flight guidance and control.
    3. It will be used in automotive travel guidance and control.

  B. It will be used as primary power.
    1. It will be used in power tools.
    2. It will be used in power appliances.
    3. It will be used in power hobbies and crafts.

III. The Variator took fifteen years to develop. (Past)
  A. Gromnich worked in microcircuitry (1953–1957).
    1. Gromnich's work was based on transistor development.
    2. Gromnich's work was based on cryogenic discoveries.

  B. It used developments in Tufflex.
    1. Tufflex was developed by XYZ Corporation (1954–1956).
    2. Tufflex was developed by ABC Corporation (1955–1957).

Question I: What is the relationship among the ideas in the following list of topics?

Existing rights of way	Kinds of industry
Future municipal funds	Present municipal funds
Future land use	Distance between residence and employment
Urban growth	Increased auto production
Traffic congestion	Present land use

6 TOPICAL STRUCTURE

Finally, as a transition from talking about natural order to the orders of thought process (which we'll discuss in the next five segments), we might take a look at what many writers and teachers call "topical structure," or order. It's a good transitional point because it can come under the heading of either natural order or thought process, depending upon how it is used.

In the simplest sense, topical order may be nothing more than the listing out of a collection of ideas, subideas, subjects, categories, and so forth, with or without relationship. In this sense, the ideas would simply occupy space, either physically or mentally. They could so exist randomly. Or, which is more likely as soon as they were listed, some relationship would be seen to inhere or emerge, even if nothing more than the space or direction between them. More than likely, the relationship would be a logical one, one of thought process.

Answer to Question I: These are headings taken from an urban development plan. They all obviously relate to each other under a single main heading or title of that nature; e.g., "urban factors," "city planning," and so forth.

Scorable Quiz: Fill in the missing word or words.

1. How many main thought–sequence patterns should a presentation have?

_____

2. What kind of structure is the simple listing of ideas? _____

3. What are the two main subdivisions of natural order? _____ and

_____

4. What are the two main divisions of the structure that we call thought processes?

_____ and _____

5. There is a Latin term that describes varying basic chronological sequence or beginning "in the middle of things." What is this term?

_____

6. What would probably be the best structure for describing the floor plan of a factory?

_____

7. Building up to a climax is a variation of what structure?

_____

8. Which structure would you classify under either natural order or thought process?

_____

Answers to Scorable Quiz (Value of each answer is in parentheses below):

1. One (10%)
2. Topical (10%)
3. Spatial structure and time or chronological structure (20%)
4. Deductive and inductive (20%)
5. "In medias res" (10%)
6. Spatial (10%)
7. Chronological or time (10%)
8. Topical (10%)

Understanding Thesis

PREMISE: That it is necessary to understand the concept of thesis as the basis for all planned thought process.

SEGMENT OBJECTIVE: That you clearly grasp what a thesis is and be able to manipulate specific theses for specific presentations and variations of idea structure.

Question A: Thesis is a common term which most people have heard. On the basis of your present experience and understanding, state here in a sentence or two what you think a thesis is. (You will be able to check your answer as you read the following text.)

Question B: State the thesis of this segment. _____

At this point, we cross over a kind of imaginary line. When we talked about natural order, we were basically speaking of how ideas might be located at places within the physical dimensions of time and space (things that can be perceived physically) as opposed to being thought out within the mind, in terms of concepts or logical relationships and processes. Now, we begin to consider the actual thought processes that occur in the perception and comprehension of ideas. And the first step is to be sure that we understand exactly what a thesis is and how is fits into the planned reasoning process.

1 THESIS: WHAT IS IT?

Most people probably think that they already know what a thesis is, and to some degree they probably do. But really knowing how to handle and manipulate a thesis is another matter entirely. Too many people do not know how to do this, although such an ability actually is the cornerstone of understanding and manipulating any form of logical structure or thought process.

We've already dropped in the idea of thesis in previous segments. As we say, we know that you have some familiarity with the concept. But let's make sure of your grasp anyway.

Some other names for thesis are:

Proposition	*Central Idea*	*Generalization*
Premise	*Main Idea*	*Deduction*

19

Contention	*Conclusion*	*Assumption*
Assertion		*Presumption*

In short, thesis is in fact the isolation of the idea being dealt with, either in your own mind and perception, or in terms of presenting that idea to someone else. It is as essential to your comprehension as it is to communicating that comprehension to someone else.

More than this, thesis is the statement, in words, of the isolated idea. Yes, we state our theses (plural) right out, because this is how it almost always should be in the teaching/learning process. Good teachers usually don't hide their premises from their students, unless such withholding is determined by plan to be a useful teaching device.

In any case, strictly from the point of view of your presentation of an idea or group of ideas to someone else, thesis is the most generalized statement that you make to your audience about what it is you're trying to tell them, teach them, convince them. It is where you tell them precisely what it is you are claiming or proving and what the details of information you are giving them support.

Answer to Question B: This is an easy one. The answer, obviously, is in the premise, as for every segment.

2 TELL THEM AT THE BEGINNING?
This is a decision you might make, as we made for this course, and for each of its segments. It certainly will give your audience a key to all that follows in your presentation to them.

Question C. But what would be a serious drawback of doing this?

There are times when this is the best way, particularly when presentations are intended to be primarily educational and informative, such as when you want someone to comprehend the "big picture," your whole idea as quickly as possible. In such a case, you probably might come right out and say at the beginning:

> *"Ladies and gentlemen, we must modernize the laboratory. Here are the data and evidence to support this contention."*

3 LEAD THEM STEP BY STEP?
But suppose instead that there is some convincing and persuading to do. Suppose you're dealing with a touchy or sensitive subject. Suppose you're selling a new piece of equipment or trying to establish a need or problem in their minds before you hit them with your idea or solution. Or, you don't, for example, want the cynic in the back row to flat–out decide against you before you have a chance to state your case.

Question D: What is a possible option here?

Remember our discussion of "in medias res" when we considered chronological structure? You have similar options here. There is nothing to say, for example, that you can't state your thesis anywhere you decide it's best: in the middle of things, or at the close of your presentation.

Question E: By the addition of a single word to the above sample thesis, you can convert from an opening statement of premise to a closing statement of premise or a conclusion that has been reached. Can you think of what that word might be?

Answer to Question C: The biggest drawback of coming right out and stating a thing at the beginning of a presentation is that you "shoot your wad." There usually will be someone who will "turn you off," figuring he's already heard your idea and doesn't need to hear the details in order to accept or reject it. Also, you run a greater risk of not being able to maintain attention.

Answer to Question D: We give you the option(s) in the paragraph following the question; namely, you can state your thesis at any time or place that you think is most strategic and propitious.

Answer to Question E: Try "thus" or "therefore."

4 OR DIVIDE YOUR THESIS INTO PARTS?

Why not? You're always in charge and control of your own presentation. The audience is allowed to touch the dials only when you decide that it suits your purposes. You thus might decide that it is advantageous to present your thesis in pieces. In this case, those pieces more than likely would be major divisions of your presentation and appear as main headings. Following is an example of a thesis divided up into the main headings of a presentation:

> I. *Data must be converted as close to its source as possible.*
> II. *Data must be stored compactly and in quickly retrievable form.*
> III. *Data must be computed and processed very rapidly.*
> IV. *Data must be displayed in a form convenient to its user.*
> V. *Data must be disseminated to its users on a timely basis.*

And, again here, your final or your beginning statement probably would be a summation of the parts of your thesis, for example, as follows:

- *Beginning: "What are the elements of an effective data–handling system?"*
- *Closing: "In conclusion, therefore, data must be converted, stored, computed, displayed, disseminated rapidly, conveniently.*

Notice above that a thesis might also be stated in the form of a question.

5 OR RESTATE IT?

Yes. There is no law against repetition. You can restate your thesis, not randomly of course, but as often and in as many different verbal, graphic, or other ways, as you, the presentation planner, deem it strategically necessary.

6 OR YOU CAN COMBINE METHODS

There is always this possibility. For added reinforcement, you can use any or all of the above methods in getting your message across. You can state it at the outset, repeat or rephrase it throughout the presentation, and then restate it at the close, perhaps in the form of an actual action step. For example,

> *"Therefore, I am asking you to authorize the modernization of the laboratory."*

7 OR YOU CAN MERELY IMPLY YOUR THESIS

There is an old saying that the highest form of communication is your ability to lead the other person to think that he has thought of your idea. What's wrong with letting your audience themselves phrase your thesis (as you intended it to be phrased) and draw their own conclusions based on data that you have given them! This is a more subtle process (one of which children and wives seem to be particularly adept) which, at the professional presenting level may take some subtlety, finesse, and other of those qualities mentioned in Segment 3.

To Summarize:

1. Your presentation must have a thesis, or it will have nothing to say.
2. That thesis can appear anywhere in the presentation.
3. It can be phrased, stated, implied, and restated in any verbal or graphic way.

Just being aware of the significance and importance of thesis statement, consciously always thinking in terms of the central idea of your presentation, in most cases, will almost force you to do something about having one. In truth, you'll not have a presentation without one, perhaps a very nice impressionistic experience for your audience, but rarely, if ever, a presentation that will accomplish a purpose.

Summary Exercise: Review and summarize (without looking back).

1. What is a thesis?

_____

_____

_____

_____

2. What are five terms that are synonymous with thesis?

a. _____   d. _____

b. _____   e. _____

c. _____

3. Name five ways of handling or stating a thesis.

_____   _____

_____   _____

_____

4. What is the thesis of this course?

_____

_____

Scorable Quiz: Fill in the missing word or words.

1. Three synonyms for the term thesis are_____,

_____, and_____.

2. Thesis is the statement, in words, of_____.

3. Where can your thesis appear in the presentation? _____

4. In an educational or informative presentation, where would your thesis be most likely stated?

_____

5. In a more persuasive presentation, where would you be most likely to place your thesis?

_____

6. Is it necessary to actually state the thesis in words? _____

7. Where would the thesis statement, "Therefore, we suggest that you adopt this program," be

most likely to appear in a presentation? _____

8. Stating your thesis at some place other than the beginning of your presentation would be

similar to what type of structure? _____

Answers to Summary Exercise:

1. Stated as simply as possible, a thesis is the verbal statement of the isolated idea with which a presentation deals.

2. Any of these: proposition, premise, contention, main idea, central idea, conclusion, generalization, deduction, assumption, presumption, etc.

3. Any five of these: statement at the beginning, statement at the conclusion, statement in parts,

restatement, any combination of methods, statement by implication, graphic or sensory statement.

4. Stated in the text of Segment 1: The main thesis of this Learning Program is that to be effective, any idea presentation must be a series of deliberate acts and contain or embody certain very specific elements.

Answers to Scorable Quiz (Each correct answer = 10%):

1. Any three of the following: proposition, conclusion, main idea, generalization, premise, deduction, contention, assumption, assertion, presumption, central idea

2. The isolated idea

3. Anywhere

4. The beginning

5. Later in the presentation (also at the end of the presentation is an acceptable answer)

6. No

7. At the end or conclusion

8. "in medias res"

ISBN 0-471-01628-4

EFFECTIVE PRESENTATION
The Kinds Of Structure

UNIT III

W. A. Mambert

Executive Director

National Communication and Education Association

Wiley Professional Development Programs

Advisory Editor

Steven C. Wheelwright

Harvard Business School

John Wiley & Sons Inc.
New York • London • Sydney • Toronto

Library of Congress Catalogue Card Number: 75-39750

ISBN 0-471-01629-2

Printed in the United States of America.

10 9 8 7 6 5 4 3 2 1

Understanding The Deductive And Inductive Processes

PREMISE: That the inductive and deductive processes are the generic elements of all thought process and the basis for any further variation in the use of thought process as a presentation device. This premise is built upon an understanding of the concept of thesis.

SEGMENT OBJECTIVE: That you clearly understand the nature of the deductive and inductive processes, see how they relate to thesis, and be able to use them in preparing and outlining a presentation.

There are only two basic processes by which ideas flow, are perceived, or transmitted. There can be only two. All other thought processes emerge from these two or are merely variations of them. These two basic processes are classically known as inductive process and deductive process, terms with which you are undoubtedly familiar. They, like all forms of idea structure, are rational processes; but for the planning communicator they also are methods of outlining idea presentations.

Many people have trouble with these processes. How about you? Can you correctly label the diagram below?

Question A: Following are four terms, the first two symbolized by their circled initials.

(MI) = Main Idea (thesis)   **Inductive Method**

(SI) = Subidea or Detail   **Deductive Method**

Also shown are two diagrams. Complete this illustration by filling in the circles with the proper initials and properly titling each of the two diagrams. Fill in all circles.

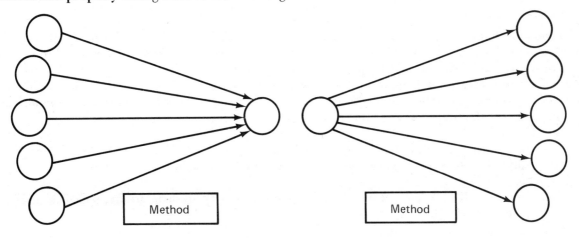

Answer to Question A:

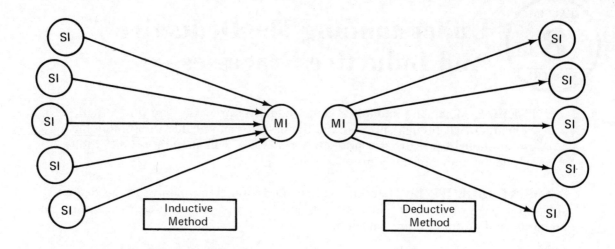

1 DEDUCTIVE PROCESS

This also is known as "a priori" reasoning, presumptive reasoning, or general-to-specific process. The deductive approach begins with a thesis, general premise, or proposition, and proceeds from the generalization through successive levels of specificity until sufficient information has been presented to support or prove the main idea. It is a traditional form of argument. It works very well in many teaching situations. It also is the basic form of almost all journalism and is usually known in that trade as the "inverted pyramid," which merely means to begin with a broad concept or idea at the top of a presentation and work downward to more specific details.

This structure has limited value in the analytical process, which normally works in the opposite direction, gathering data empirically and then formulating the idea. However, one might formulate a hypothesis or assume a certain generalization to be true and then examine or present the random data to see if it proves the assumption. But care and open-mindedness must be exercised in such a case because the data may dictate or prove an entirely different generalization than the original hypothesis. Thus, in problem solving or information receiving, always suspect the deductive process.

Question B: Let's see how well you can work with the deductive or general-to-specific process. Following is a series of ideas. Also shown is our inverted pyramid. The broadest level represents where the broadest idea should be placed. The next narrower level, the next narrower idea, and so on. Study the listed ideas and place them in proper general-to-specific order within the pyramid. To save you writing time, the ideas are numbered and you may simply place the number for each idea in the proper level of the pyramid.

1. In response to pleas from several civic groups, a committee of experts has been formed to develop a "Year 2001" urban-development plan.

2. Mr. John R. Jones, prominent author and authority in civic affairs, will head the group consisting of . . .

3. Mayor hires urban experts to aid Maintown.

4. The new group will study major traffic entry arteries.

5. The new group will study future streets.

6. The new group will study existing streets.

7. The new group will study building plans.

8. The study will consist of four phases.

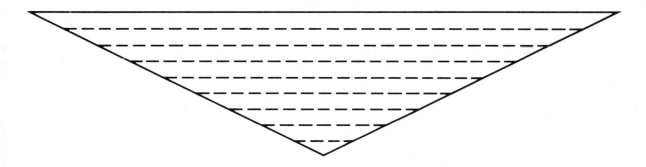

As an information-transmitting process, the order of general to specific does have some distinct advantages. It is a direct approach, clear and easy to follow.

Since it always gives the main or general idea early in the presentation, the other person has a clear idea of the mental pathway to be followed. Wherever the presentation stops, he at least will know what you are trying to show or prove, even if he does not have sufficient evidence to believe, act, or be convinced. Variations of this technique include such devices as:

- *Setting up an argument and knocking it down*
- *Giving a rule and showing its exceptions*
- *Following a process of elimination*
- *Showing a process of deterioration*
- *Following a process of decrease or descending order*

On the other hand, the main disadvantage of such an approach is that the speaker or writer may have difficulty in retaining attention and interest throughout the presentation of his supporting detail, since the other person always will know his whole story and will tend to reach a conclusion on the basis of the generalization, or lose interest before hearing all of the idea support. You usually will have to reinforce this basic structure with other devices to retain audience interest and contact. Another disadvantage is that if the generalization is wrong, all of the information supporting it will be wrong too.

Answer to Question B:

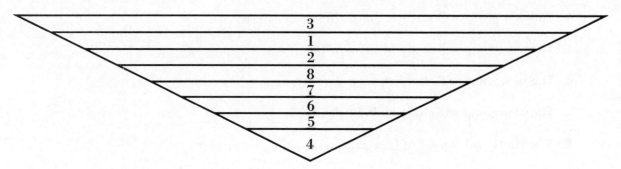

ANOTHER EXAMPLE OF DEDUCTIVE OR GENERAL-TO-SPECIFIC PROCESS IS:

1. *The U.S. Council on Economic Statistics has effectively applied the principles of PERT to the world's longest statistics gathering tasks.*
2. *The Council has the task of compiling most of the figures behind the familiar economic trend forecasts in the nation's newspapers.*
3. *These familiar news items are only a part of the Council's statistics*
4. *The whole program encompasses the labor force, the financial world, agriculture and industry.*

2 INDUCTIVE PROCESS

Once you have a good grasp of the general-to-specific process, simply turn the pyramid around, and you have another common idea-handling structure known variously as "a posteriori" reasoning, inductive thought, the empirical approach, or scientific method. It is the direct opposite of the foregoing approach and also has many variations. It begins with the details and leads to the generalization, obviously a more reliable analytical and problem-solving approach. This structure also affords more flexibility in the transmitting of ideas. It is easier, for example, to build a more convincing story using this method, to develop more effective moods, to be sure that the main idea will get a fair hearing—to get all of the facts in before permitting a conclusion to be drawn.

Variations of this process include such devices as showing:

- *Growth or development*
- *Accumulation and refinement*
- *Increase or addition*
- *Step–by–step procedures*
- *Building, constructing, or composing*
- *Process and function description*
- *Intensification, aggravation, or enhancement*
- *Addition, enlargement, or expansion*
- *An incremental process*

Note the similarity between this method of developing a structure from details and the basic analytical process of isolating your idea as well as the development of spatial structure. This is because it is the structure of scientific method and problem solving. Actually, this empirical approach, by its very nature (that of seeking to arrive at a generalization from details) might lead to any other structure as the individually gathered details fall into place. Often, the generalization reached may in fact be that this or that pattern exists or appear as inherent, as the data refines itself.

Question C: Following is a random list of specific details. Also included somewhere in the list is the generalization to which these specifics would logically lead. We're feeling generous at the moment, so we'll give you another hint. There are at least three levels of specificity here also. That is, your outline will have at least this many levels:

1. _____
   A. _____
      1. _____

Let's take the problem in steps, just as would be done if you were actually sorting down this random data to get it into some kind of order for meaningful presentation to someone.

Step 1: Find the most generalized term or statement.
Step 2: Find the major categories.
Step 3: Find the sub-ideas that group within the major categories.
Step 4: Find the next level of detail to fit under the second-level headings.
Step 5: Arrange all of these into a logical outline which will lead to and prove the generalization.

Insurance deductions
Retirement deductions
Bond deductions
Voluntary deductions
Allowances
FICA deductions
Night pay

FIT deductions
State tax deductions
Payroll accounting is a
  complex process
Deductions
Meal allowances
Travel allowances

Housing allowances
Holiday pay
Statutory deductions
Overtime pay
Kinds of pay
Special pay
Regular pay

5

Answer to Question C:

Step 1:
Generalization (Thesis)

Step 2:
Level 1 detail

Step 3:
Level 2 detail

Step 4:
Level 3 detail

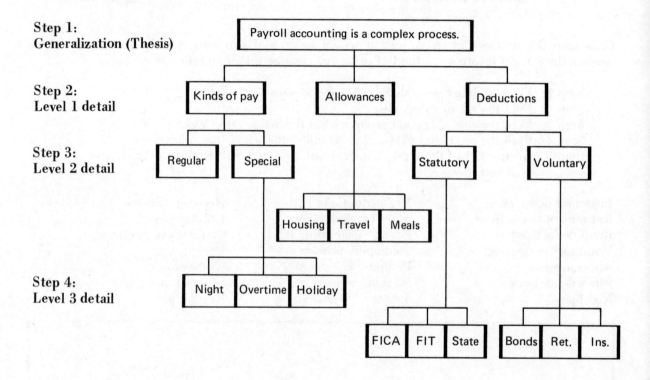

Now, let's go a step farther and develop an actual general-to-specific presentation outline from our sort.

   I.   Kinds of pay
       A.   Regular pay
       B.   Special pay
           1. Night pay
           2. Overtime pay
           3. Holiday pay

  II.   Allowances
       A.   Housing allowances
       B.   Travel allowances
       C.   Meal allowances

6

III. Deductions
  A. Statutory deductions
    1. FICA deductions
    2. FIT deductions
    3. State tax deductions
  B. Voluntary deductions
    1. Bond deductions
    2. Retirement deductions
    3. Insurance deductions

Generalization: Therefore it can be concluded that payroll accounting is a complex process.

Summary Exercise: If you've successfully completed the exercises that we've given you in this segment, you don't really need much of a summary exercise. So we'll go fairly easy on you and ask you a single question: What is the relationship and difference between the inductive and deductive processes (or structures) and spatial structure as discussed in Segment 6?

_____

_____

_____

_____

_____

Scorable Quiz: Indicate true (T) or false (F)

1. The structure that begins with the gathering of specific details and works toward a generalization is sometimes called the inverted pyramid. _____

2. Setting up an argument and knocking it down is a form of deductive reasoning. _____

3. A main disadvantage of deductive process is that it may reveal too much too soon. _____

4. Inductive process and scientific method are synonymous. _____

5. Showing a process of growth, development, accumulation, and so forth, would be the deductive process. _____

6. The drawing of a conclusion would likely be a result of the inductive process. _____

7. The forming of a hypothesis and proving it would follow the inductive process. _____

8. Ideas presented by either the inductive and deductive method might also be presented chronologically or spatially at the same time. _____

9. The word "therefore" would be quite likely to indicate that the deductive process was in use. _____

10. A process of decreasing or descending order would be inductive. _____

Answer to Summary Exercise: The basic relationship here is that the detail which leads to the conclusion (inductive) or the detail that supports the proposition (deductive) does exist in space; that is, they could very well simply be arranged in a spatial pattern or order. The basic difference is that the deductive (general-to-specific) and the inductive (specific-to-general) processes are in fact thought, or logical, processes; whereas the spatial structure simply has to do with physical location.

Answers to Scorable Quiz (Each correct answer = 10%): (1) F, (2) T, (3) T, (4) T, (5) F, (6) T, (7) F, (8) T, (9) F, (10) F.

LEARNING

9

SEGMENT

Understanding Causal Structure

PREMISE: That causal structure is a refinement of either the inductive or the deductive process.

SEGMENT OBJECTIVE: That you understand causal structure as a thinking process and as a presentation method and be able to use it as an option in outlining your idea presentations.

Question A: Put a check in the appropriate boxes to identify the following as either possible causes or possible effects or as embodying both possibilities:

	Cause	Effect
1. Maintenance		
2. Faculty maintenance		
3. Employee lateness		
4. Position of a satellite		
5. Accidents		
6. Good personal relationships		
7. Effective presentations		
8. This self-teaching guide		
9. God		
10. Man		

1 IDENTIFYING CAUSAL RELATIONSHIPS

In dealing with a body of information, a key analytical step often is to determine whether or not there is a causal relationship between or among individual ideas, events, or circumstances, especially when they occur in proximity to each other because that proximity may not necessarily indicate relationship. Sometimes, even the determination of a lack of causal relationship can be a significant clarifying step. When confronted with a body of information, it frequently will be wise to at least put it to the cause-effect test by asking such questions as:

- *Is there a causal relationship here?*
- *Is this particular item a cause or an effect?*
- *What does this cause?*
- *What can it cause?*
- *If this is an effect or result, what caused it?*

9

- *Is the cause present or known here?*
- *Is the effect present or known?*
- *What if this cause or effect were not present?*
- *Is there an assumed but invalid cause–effect relationship?*

Answer to Question A:

	Cause	Effect
1. Maintenance	√	√
2. Faulty maintenance	√	√
3. Employee lateness	√	√
4. Position of a satellite	√	√
5. Accidents	√	√
6. Good personal relationships	√	√
7. Effective presentations	√	√
8. This self-teaching guide	√	√
9. God	√	√
10. Man	√	√

That's right, all of the items given as they are singly given could be interpreted as either causes or effects. Why? Simply because cause-effect does signify relationship. When you put something to the cause-effect test, you are in fact asking the question: Do these ideas have relationship? Thus, you would have to have at least two ideas before you could even make the test. Notice, too, the speculative nature of some of these questions. Often, information not present, known, or existent is significant in understanding the actual information under consideration. This, of course, goes for dealing with or attempting to use any form of idea structure, not just cause-effect. The average, perhaps noncreative person tends to ignore what he does not see. Not so with the truly analytical communicator. His approach is multidimensional, which often includes the dimension of nonexistence. It may be your key to isolating the idea and to clarifying the borders and limitations of exactly what it is that you are dealing with, toward establishing your communicative increment. Such questions also help the thinker to avoid some of the common fallacies and pitfalls in the reasoning process, jumping to conclusions and closed-mindedness.

Question B: In attempting to determine the presence or absence of a causal relationship there are two basic thinking approaches. See if you can name what those are before reading on.

Approach 1: _____   Approach 2: _____

_____   _____

_____   _____

_____   _____

_____   _____

10

Answer to Question B: The two obvious possibilities in causal structure are to work from cause to effect or from effect to cause. Thus:

Approach 1: Examine or present certain conditions or ideas and then analyze their real, possible or probable causes.

Approach 2: Examine or present certain causative events or ideas; and then show, analyze, or discuss their real or hypothetical results.

Question C: There also is a very obvious danger in dealing with information or ideas in terms of cause-effect; this is that it often is very easy to mistake _____ for a _____ relationship.

2 CAUSE AND COINCIDENCE

There are many coincidental happenings in life, unrelated from a causal point of view, and not caused by each other, and yet which may quite validly seem to have meaning or a cause-effect relationship, especially when viewed in retrospect. In the metaphysical world, this phenomenon is known as "synchronicity." In the world of reason and logical thinking, coincidence of events can represent a thinking pitfall because it sometimes is very easy to impute a cause-effect relationship where none exists. Thus, one must always approach causal reasoning with caution and scepticism.

On the other hand, in the communication of information, once a valid, causal relationship is established, cause-effect represents a method of giving presented ideas a meaningful structure. In transmitting information, effect-to-cause adapts well to many forms of analysis, reporting, evaluation, and so forth. The opposite cause-to-effect, often forms the structure of a forecast, a discussion of probability, a speculation, and so forth. Causal reasoning is an excellent educational device because, properly used, it establishes or clarifies relationships between ideas, and, more important, it eliminates relationships where they should not exist or be assumed.

Answer to Question C: It is easy to mistake coincidence for a causal relationship.

Question D: Below are outlines. (1) Identify which represents a cause-to-effect pattern, and which is an effect-to-cause pattern; (2) Identify the causes and effects at the Roman numeral level.

Check One	Outline 1	Cause/Effect

____ Effect to Cause
____ Cause to Effect
	I. Vast amounts of orbital data are transmitted at high speeds
	  A. Speed of satellite
	  B. Position of satellite
	  C. Function of systems	

	II. The data must be received and refined at equally high speeds
	  A. For feedback and control
	  B. For position and life prediction
	  C. For recovery calculation	

Check One	Outline 2	Cause/Effect

___ Effect to Cause
___ Cause to Effect
	I. 65% of the students in this class received failing grades
	   A. They did not know the answers to two key questions.
	   B. They all misinterpreted the other three questions.	

	II. Why?
	   A. The instructor had not discussed the two major principles in class.
	   B. The examination was not written clearly.	

NOTE . . .
Don't look at our answer until you've figured out your own.

Answers to Question D: The first outline is an example of cause to effect; the second of effect to cause. This means that in outline 1, "I" is the cause and "II" is the effect, in Outline 2, "I" is the effect and "II" the cause.

Summary Exercise: Here is a list of ideas:

- Maintenance of communications equipment affects operational readiness.
- Communications is the basis of operational readiness.
- Speed is important in communications.
- Broad coverage is important in communications.
- Operational readiness consists of several elements.
- Trained personnel are important to operational readiness.
- Reliability is essential to communications.
- Operational readiness depends on good supply lines.

Arrange these ideas in a logical, properly subordinated (the right levels of detail), cause-to-effect outline. (Hint: Identify your major levels first: the *cause* and the *effect*.)

Cause:

I. _____

   A. _____

   B. _____

   C. _____

Effect:

II. _____

    A. _____

    B. _____

    C. _____

Scorable Quiz: Fill in the missing word.

There are many (1) _____ happenings in life, unrelated from a (2)

_____ point of view, and yet quite validly (3) _____

to have (4) _____ or a cause-effect (5) _____ ,

especially when viewed in restrospect. In the metaphysical world, this would be known as

(6) _____ . In the world of reason and logical thinking (7) _____

_____ of events can represent a thinking (8) _____ , because

it sometimes is very easy to impute a (9) _____ relationship where none

exists. Thus, one must always approach causal reasoning with (10) _____ .

Answer to Summary Exercise: With the parameters we gave you, there is only one way to go with this outline. "Communications" is clearly stated as the "basis" (cause) of operational readiness. From there on, you're home free simply by applying the principles of parallelism. For every sub-item is clearly identified in terms of whether it relates to communications or operational readiness. Thus, with the possible exception of your having a different sequence for the lettered (A, B, C) items, you would have to put them under the right headings. Following is the correct cause-to-effect outline.

I. Communications is the basis of operational readiness.
    A. Reliability is essential to communications.
    B. Speed is important in communications.
    C. Broad coverage is primary to communications.

II. Operational readiness consists of several elements.
    A. Operational readiness depends on good supply lines.
    B. Trained personnel are important to operations readiness.
    C. Maintenance of communications equipment affects operational readiness.

Answers to Scorable Quiz (Each correct answer = 10%): (1) coincidental **(2)** causal **(3)** seem **(4)** meaning **(5)** relationship **(6)** synchronicity **(7)** coincidence **(8)** pitfall **(9)** causal **(10)** caution.

Understanding The Order Of State, Condition, Quality, And Degree

PREMISE: Basically that of Segment 9, with the possible difference that this represents a further refinement of the capability to perceive and structure ideas for presentation.

SEGMENT OBJECTIVE: Similar to that of Segment 9: that you possess additional options for structuring and composing your presentations and know how to take advantage of those options.

Question A: There really is no better way to learn idea structuring than to practice it. If you're getting a little tired of practice in structure, remember how important it really is to your making effective presentations. There is only one more segment dealing with structure after this one, and we're trying to make your exercises as quick, painless, and profitable as possible. For a change, however, we'll begin this segment simply by asking you a few questions.

1. What do you think is meant by the term "the order of utility"?

_____

_____

_____

2. What do you think is meant by the term "the order of familiarity"?

_____

_____

_____

3. What do you think is meant by "the order of acceptability"?

_____

_____

_____

1 AN OUTGROWTH OF OTHER STRUCTURES
Remember, we said that there really are only two basic forms of thought process.

Question B: Just to review, what are these two basic forms?

1. _____ 2. _____

In reality, the order of state, condition, quality or degree is an outgrowth of either the inductive or deductive processes, or perhaps some combination of both. This order has to do basically with what sequence ideas flow within either the inductive or deductive process. That is, it reduces the random nature of the flow of ideas or parts of them, thus giving the idea presenter greater control over how and when they are perceived.

If you were giving someone a presentation on how to repair a machine, a typewriter, for example, it would be very important for you to provide the instructions in the order of, shall we say, the learner's "need to know." You wouldn't, for example, begin by discussing a typebar cam mechanism and how to repair it before giving instructions for removing the machine cover. Ridiculous as such may sound, we have actually seen such instructions in print and many an inept instructor begin at the wrong place and hopelessly confuse his students. Giving information in the order of utility is only one of many possibilities within this general category of structures. An example of an outline in the order of utility is:

> I. *Define objective*
> II. *Convert to thesis*
> III. *Choose basic structure*
> IV. *Develop outline*

Question C: Before reading on, list here as many possibilities for this type of structure as you can think of. We'll give you a beginning hint. Look at items 2 and 3 under Question A.

_____ _____

_____ _____

_____ _____

_____ _____

_____ _____

Answers to Question A:

1. The order of utility would give information and ideas in the order in which they are needed in order to understand or use succeeding information.
2. The order of familiarity would give information and ideas in the order in which they are most familiar to an audience. This frequently is used in education and informative presentations or announcing something new.
3. The order of acceptability is very similar to the order of familiarity. Frequently, when you are trying to convince or persuade someone of something, it's "good psychology" to start with ideas they already accept, and to "work up" to what they might not accept so readily.

Answers to Question B: Inductive and deductive, of course.

Answers to Question C: This category represents what might be called a family of structures that is very open ended. Generally it is typified by the presence of word endings such as "-ity," "-ance," "-ence," "-ness," "-ent," and "-age." For example, ideas, events, conditions, or concepts can be perceived or presented in the order of their increasing or decreasing, ascending or descending.

Absence
Acceptability
Accomplishment
Achievement
Acquisition
Advantage
Agreeability
Applicability
Assimilation
Attraction
Believability
Coexistence
Comprehensibility
Complexity
Composition
Conduciveness
Convergence

Correlation
Credibility
Decomposition
Disadvantage
Divergence
Dominance
Effectiveness
Excellence
Expedience
Familiarity
Feasibility
Fragmentation
Frequency
Immensity
Implementation
Importance
Impression

Improvement
Inoffensiveness
Largeness
Manifestation
Meaningfulness
Necessity
Occurrence
Parallelism
Pleasantness
Possibility
Presence

Probability
Progression
Proximity
Recession
Relevance
Similarity
Significance
Smallness
Timeliness
Utility
Visibility

Nor is this a complete list of the possibilities.

2 TWO DIRECTIONS

As you can go from cause to effect or effect to cause, so also in this order is it possible to go in two directions. That is, if it is possible to give ideas in the order of their increasing complexity, for example. It is also possible to present them in the order of their decreasing complexity. If it is possible to present ideas beginning with those most believable and moving toward the least believable, it also is possible to go in the other direction. Thus, ideas can be structured in the order of their increasing or decreasing: ascending or descending order of state, condition, quality, or degree. An example of outline giving ideas in the order of their increasing complexity is:

> I. Punched card coding principles
>   A. Punching zones
> II. Magnetic tape storage
>   A. Channels and bit structure
> III. Random access disk storage
>   A. Addressing
>   B. Formatting

Question D: How is this structure similar to (or how can it be seen as) inductive or deductive process?

_____

_____

_____

```
NOTE . . .
Don't look at our answer until you've figured out your own.
```

Answer to Question D: The inductive and deductive processes have to do with details either flowing toward a main idea or from a main idea. The order of state, condition, quality or degree has to do with the sequence of the flow of those details. That is, if you had five subideas leading to a conclusion, you might arrange those ideas in any sequence. The same would apply if you stated your thesis and then presented the five subideas to prove it. Thus, in reality, the order of state, condition, quality, or degree is a refinement of the inductive and deductive processes.

3 GETTING A LITTLE MORE SOPHISTICATED

It is in this type of structure that you'll also start moving into some of the more sophisticated aspects of presenting ideas in terms of building in psychological or emotional appeal. Some of the things we're talking about here are best used with subtlety and finesse. Frequently, an audience may not and should not necessarily know what devices you are using. Take the idea of presenting ideas to someone in the order of their acceptability to him. It rarely would serve your interests as a presenter to come right out and tell an audience that this is what you are "using" on them.

Many sales presentations use some variation of this kind of structure, which essentially works on points of agreement, gradually eroding points of disagreement, ultimately, hopefully, bringing the audience or prospect around to complete agreement or acceptance of your idea (i.e., your thesis).

Question E: What is the basic structure of this self-teaching guide?

_____

_____

Question F: Let's see how good you are at arranging ideas in the order of their acceptability. Let's say that you are with your city or county government. Your task is to make a presentation to a civic group to justify the installation of a new traffic control system in their neighborhood, which, incidentally, is going to increase their property taxes. Here's your familiar list of ideas. Your job is to outline your presentation of these ideas in the order of decreasing acceptability. (Start with the most acceptable ideas and work toward those least likely to be accepted.) We've again built in some parallelism to facilitate your sorting jobs. The ideas for you to manipulate are:

18

- A good traffic-light control system has two requirements.

- Good traffic lights are fair to pedestrians.

- The streets must be made safe for our children.

- It's pretty well accepted that policemen cannot control all intersections.

- A good traffic-light control system is the real answer.

- Good traffic light control must include reliability.

- Good traffic light control must include flexibility.

- Good traffic lights are fair to auto traffic.

- The planned system operates for months without maintenance.

- The city's planned system meets the requirements.

- The planned system automatically adjusts to flexible requirements.

- The planned system will cost a little more.

Answer to Question E: We like to think that it's presented basically in the order of utility. That is, we believe that each segment is cumulatively a foundation for the next.

Answer to Question F:

I. The streets must be made safe for our children.
II. It's pretty well accepted that policemen cannot control all intersections.
III. A good traffic-light control system is the real answer.
   A. Good traffic lights are fair to auto traffic.
   B. Good traffic lights are fair to pedestrians.
IV. A good traffic-light control system has two requirements.
   A. Good traffic-light control must include reliability.
   B. Good traffic-light control must include flexibility
V. The city's planned system meets the requirements.
   A. The planned system operates for months without maintenance.
   B. The planned system automatically adjusts to flexible requirements.
   C. The planned system will cost a little more.

Scorable Quiz: Circle the correct answer or answers for each question.

1. The order of state, condition, quality or degree might follow
  a. The inductive process
  b. The deductive process

2. Presenting ideas in the order of utility gives information
   a. In order of decreasing complexity
   b. As it is needed
   c. In the order of decreasing utility

3. A salesman would be most likely to use
   a. The order of decreasing applicability
   b. The order of increasing visibility
   c. The order of decreasing familiarity

4. A teacher would be most likely to use
   a. The order of proximity
   b. The order of utility
   c. The order of agreeability

5. The order of state, condition, quality, or degree is similar to the inductive process because
   a. It would be likely to present ideas in a basic specific-to-general process
   b. It would be likely to present ideas in a general-to-specific process
   c. Neither

6. The order of utility could be considered a refinement of
   a. Chronological structure
   b. Spatial structure
   c. Topical structure

7. Which of the following would lend itself *best* to presentation in the order of acceptability?
   a. A research report
   b. A political speech
   c. A floor-plan description

Answers to Scorable Quiz (Each correct answer = 10%): (1) a, b (2) b (3) c (4) b (5) a
(6) a, b, c (7) b

Understanding Two-Sided And Other Structure Combinations

PREMISE: The same as for Segment 10 with respect to these structures.

SEGMENT OBJECTIVE: The same as for Segment 10 with respect to these structures.

Question A: We're not "psychoanalyzing" you, but let's open this segment with a little word association game. Complete the following equations:

SIDE ONE	SIDE TWO
Problem	
Need	
Desire	
Question	
Requirement	
Advantages	

1 MANY VARIATIONS

Two-side structure is not a particularly esoteric or difficult structure to understand. Basically, the process or method consists of stating or establishing certain conditions or requirements as one side of an idea pattern, and then meeting, answering, or fulfilling those conditions as the other side of the pattern. For example, you might

- *Ask a question(s) and answer it (them)*
- *Arouse a desire and fulfill it*
- *State a problem and solve it*
- *Create or discover a need and meet it*
- *State the requirements and meet them*
- *Contrast two ideas*
- *Compare two ideas*
- *Give the advantages and disadvantages*

or, set the structure up in terms two opposite, bilateral, contrasting, or comparative sets of conditions.

Your statements of either side of the situation can be made using almost any of the forms of structure we've discussed. This is a very common structure in business, selling, technological discussion, education, and similar situations, simply because much of business and technology concerns itself with solving problems and meeting needs. It is probably the most traditional form of selling. What a trained salesman actually does is to establish a problem, need, or desire and then show you how his product or service solves, meets, or fulfills your problem or need.

The pitfalls in this kind of approach are pretty obvious, just as in causal reasoning as we've already seen. It's very easy for an audience or prospect to be "set up." That is, the solution to a problem, for example, can be made to seem like it matches the problem even if it doesn't really match. So, caution is recommended, not only when you're on the receiving end but also when you're trying to set someone else up.

Answers to Question A:

SIDE ONE	SIDE TWO
Problem	Solution
Need	Fulfillment
Desire	Fulfillment
Question	Answer
Requirement	Meet
Advantages	Disadvantages

Question B: Now let's do a little exercise with two-sided structure. Following are some outline segments. This time, we won't make you sort them down at the single-item level.

Segment 1: Daily Manpower Consumption
  A. Time per job
  B. Cost per job

Segment 2: Material Use and Inventory Restocking
  A. Recording items used
  B. Forecasting future needs

Segment 3: Machine-Readable Worker Badge
  A. Will activate job timer
  B. Will enter worker pay rate

Segment 4: Machine Tool Usage Reporting
  A. By time consumed
  B. By type of job

Segment 5: Worker Will Insert Badge and Job Part Card
  A. Badge and card will create inventory record
  B. Badge will create forecast base

Segment 6: Badge Will Report Tool Usage
  A. By time consumed
  B. By type of job

Segment 7: Job Shop Control

Segment 8: Machine Readable Worker Badge

Segment 9: Side One: The need, conditions, problem, or question

Segment 10: Side Two: The answer solution or fulfillment

Your Task: In the box below, set these segments up in outline form, in a two-sided structure.
Hint: Look for parallelism and tenses.

_____   _____

_____   _____

_____   _____

_____   _____

_____   _____

_____   _____

_____   _____

_____   _____

_____   _____

_____   _____

_____   _____

_____   _____

_____   _____

_____   _____

_____   _____

Examine the following two-sided structure outline before you check your answer.

Side One. The question, need requirement, or problem.

Material Transportation and Control

   I. Receipt control

  II. Shipment processing
     A. Planning
     B. Warehousing
     C. Transportation

 III. Post shipment recording
     A. Identification and location
     B. Issuing
     C. Custody recording

Side Two. The answer, fulfillment, or solution.

Unified Material Transportation and Control Procedure

   I. Three-part standardized record
     A. Recorded once at receiving point
       1. Eliminates repetitious recording
       2. Reduces clerical cost and manpower

  II. Duplicate copy
     A. Furnishes statistics
     B. Serves as warehouse receipt
     C. Contains data for trans-shipment

 III. Shipment copy
     A. Filed for bin location
     B. Serves as packing ticket, issue receipt, and custody record

Answer to Question B:

Segment 9: Side One: The need, conditions, problem, or question

Segment 7: Job Shop Control (Problem)

  I. Segment 1: Daily Manpower Consumption
     A. Time per job
     B. Cost per job

 II. Segment 2: Material Use and Inventory Restocking
     A. Recording items used
     B. Forecasting future needs

III. Segment 4: Machine Tool Usage Reporting
     A. By time consumed
     B. By type of job

Segment 10: Side Two: The answer solution or fulfillment

Segment 8: Machine Readable Worker Badge (Solution)

  I. Segment 3: Machine-Readable Worker Badge
     A. Will activate job timer
     B. Will enter worker pay rate

 II. Segment 5: Worker Will Insert Badge and Job Part Card
     A. Badge and card will create inventory record
     B. Badge will create forecast base

III. Segment 6: Badge Will Report Tool Usage
     A. By time consumed
     B. By type of job

Quite simple, when you sort it down and put it back together. The clue, of course, is that the problem—*Job Shop Control* and its three subsets—is stated in the present tense. The solution, our magnificent new machine readable worker badge, is stated in the future tense. And, of course, there is a subset solution for each subset of the problem, stated in parallel terms. This parallelism, by the way, would rarely be an overexaggeration of the way it should be in real presentations. The simple truth is that simplicity is always better than complexity. Would that all real-life problems were this easy to solve.

2 COMBINING STRUCTURES

Sometimes a presentation won't be simple enough to use only one pattern in the development of its ideas. One pattern must govern the total organization, and numerous other structures might be used to develop the individual divisions and details. Once you learn to distinguish the various patterns and their use you will gain a new insight into the handling of your own ideas, and often will see them far more clearly: a primary key to making them clear to someone else. There are several patterns used in the following example outline. Learning to recognize thought patterns such as these is one of the primary building blocks of idea handling.

Question C: Examine the following outline and try to identify its main thought sequence pattern and as many subpatterns as possible. Then look at the annotated copy of the same outline and compare the results.

ONE: RAPIDLY MACHINE-DRILL PARTS FOR STORAGE AT ASSEMBLY POINT

I. Elements of machine drilling
  A. Get part to worktable
    1. Secure part
    2. Secure worktable
  B. Control worktable
    1. One-axis movement
    2. Two-axis movement
    3. Three-axis movement
  C. Test part
  D. Remove part
    1. Extraction
    2. Moving
    3. Storage

II. Present methods
  A. Hand operation
    1. Disadvantages
      a. Slow
      b. Dangerous
      c. Inaccurate
      d. Costly
  B. Partial automatic control
    1. Disadvantages
      a. Wastes material
      b. Unutilized operator time

TWO: A NEW SYSTEM FOR FULLY CONTROLLED AUTOMATIC PRECISION DRILLING

I. Combined two-phased operation
  A. Automatic conveyor moves part to table
    1. Special attachment secures part
      a. Simultaneously securing table
  B. Tape unit permits variable axis control
  C. Depth and diameter control eliminates testing
  D. Conveyor access transport
    1. Removes
    2. Conveys
    3. Packages

II. Advantages
  A. Load time reduced 50%
  B. Operator danger removed
  C. Errors reduced to .002%
  D. Cost reduced
    1. No waste
    2. One operator per two machines
  E. Compatible with future developments

Write your comments here:

_____

_____

_____

_____

_____

_____

_____

_____

Answer to Question C:

I. RAPIDLY MACHINE-DRILL PARTS FOR STORAGE AT ASSEMBLY POINT (NEED)

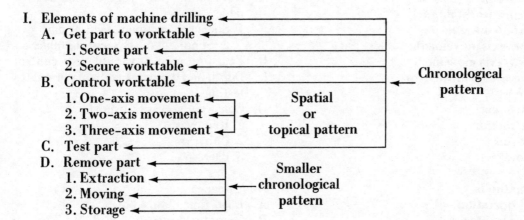

I. Elements of machine drilling
  A. Get part to worktable
    1. Secure part
    2. Secure worktable
  B. Control worktable
    1. One-axis movement
    2. Two-axis movement
    3. Three-axis movement — Spatial or topical pattern
  C. Test part
  D. Remove part
    1. Extraction
    2. Moving
    3. Storage — Smaller chronological pattern

Chronological pattern

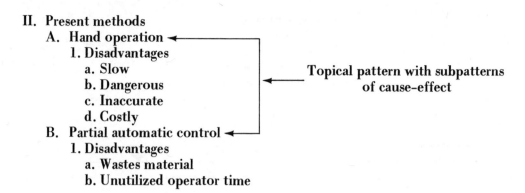

II. Present methods
- A. Hand operation
  - 1. Disadvantages
    - a. Slow
    - b. Dangerous
    - c. Inaccurate
    - d. Costly
- B. Partial automatic control
  - 1. Disadvantages
    - a. Wastes material
    - b. Unutilized operator time

Topical pattern with subpatterns of cause-effect

II. A NEW SYSTEM FOR FULLY CONTROLLED AUTOMATIC PRECISION DRILLING FULFILLMENT

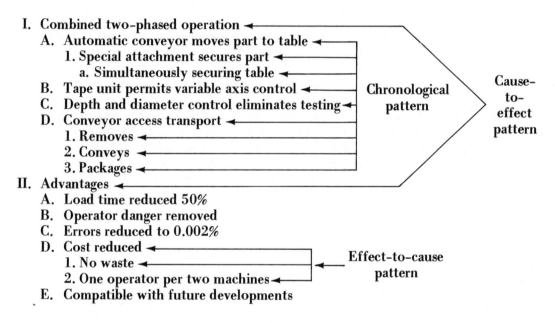

I. Combined two-phased operation
- A. Automatic conveyor moves part to table
  - 1. Special attachment secures part
    - a. Simultaneously securing table
- B. Tape unit permits variable axis control
- C. Depth and diameter control eliminates testing
- D. Conveyor access transport
  - 1. Removes
  - 2. Conveys
  - 3. Packages

Chronological pattern

Cause-to-effect pattern

II. Advantages
- A. Load time reduced 50%
- B. Operator danger removed
- C. Errors reduced to 0.002%
- D. Cost reduced
  - 1. No waste
  - 2. One operator per two machines
- E. Compatible with future developments

Effect-to-cause pattern

Summary Exercise: Remember our "structure genesis" chart in Segment 6? This will serve as an excellent review of our whole discussion of structure, which we're wrapping up here at the close of this segment. We've reproduced it below, with a couple of variations. First, you'll notice its blank. Guess why. Second, you'll notice there now are a few more boxes added (but don't look back to check it, you'll spoil the exercise). Yes, we'd like you to fill in this chart as best as you can and then compare your answer with ours. Go!

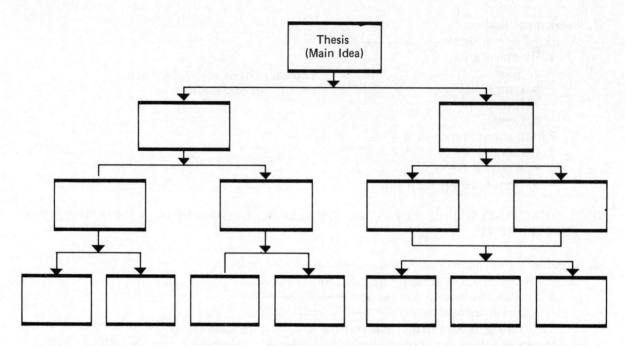

We, of course, didn't tell you at the outset, but many students consider idea structure the dullest part of learning how to make presentations. We don't really think it's all that dull. It actually can be exciting because one is really learning how to comprehend and handle ideas more clearly, with greater insight. And the comprehension and transfer of ideas, human communication, has got to be one of the most exciting things that humans can do. So we hope you haven't found the foregoing few segments overly taxing. Believe us, if you've really grasped what we've been trying to tell you, you've acquired a very powerful and useful tool that will stand you in good stead the rest of your career.

3 SUMMARY

In summary, remember that you are always seeking a meaningful and workable answer to one simple question:

How can my idea be structured to accomplish my specific objective?

If you cannot isolate and structure an idea, or at least recognize when it is "unisolatable" or "unstructurable", you do not sufficiently understand that idea yourself and certainly are in no position to try to make someone else understand it. The main things to remember when structuring an idea are:

- *Let the maxim "form follows function" be your guiding light.*
- *Always seek to establish a point of reference and external boundaries. No matter how intimately related the idea at hand may be to other ideas, in order to be dealt with in an intelligible way, it must be isolated from the total body of knowledge and experience and dealt with as something finite.*
- *Think both broadly and narrowly. Learn to step in and out of the idea, to shift point of view.*

Following are some additional analytical questions that will help you to do these things. Ask yourself:

What is this idea a part of?

What are its dimensions? Where, When, and how does it begin and end?

What is larger?

What is opposite?

What is like it?

What does it influence or cause?

What coexists with or without relationship?

How can it be permuted?

What can be added to it, with or without changing it?

Is this all of it?

What is unknown?

What are the alternatives to this idea?

What are the false, assumed, imputed, irrelevant, erroneous relationships?

Where am I with respect to it?

What comes before, around and after it?

Where is the other person with respect to it?

What is smaller?

What is near?

Can it be larger or smaller?

What influences or causes it?

What if I shifted point of view (inside or outside the idea)?

What if it did not exist?

What if it were placed in a different setting?

How many ways can it be stated or described in its simplest form?

Am I subjective or objective in relation to this idea?

Remember that:

- *Almost all ideas have some kind of inherent or natural pattern. However, this natural structure usually can be improved upon or reinforced in order to make the idea accomplish a specific function.*

- *No matter how complex an idea is, its basic framework must remain simple.*

- *No matter how many sub-patterns an idea has, it should have only one main pattern.*

- *You should always be able to distinguish in your mind the difference between the idea and its parts.*

Remember to control the idea: do not let it control or confuse you.

Answers to Summary Exercise: This is the full graphic story of idea structure. Notice particularly the dotted line showing the relationships between spatial and time structure and the thought-process structures. That is, any information, data, or details presented in any thought process structure can be controlled in terms of the time or spatial sequence in which they're given.

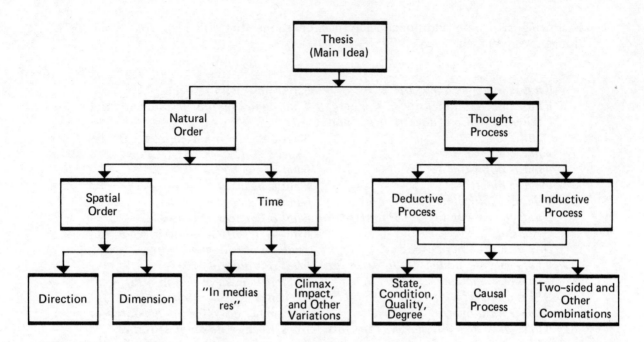

Scorable Quiz: Fill in the missing word or words.

A. The structure which states or establishes certain conditions and then meets, answers, or fulfills them is known as (1) _____ structure. One might, for example, state a problem and (2) _____ it, create a desire and

(3) _____ it, merely (4) _____ or

(5) _____ two ideas.

B. The main pitfall in using two-sided structure is similar to that in using causal structure; namely, the imputing of false or invalid (6) _____.

C. Many presentations turn out to be (7) _____ of structures.

D. At the overall level, according to our structure-genesis chart, the two main kinds of structure are (8) _____ order and (9) _____ process.

E. The primary question in the use of any structure always must be:

Will it (10) _____?

Answers to Scorable Quiz (Each correct answer = 10%): (1) two-sided, (2) solve it, (3) fulfill, (4) compare, (5) contrast, (6) relationships, (7) combinations, (8) natural, (9) thought process, (10) accomplish the objective.

ISBN 0-471-01629-2

EFFECTIVE PRESENTATION
The Functional Approach

W. A. Mambert

Executive Director

National Communication and Education Association

Wiley Professional Development Programs

Advisory Editor

Steven C. Wheelwright

Harvard Business School

John Wiley & Sons Inc.
New York • London • Sydney • Toronto

Professional Development
University of Dayton
Dayton, Ohio

Library of Congress Catalogue Card Number: 75-39750

ISBN 0-471-01630-6

Printed in the United States of America.

10 9 8 7 6 5 4 3 2 1

Understanding The Functional Approach And Formulating A Presentation Objective

PREMISE: That the purposeful idea presenter is in business to do and accomplish specific things, and that such cannot be done without a working grasp of the functional approach to human communication.

SEGMENT OBJECTIVE: That you understand the functional approach, realize its significance, and be able to apply it in the preparation of your own presentation objectives.

Question A: As we're sure you're aware by now, every segment of this course has a clearly stated learning objective at its beginning. Go back now and look at the stated objective on the first page of each segment. State below what you think all of these objectives have in common.

_____

_____

_____

_____

Make Your Own Headings: Let's try another learning-reinforcement device in this segment, which is really no more than a technique of effective reading and also a good practice for you in isolating and distinguishing main ideas. Notice that the numbered main headings for each of the subject divisions have been left blank. As you read each section, summarize in your mind a heading that you think expresses the content of that section, and write it in the numbered blank heading space. You'll find our headings at the end of the segment for comparison.

1 ———————————————

As in most fields and disciplines, there are many places where you can see the difference between the professional and the amateur. Suppose we were pressed to the place where we would have to answer the question:

> *In the business of idea handling and communication, what one thing, more than any other, separates the professional from the amateur or novice?*

We would have to answer that it would be here: it would be in the realm of how that person deals with the matter of objectives. For, the truly purposeful presenter of ideas most definitely takes a different turn of mind in this matter than does your run-of-the-mill purveyor of ideas. And we're going to take a pretty close look at that turn of mind in this segment. Let's start with another question, whose answer has great bearing on everything said in this segment.

1

Question B: You've undoubtedly heard many definitions of the term "communication," many of which no doubt have much validity and express some nice thoughts. But, really, what is communication? Write your definition here before reading on.

_____

_____

_____

Answer to Question A: You will find that every statement of objective, including the objective of the course as a whole, is stated in terms of some action, behavior, activity, or change in you, our audience. Each is stated in terms of what we want to happen to you; not in terms of us or what we are going to do. You may or may not fully grasp the significance of this at this point, but you should as you study on.

Answer to Question B: For the planning, purposeful idea presenter, communication is a change in a human being.

2   Remember that we said earlier that the person who just naturally has the urge to ask, "to what account have I turned this particular effort or time?"—who instinctively seeks to measure the results of what he does, as opposed to the machinations that he engages in—is better predisposed toward being an effective idea presenter in the context of this course.

This is the true beginning point. Start with the fundamental premise that:

You are in business to do and accomplish specific, identifiable things.

This then means that any presentation that you engage in, if at all possible, must seek to do or accomplish something that is specific, that is identifiable, and, if possible, that can be measured. In short, a presentation must serve a function: there is no other reason for making one. If it does not, nothing has been accomplished. That function is always the same: to affect human beings, to get others to respond or change in some way. The change itself may take many forms. It can be a temporary or permanent audience response, a single decision or act. It can range from the highest intellectual or emotional communion to simple entertainment. In some forms of communicating it may be perfectly valid to seek an undefined "expressionistic" response without necessarily knowing beforehand what the desired response is. Yet even in that situation the presenter's objective, stated or unspoken, is to evoke a response.

But you, as a purposeful idea presenter, must be far more specific. You must consciously attempt to describe the response that you want in terms of a concrete audience activity. Sometimes it will be difficult for you to articulate, but if you look closely enough, even at the generalized presentation to "inform" or to "familiarize," you will find a definable response. You will find something that expresses action or behavior. The audience acts or becomes. In human beings action is behavior. This behavior takes many forms, but the response a purposeful presenter always seeks is in fact behavior. This is extremely important. If the function of a presentation cannot be expressed in terms of audience behavior, one should examine the validity of giving it in the first place. The truth is that many presentations today might just as well be given, since they really don't accomplish anything.

Question C: All presentation objectives ought to be expressed in terms of what is supposed to happen to _____ .

3
If a presentation must be functional, that is, if it is to actually do something, it stands to reason that knowing what that something is is of utmost importance. This, in fact, is the whole key to getting any presentation off on the right foot from the very beginning of its planning. Until you identify what you are trying to do, it's going to be very difficult for you to do anything else right. For, you'll never have anything to measure that rightness against. Right in terms of what?

So, to effectively plan any functional presentation, you'll find that the true beginning point is where you want to end up. Yes, the end is the beginning. A properly formulated and stated objective actually is nothing more nor less than a description of conditions as you want them to be after you have finished. The whole planning and execution of your attempt to communicate then becomes a matter of "working backwards" to construct the most effective mechanism that leads to that result. Obviously, the more clearly and explicitly that you can describe how you want things to be after you have finished, the greater your chances of accomplishing them. If nothing else, the greater become your chances of knowing whether or not you have accomplished what you set out to do, a far better posture than not even being able to determine whether you have succeeded or failed.

The next logical question then is:

What is the best possible way that I can state or describe where I want to end up?

We're here to tell you that there are indeed specific things that you can do to make your description of the conditions after your presentation meaningful and measurable. That is, your statement of objective can and should have some very specific characteristics.

4
The very first characteristic that a good presentation objective will have is narrowness and specificity. One of the biggest mistakes that novices make is to try to do too much in too little time or space. The professional, on the other hand, thinks and deals in workable increments.

Question D: The whole key to effective planning of a presentation objective is to _____ at the _____ .

This does not mean that you should forget that each individual situation is a part of a larger relationship or life process. It merely reduces what may on first examination seem like a formidable, perhaps confusing, hodgepodge to a solvable level. By all means, establish what a particular interchange is supposed to do in terms of the larger relationship. But, aside from that, form the habit of compartmentalizing. If you are making a telephone call, for example, or having a conversation, or making a speech, think of each as a single entity. Identify something that begins, ends, and has borders. Establish its objective and concentrate on controlling and structuring the single situation to meet that specific objective. If you do this often enough, you will indeed also find the larger relationship or problem resolving itself. There is no other way.

The second reason for thinking and dealing in small increments is that amount of information and detail involved in handling and communicating almost any idea. This almost always automatically precludes the problem of not having enough to fill whatever time or space is allotted. The opposite usually will be true. It will almost invariably be a problem of having too much information and not enough time or space, necessitating a high degree of selectivity.

Perhaps the most important reason of all is people themselves. For, human beings simply are not geared to big steps. They do not learn complicated subjects in one fell swoop, nor do they make large sweeping changes in their attitudes, beliefs, personalities, or behavior. The wise communicator, therefore, concentrates on getting his audience to do very small things, usually one at a time. And he sees his bigger successes as actually chains of smaller ones all linked together.

Answer to Question C: the audience.

Answer to Question D: begin at the end.

Question E: Give three reasons for making presentation objectives very small and narrow.

1. _____

2. _____

3. _____

5 Sometime, no matter how much time or space you have or what facilities are available to you, you could meet a situation whose outcome is hopeless before you even begin. The astute presenter, therefore, also gives conscious consideration to whether or not his objective is actually accomplishable in terms of the physical, emotional, and rational capabilities of his audience. If, for example, you are leading a person to make a decision, he must have the decision-making power or capability. If you are teaching him something, he must already be at a point where he is capable of learning that particular thing. It is silly to ask a person to buy something if he has no money (or credit) to buy it, to give up certain beliefs or allegiances, to feel something that he is incapable of feeling, and so on. A properly selected communicative increment, of course, could well be to change a person to the point where he would have a given capability.

Question F: Let's take a very simple example of incremental presentation. Assume that your task is to sell a $10,000 product or program to a company. We know that it would be rare that you could call on a prospect and get him to commit this kind of money in a single visit. So, the wise marketing representative will actually sit down and plan an incremental marketing program, probably a series of presentations. We've furnished you the increments below. Your task is to formulate a handleable and workable objective for each increment.

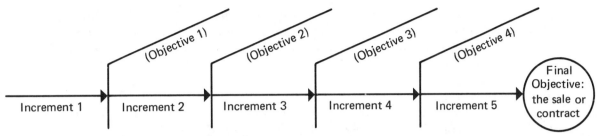

Increment 1 | Increment 2 | Increment 3 | Increment 4 | Increment 5 | Final Objective: the sale or contract

(Objective 1) (Objective 2) (Objective 3) (Objective 4)

Fill in the four objectives as indicated.

Education affords another example of the need for limited and accomplishable communicative objectives. Teachers have long known that they not only must divide their subjects into digestible segments, but that they must also be sure that their students are ready for each segment. Another good example can be seen in what it takes to sell or put across some of our more elaborate technology and ideas in business today.

Marketing people, for example, know that it is virtually impossible to close sales for millions of dollars' worth of equipment in the first ten-minute visit with a prospect. So, if they know their business, they split their marketing programs up into many smaller phases, each designed to accomplish a specific change in a prospect's thinking or actions. A brochure, for example, is designed with one very narrow purpose: to get some kind of reaction, such as an inquiry or telephone call, from the reader. The telephone call has a very narrow and specific objective, such as arranging an appointment. The first visit's objective in all probability will be little more than to get an invitation to come back for a longer discussion. The longer discussion's objective may be merely to get a very simple response from the prospect (audience) in the form of an invitation to submit a detailed written bid. The transmittal letter for the bid will have the very narrow objective of getting the prospect to read the bid. And the final visit's objective will have the also very narrow objective (albeit the most significant one) of finally getting a signature on a contract.

There are many other examples of how this incremental approach works. A manager who wishes to communicate successfully with his subordinates attacks his overall problem in the same way, if he is a good manager. He never loses sight of his general objective of continually motivating and guiding his subordinate. But his total success will be measured in terms of numerous individual, day-by-day achievements. Even a successful marriage or friendship is based on countless successful small interchanges that gradually build into the larger successful relationship. Time and again, in all walks of business, professional and personal life, wherever progressively successful communicative programs and relationships occur, you will find that this basic, incremental, problem-solving approach has been followed. And you will find, wherever individual human beings count long lists of achievements after their names, that those achievements were made by concentrating on each task in its turn.

Answers to Question E: (1) It reduces the big problem to meaningful and workable increments. (2) The amount of information and details present in most presentation situations dictates it. (3) Humans take small steps much more readily and easily than they take big ones.

Answer to Question F: (Paraphrases of the following ideas are, of course, acceptable.)

Objective 1: Make an appointment to discuss in more detail.

Objective 2: Even on the first visit with a product like this, you'd probably not be able to close the deal. So you'd still shoot for an intermediate action; probably something like getting an invitation to make a more detailed presentation.

Objective 3: Again, such a prospect would probably want a written bid or proposal; so in all probability your incremental objective here would be stated as, "to obtain an official invitation to bid or propose."

Objective 4: Although we're talking basically about live presentation here, there would quite likely be some written presentation in the series as well (which, incidentally could have its own set of increments). The objective could simply be stated as, "to get official acceptance of our program or product and an invitation to come in and sign the contract."

Objective 5: Finally, the big day. And here, too, if you carry your incremental communicating task through, you'll treat and plan this as a presentation in its own right, violating none of the rules. The stated objective will be, "to get the right signature on the contract."

6

In functional communicating, the way that you state your objective is extremely important. "Objective" is just another way of saying function, the whole reason for the existence of the attempt in the first place.

There are few exceptions to the rule that you should always:

Seek to state your objective in terms of audience behavior.

There is no need to adhere to a rigid format for actually writing the statement. It is a highly personal matter, and what may suffice for one presenter might hardly do for another. It should minimally include an accurate description of the desired audience response, almost without exception containing a verb with the audience as its subject. Thus, the statement, "To explain circuit X," is not a true objective, because it is not stated in terms of audience response. There is nothing to measure. How will you know when you have explained circuit X? The presentation will be open-ended. What you think is sufficient explanation will have no basis for comparison. Yet if you simply alter the statements and say, "To enable the audience to recognize circuit X when they see it," "To construct circuit X," or, "To differentiate circuit Y," you immediately give your objective a measurable quality. Every time an audience member "recognizes," "constructs," or "differentiates," you will have a "hit" on objective accomplishment.

Be explicit. If, for example, you want someone to know something that he does not now know, you should be able to describe exactly what it is that you want him to know. Frequently you may want to list things out in some detail. For instance, a history teacher's statement of objective could very well include his whole history text, although in all likelihood he would reduce that text to a symbolic statement or two. You should be able to see here that the importance lies in your point of view. What, exactly, is it that you want to get into the mind and being of the other person? What do you want him to know that he does not now know? What do you want him to feel that he does not now feel, to believe that he does not now believe, or to do that he has not, cannot, or will not do? When dealing with intangibles, such as feelings and attitudes, you still should seek to describe your objectives as concretely as possible. You will want to describe, as explicitly as you can, the attitude or feeling that you wish to produce. Do not be concerned with fancy words. Remember: you usually will be the only one who needs to see your objectives. You are merely seeking a meaningful understanding of your own goals. For example, you might simply say, "I want this person to feel as loyal, or as positive, or as upset as I do after I have finished." You know how you feel.

Question G: On the basis of what you have just read, complete the following two equations:

1. Objective = _____

2. Objective accomplishment = _____

7   A true objective almost invariably should be individual–oriented. Assume that the objective of a presentation is the following:

> *To make an audience understand the circuitry of component X.*

A member of the group arrives before the presentation starts, with a perfectly constructed circuit X, which he has designed and assembled himself. His performance indicates that he understands circuit X.

> *Objective: understand circuit X*
> *Audience behavior: understands circuit X*

For this person, although the presentation hasn't even been given, its objective already has been accomplished. Rarely will an objective be accomplished in every member of an audience. You are seeking individual responses most of the time. In the ultimate sense you are aiming for a total audience response, but each time an individual responds, the objective is accomplished. This may be quite disappointing for the inexperienced presenter who is usually seeking a total audience response. But experienced presenters always know that they are "working percentages" and that a single response out of an entire audience is in fact objective accomplishment.

Answer to Question G: Objective: specifically planned audience response. Objective accomplishment: the actual response.

8   If what you are seeking cannot be put into words on paper, the chances are very strong that it is not real enough to you for you to even bother going through any kind of concerted effort to accomplish it. There is a reality about putting your goals down in hardened form that will always be lacking in merely having a purpose in mind. Getting your aim out into the light of day, so to speak, helps you to see just how real and accomplishable it is to distinguish between your hopes and wishes, perhaps even fantasies, and what really can be done. It helps you to see weaknesses and revise, strengthen and narrow down to something that is realistic. A good objective, therefore, is always written down.

9 It's time now to link the idea of objective development with another important idea we've already covered.

Question H: Can you think of what that subject is? _____

We'll not make you turn the page for the answer to this one. It is "thesis." When you speak in terms of "objective," you're always talking about "what the boys in the back room are doing." That is, you're talking about your private planning processes, which you may or may not want to reveal to your audiences, depending on your strategy, need for leading them, and so forth. On the other hand, your thesis has to do with the actual content of your presentation with the actual words you speak to your audience. In a word, your thesis is your private objective "converted for public consumption."

As we've seen, thesis is the main idea or central thought of the presentation itself. It may be stated exactly like the objective, but usually it will not be; for example, a saleman's objective is to sell his product, but his thesis is that the product is better for his customer. An instructor's objective might be to train his audience in the use of a certain device, in behavioral terms—to enable them to operate device X. His thesis could well be: "By learning how to operate device X, you will be better qualified to advance in your job, since foremen must know how to operate it." Notice here that the thesis also is motivationally reinforced by linking it to a basic emotional channel. Intellectually it uses a cause and effect pattern. The outcome is behavioral.

All of the "rules" concerning how, when and where you state or develop your thesis as discussed in Segment 7 apply. For example, you may or may not wish to state you thesis until later in the presentation, leading your audience to a conclusion instead of telling them what it is in the beginning. You may wish to build and reveal your main idea gradually, giving portions of your thesis as you go and concluding with, "Now, you can easily see that it is necessary to convert data at its source if the entire system is to be efficient."

Question I: A _____ **is a private** _____ **converted for** _____ **.**

10 The next natural question that comes to mind is: "So, I've described this thing I want to accomplish to my own satisfaction. Now, how do I know whether or not I've accomplished it?"

The answer to this is that you must try to find out. This is done through a communicative device known as an action step, which every functional attempt to communicate should have. Action step is one of the last things done in the planned, functional idea presentation. For this reason, we'll cover it in detail a little later. The important thing to keep in mind at the moment, and while constructing any functional attempt to communicate, is that you will reach a point in your message when you must attempt to precipitate the outcome you desire, or to get some evidence that it has, can or will take place. When the time is ripe, you must appropriately force the issue. You

8

may force it gently, secretly, authoritatively, harshly, as circumstances dictate. But you must seek to know whether you have succeeded or failed. For, if you do not seek to measure, the whole philosophy of functional communication remains open-ended.

11 In summary, seek function above all else, and suspect yourself, any ideas, any interchanges in which it is not clearly identifiable. For, without it, what you are very likely to be up against is consumption, not communication.

Your quest for function then will dictate that you do something about it: namely that you develop sound specific objectives for your individual presentations. Then, too, your objectives will become the very heartbeat of your truly functional attempts to communicate. Like guiding stars, they will shed their light and touch upon everything else that you feel, think, do, and say. Your objectives will be the main guiding force for your own motivation. They will dictate the general mood, structure, and approach of your attempts and be the main criterion and measurement for the inclusion or omission of any specific item of information, detail, device or technique.

Finally, accomplishment of your objective is the only valid measurement of your success or failure. In short, a truly functional attempt to communicate is a process of objective development. It therefore should be fairly obvious that the initial statement of one's objective is far more than a matter of just putting some words down on paper, or simply having them in mind in some unverbalized form.

Answer to Question I: Thesis is a private objective converted for public consumption.

Check your headings:

1. A Different Turn of Mind
2. In Business to *Do* Something
3. The End is the Beginning
4. Think and Deal in Increments
5. An Objective Must Be Accomplishable
6. Think Behavioristically
7. Be Individual-Oriented
8. Always Write It Down
9. Convert Your Objective to a Thesis
10. You Must Seek to Measure
11. Summary

Summary Exercise: Fill in the missing word or words.

1. A function-oriented idea presenter thinks of himself as being "in business" to _____

_____

2. To do and accomplish something specific, it stands to reason that one ought to at least know

_____

3. In preparing objectives for functional idea presentations, the proper beginning point always is

_____

4. The key to any form of problem solving, and particularly to the task of presenting ideas to some purpose, is always to think and deal in _____ .

5. It is foolish and wasteful to ask an audience to do something that _____ _____ . Therefore, a key question to ask about any presentation objective is: "Is it _____ ?"

6. Good presentations invariably will be stated in terms of _____ behavior and will describe that behavior in very _____ terms.

7. There may be a hundred people in an audience, but the function-oriented idea presenter always will think in terms of _____ .

8. A good objective always will be _____ , because if it can't be so stated, it probably isn't sufficiently known.

9. Private _____ must be _____ for _____ consumption.

10. In the final analysis, the function-oriented presenter will always seek some _____ of whether or not he has actually accomplished his objective.

Scorable Quiz: Indicate true (T) or false (F).

1. As long as you have a good mental grasp of your presentation objective, there is no particular need to write it down. ____

2. Your objective and thesis always are identical. ____

3. A key to formulating a good incremental objective is to have a clearly articulated final objective. ____

4. Intangible objectives such as changes in feelings and attitudes cannot be stated or dealt with in measurable terms. ____

5. One should always try to compare the objective with the final results of the presentation. ____

6. A true objective invariably will be stated in terms of audience behavior. ____

7. Some presentations may merely consume time, which on occasion might be quite acceptable. ____

8. Success or failure of a presentation ultimately must be measured in terms of correct choice of idea structure. ____

9. If you cannot put your objective in actual words prior to beginning to compose your presentation, it would still be all right to proceed, since a valid objective might emerge from the structure you select. ____

10. At times, it might be perfectly acceptable to have secondary or alternative objectives in addition to your main one. ____

Answers to Summary Exercise:

1. Do and accomplish specific things
2. What he or she is trying to do
3. Where you want to end up
4. Workable increments
5. They cannot do . . . accomplishable
6. Audience . . . specific
7. Individual persons
8. Written
9. Objectives . . . converted . . . public
10. Measurement

Answers to Scorable Quiz (Each correct answer = 10%.) (1) F, (2) F, (3) T, (4) F, (5) T, (6) T, (7) F, (8) F, (9) F, (10) T.

ISBN 0-471-01630-6

EFFECTIVE PRESENTATION

Idea Support And Reinforcement

W. A. Mambert

Executive Director

National Communication and Education Association

Wiley Professional Development Programs

Advisory Editor

Steven C. Wheelwright

Harvard Business School

John Wiley & Sons Inc.
New York • London • Sydney • Toronto

Center for
Professional Development
University of Dayton
Dayton, Ohio

Library of Congress Catalogue Card Number: 75-39750

ISBN 0-471-01631-4

Printed in the United States of America.

10 9 8 7 6 5 4 3 2 1

Understanding Idea Support

PREMISE: That the capability to distinguish between ideas and their "parts," that is, between a thesis or main idea and the evidence or persuasion that supports it, is another key to the effective handling and presentation of ideas.

SEGMENT OBJECTIVE: That you clearly grasp the concept of idea support and thereby be able to effectively incorporate the right amounts and kinds of detail into your presentation structure.

Question A: Following is a list of ideas, data, thought segments, details, and so forth. In the columns provided indicate whether you think each item would be more likely to represent a major point in the outline of a presentation, or merely a subelement or division of a main idea. We know that some of the things listed could be construed as either; however, we are asking you to stick with just the two choices for the moment.

ITEM	MAIN IDEA	SUPPORTIVE ELEMENT
An analogy		
A statistic		
There are ten steps in effective presentation		
A joke		
A picture		
An exclamation		
The kinds of idea support		
A parable		
The order of acceptability		
Understanding idea support		

1 DISTINGUISHING BETWEEN IDEAS AND THEIR PARTS

As a knowledge of idea structure is essential to grasping an idea in its total form and relationships, so is an understanding of how to handle detail necessary in order to fully understand the individual parts of that idea and how they relate to the whole.

The primary capability that you must develop is to distinguish between an idea and its parts; to see the difference between a principle or concept, for example, and the evidence or persuasion that supports it: between a proposition and its proof, or simply between a main idea and the individual elements that compose it. You might describe this capability as a refinement of the basic ability to shift point of view beyond merely shifting from one person or major element of the communicative interchange to another, down to the smallest parts of any given idea.

1

Answers to Question A:

ITEM	MAIN IDEA	SUPPORTIVE ELEMENT
An analogy		✓
A statistic		✓
There are ten steps in effective presentation	✓	
A joke		✓
A picture		✓
An exclamation		✓
The kinds of idea support	✓	
A parable		✓
The order of acceptability	✓	
Understanding idea support	✓	

Question B: Give some synonyms for the term "idea support."

_____   _____   _____

_____   _____   _____

_____   _____   _____

2 IDEAS WITHIN IDEAS

One of the best aids to clear thinking and orderly construction of individual communicative messages is to think of any message or attempt to communicate as a succession of ideas within ideas. Once you have established a main structure for the idea you are handling, think of the details and subideas as building blocks. If you do the job right, each subidea will have its own structure, and the principle, form follows function, will carry through. Each element of your idea will be a distinctly functional module designed to perform one of the following supportive functions with respect to your main idea:

- *Define or identify part or all of the idea.*
- *Clarify part or all of the idea.*
- *Prove part or all of the idea.*
- *Strengthen or reinforce part or all of the idea.*
- *Generate, increase, or decrease mood, overtone, or undertone.*

The function and framework of each subelement in turn will have a clear, strong and meaningful relationship and connection within and to the main function and structure of your idea. In fact, once a good idea presentation is put together, the structures of the parts may merge so smoothly and imperceptibly that it might be difficult for anyone other than the builder himself to distinguish exactly where the main framework takes up and the framework of a particular part leaves off. This is as it should be, for a well–constructed idea is, in fact, an integrated entity.

Many writers and teachers refer more formally to the details and subelements that make up main ideas. Some call such details "forms of evidence," "rhetorical elements." "substantiation," "idea support," or "idea reinforcement." Others refer to them as forms of "figurative and literal reasoning," or merely group them along with the various forms of idea structure. It is equally valid to speak of them collectively as "idea enhancement" or "idea conduciveness." All such terminology is quite valid so long as the term used serves as an adequate linguistic symbol for the concept within the mind of its user, and so long as the user understands that they refer to the divisions of main ideas or to the units of expression that make up a total message.

Like the basic forms of idea structure, the basic forms of idea support (evidence, persuasion, proof, and so forth) are quite classic. Although knowing the technical names (and they all do in fact have names that are well known) is obviously desirable. it is not absolutely necessary to be able to catalog them in order to be adept at their use. But it always is helpful to be able to identify what you are doing. Any English composition, speech, or rhetoric textbook will give you these "official names." Because they are so commonly available, we are not going to take up valuable space defining each here. We will, however, give a fairly complete list and suggest that if you do not know what each of these terms means, you obtain a good textbook and become familiar with them. The basic forms of idea support (in the rhetorical sense) are:

Alliteration	*Example*	*Oxymoron*
Allusion	*Exclamation*	*Parable*
Analogy	*Explanation*	*Paradox*
Anecdote	*Facts*	*Pause*
Anthropomorphism	*Humor*	*Personification*
Anticlimax	*Hyperbole*	*Play on words*
Antithesis	*Idiom*	*Punctuation*
Apposition	*Illustration*	*Puns*
Assertion	*Imagery*	*Quotations*
Association	*Interrogation*	*Repetition*
Colloquialism	*Irony*	*Satire*
Definition	*Litotes*	*Simile*
Description	*Metaphor*	*Statistics*
Diction	*Metonymy*	*Synecdoche*
Emphasis	*Narrative*	*Testimony*
Enigma	*Onomatopoeia*	*Understatement*
Evidence	*Opinion*	*Words*
Exaggeration	*Overstatement*	

Come to a place in your own mind where you can see how each of these forms would function as an idea within an idea, thereby supporting a main idea by defining, clarifying, proving, strengthening, reinforcing it; or by generating a certain mood, overtone, or undertone with respect to that idea.

Question C: Let's take one of the forms from the above list and work with it a moment. Take "anecdote," for example. What is an anecdote? And how would an anecdote function as a sub-idea within a presentation?

Question D: Let's try another. What is an "example"? And how would it function as an "idea building block"?

_____

_____

_____

_____

_____

_____

Answers to Question B: (1) Evidence, (2) Persuasion, (3) Substantiation, (4) Proof, (5) Idea reinforcement, (6) Rhetorical elements, (7) Idea enhancement, (8) Subelements, (9) Subideas, (10) Subpoints, (11) Idea building blocks, (12) Ideas within ideas.

Answer to Question C: An anecdote is a short narrative, e.g., a story exemplifying an idea. It normally is relatively short. Since its role almost always would be to clarify an idea, it hardly ever would be a main point in a presentation. More than likely, you would make your point and then "tell a story" to illustrate or clarify the point you're making.

Answer to Question D: Literally, "example" means "something taken out of a larger quantity to show the quality of all." Examples rarely prove anything. Their main purpose is to clarify ideas. Rarely, too, would you ever make an example a main point in your main idea structure.

3 HOW TO SELECT EFFECTIVE "IDEA BUILDING BLOCKS"
Only you, of course, can be the final judge of whether your message includes the right amounts and kinds of evidence, persuasion, and other subelements. There are, however, certain minimum criteria by which any form of idea support should be judged, and which will help you to greatly improve your capability to choose effective "idea building blocks." These criteria follow:

- *Is it, of course, functional? Does it actually contribute to your main objective and advance your idea presentation closer to that objective?*
- *Is it relevant and applicable? Does it have a valid relationship to your main idea?*
- *Is it clearly stated and perceivable? If it isn't, no matter how relevant it is, no one will know it.*
- *Is it appropriate and consistent? Does it fit the occasion, overall mood, and level of formality?*

4

- *Is it efficient? Does it prove, reinforce, and substantiate in as quick, concise, and concrete a way as possible?*
- *Is it subjective or objective? Either is valid, but you should know whether what you use is, for example, a fact or an opinion and from whose point of view it is used or given.*
- *Is it in the right position and proportion? Have you picked not only the right amount and kind of evidence, but is it presented at the best time and place in your overall idea flow as well?*
- *If you use a fact, statistic or similar evidence, is it accurate and reliable?*
- *Finally, always ask yourself what the alternatives are. Is an anecdote or example better than a fact or figure? Is a metaphor or simile better than an assertion? Is a rhetorical question better than a statement?*

> *NOTE . . .*
> *Your capability to select and deal with idea support grows out of your basic ability to handle detail as shown by our "tree" analogy in Segment 3. It also will have direct bearing on your data-gathering and notetaking ability which we'll discuss in Segment 18.*

In summary, the foregoing, of course, merely demonstrates the forms of idea support. Where do you get a repertoire of specific content for applying the concept in constructing specific messages and idea presentations? There is only one source. It can only be a product of your own personal exposure to the actual possibilities in the rational, physical, and emotional realms of real life. Your best source of specific idea support is undeniably an eclectic, peripatetic self-education—your own intellectual, sensory, and emotional development which no one can do anything about but you—which, in turn, is nothing more nor less than a refinement of your own intellectual freedom.

Question E: Let's review something we've already discussed. What are the three dimensions in which all human communication takes place?

_____   _____   _____

4 THINK MULTIDIMENSIONALLY
This is where the existence of these three dimensions starts to get really important. For, although the verbal is the means by which ideas are conceived in the mind, (in the rational dimension), and is an extremely versatile medium for conveying ideas: it is only one of many possible ways in which ideas can be transmitted to and perceived or experienced by your audience. The truly professional presenter will invariably think in terms of all three dimensions. He will think not only in terms of the three, but in terms of the almost limitless variations and possibilities for communication that exist within each.

Did you ever stop to think, for example, that we have five senses through which ideas and feelings can be perceived? But go a step farther. There actually are thirty-one possible combinations of the five senses. Go yet another step and you will find that there are four hundred and fifty-six permutations or possible combinations and sequences in which the human senses can perceive. This is how multidimensional your thinking can really be. The multidimensional-thinking idea presenter always will ask such questions as:

> *If I can state this idea in words, cannot I also state it, reinforce it, clarify it, and enhance it with not only other words, but with other sights, sounds, tastes, sensory feelings, or even odors?*

But now, add to this the emotional dimension of human communication, such things as a person's fears, anxieties, psychological needs for recognition, belonging, and so forth, and you suddenly have opening up to you a repertoire of communicating channels that you may never have considered before.

Answers to Question E: The rational, the physical, the psychological.

All of these things come under the heading of idea support and reinforcement in the context of this course. Your key will be to continually think multidimensionally.

Question F: Following is a list of ideas that might be found within a presentation. Create for each a means, other than verbal, by which each might be expressed to or experienced by an audience.

Item	Multidimensional Expression
1. A new solid-state pluggable circuit	
2. The need for new traffic lights	

3. A new food item	
4. The importance of their attention	
5. How a new model typewriter works	
6. A great distance	
7. A statistic	

Item	Multidimensional Expression
8. The illustration of the inductive/deductive methods in Segment 8	
9. A microsecond (a millionth of a second)	
10. The statement, "I am friendly"	

Answers to Question F: These are some ideas. There are, obviously, many possibilities. Compare your ideas with ours.

1. Try just getting a sample and passing it around.

2. Try showing a picture of a child just run over by a car.

3. Try passing around samples.

4. Try anything: e.g., fire a gun, stand on your head, pound the rostrum, "accidentally" kick a trash can, or just be silent for a moment.

5. Get one and let them have "hands on" experience.

6. Try a string with knots in it.

7. This is a good candidate for graphics; e.g., a bar graph; or, how about a handful of sand if it's a huge statistic.

8. Try using live people and strings.

9. Just tap a pointer on a table and say, "That's about a second: can you conceive of one million things happening in the time it took me to tap this point?

10. Would you believe a smile, or even passing through the audience shaking hands.

Summary Exercise: Answer briefly.

1. What is "idea support"?

_____

_____

_____

_____

2. What primary guiding rules should you follow when thinking about idea support?

_____

_____

3. What are the major functions of idea support?

_____

_____

_____

_____

4. What are the three basic forms or dimensions of idea support?

_____   _____   _____

5. In total, how many variations of idea support are there among the three dimensions?

_____

6. Go back, now, to the list of the forms of idea support given earlier in this segment. List below
   the ones that you do not know or understand as forms of idea support, and take the time to
   look them up in an English textbook or dictionary.

_____   _____

_____   _____

_____   _____

_____   _____

Scorable Quiz: Fill in the missing word (or words).

1. The three basic dimensions of idea support are _____ ,

_____ , and _____ .

2. Into what dimension of idea support would an analogy normally fall?

_____

3. Into what dimension of idea support would a rhetorical question normally fall?

_____

4. A shocking photo probably would come under the heading of _____
support as opposed to physical/sensory support.

5. How many combinations of the five senses are there? _____

6. An exaggeration for effect is called a _____ .

7. What is something taken out of a larger quantity to show the quality of all?

_____

8. The basic guideline for selection of any form of idea support must be: Does it

_____ ?

Answers to Summary Exercise:

1. By our definition here, the term distinguishes between main idea and subidea or similar element within the body of a presentation. Outlinewise, the supportive element rarely will be a major heading, sometimes a second-level heading, but usually a lower level heading.
2. There are at least two. They are:
   a. Form follows function.
   b. Think multidimensionally.
3. a. To define or identify part or all of an idea
   b. To clarify part or all of an idea (e.g., often by restating in a different way or dimension)
   c. To prove part or all of an idea
   d. To strengthen or reinforce part or all of an idea
   e. To generate, increase, or decrease mood, overtone, or undertone
4. Rational, physical, emotional
5. Trick! There may be a finite number, rhetorically (rationally or verbally) speaking; but when the physical and emotional are added, with their infinite variations, nobody could actually fix a number. (Sorry.)
6. Don't forget to do it!

Answers to Scorable Quiz: (Each correct answer = 10%.) (1) a. Rational, b. physical/sensory, c. psychological/emotional, (2) Rational, (3) Rational, (4) Psychological/emotional, (5) Thirty-one, (6) Hyperbole, (7) Example, (8) Perform a function.

Understanding Physical/Sensory Communication

PREMISE: That the physical/sensory dimension offers the idea presenter a great many often–overlooked communicative devices and that this dimension should be taken into account by the purposeful idea presenter.

SEGMENT OBJECTIVE: That you become more sensitive to and aware of the possibilities for reinforcing your idea presentations through the physical sense and strategic manipulation of the physical environment of your presentations, and that you know the basic principles that apply in such use.

Question A: Name ten factors in the physical environment of a presentation room that you think might affect your presentation.

1. _____   6. _____

2. _____   7. _____

3. _____   8. _____

4. _____   9. _____

5. _____   10. _____

1 A VAST AND VARIED POTENTIAL

The average person tends to ignore the true communicative potential in the simple fact that people are physical, as well as rational beings, and that they live in physical environments that profoundly affect everything that they think and feel. The strategic communicator, however, has a heightened sensitivity to these facts. He recognizes that the human sense, the physical instincts, and the physical environment of his presentation in the broadest sense offer a vast and varied storehouse of possible communicative devices that can contribute to the accomplishment of his communicative objectives. He also recognizes that he must, in fact, not only be aware of the physical aspects of his presentation, but he must invariably do something about it. That is, the physical doesn't "just go away" if it is ignored. There, in fact, are many physical things that actually will work against the effectiveness of a presentation, will function as barriers if some attempt is not made to control them. In many cases, it will be a case of control or be controlled. Thus, what you really are seeking is to take the physical aspects of your presentations out of the realm of happenstance as much as you possibly can, to make them work for you, instead of against you, or merely allowing physical factors to be there.

Question B: There is a principle, or maxim, which we have stated and referred to several times in preceding segments. It applies here, too. Can you think of what it might be?

_____

_____

_____

Answers to Question A: Here are a few of the most obvious. You may have thought of others. Compare yours with ours.

1. Time of day	9. Auditory distractions
2. Air quality and ventilation	10. Visual distractions
3. The lighting	11. Your attire
4. Seating arrangement	12. Your location and visibility to the audience
5. Room decor	13. Your voice
6. Comfort of audience seats	14. The length of your presentation
7. The acoustics	15. The audience's hunger, thirst, and so forth
8. The temperature	16. The weather

Answer to Question B: "Form follows function," what else? The guiding rule still must be to evaluate whether or not whatever you do or don't do contributes to your stated presentation objective.

2 A VERY SPECIFIC HIERARCHY OF STEPS

Remember, we're talking about a very deliberate, strategic approach here, not about merely taking a quick glance around the presentation room. And, we're not talking about the presentation room only, but the whole range of physical and sensory dimensions.

The amateur or novice presenter tends to think randomly. The professional thinks strategically. He actually goes through mental checklists in his planning. He establishes "lines of defense," knows when to "fall back" on his next line, thinks in terms of nullifying adverse effects, compensating for weaknesses, and so forth. And what we're telling you is that you ought to start thinking this way, if you don't already do so. What does this strategic approach consist of? It is a very specific hierarchy of steps, a mental checklist, if you will, that you can and should go through to establish the most effective physical and sensory reinforcement for your idea presentation. We're going to give you this checklist in a moment, but before we do, to get yourself thinking in this direction, and before reading on, answer . . .

Question C: Make your own checklist. In the order of utility, what should a presenter think about with respect to the physical dimension of his presentation?

_____

_____

_____

_____

_____

_____

_____

_____

_____

_____

3 **WHAT ARE THE STEPS?** **(Answers to Question C.)**
   1. Start at the very beginning. Ask the question, "Is it physically possible for me to communicate in this instance (be it the whole presentation or any part or specific device within it)? Can the message be seen, heard, and so forth?"

   2. After establishing the most fundamental possibility, the next question to ask is: "How can I increase the probability that the message will be perceived in the most effective possible way?" Or, "How difficult is it for the message to be perceived?"

   3. Then, identify anything in the physical environment that will work out and out against you.

   4. Then, eliminate any such counterproductive or negative factor that you can. Just get rid of it if it is at all possible.

   5. If you cannot eliminate a negative influence, the next line of defense is to neutralize it, equalize it, or compensate for it. This can be done simply by increasing your vocal volume, covering up distractive material, increasing or decreasing the light, and so forth.

   6. Consider also the possibility of converting what may seem to be a barrier into a useful device or channel for conveying or reinforcing your message.

   7. Your next line of defense is to take the offensive. Now observe the physical aspects and ask: "What is already present in the physical environment that can effectively serve as a planned communicative device?" For example, chairs are usually present. You can control their location. You can control the lighting. You can control where you stand. You can control almost anything in a room that you want an audience to perceive or not perceive.

   8. Your next line of defense, after nullifying, using, or seeking control of everything in the physical situation that you can, then would be to seek other physical or sensory devices that can be created or brought into the situation to fulfill specific sup-

portive roles; e.g., pictures, actions, gestures, dress, colors, shapes, visual aids, and so forth. This, in fact, is the point where you'll start thinking about visual aids.

9. And, of course, the dictum, "form follows function," always will adhere. The only justification for including any sight, sound, or other sensory stimulus in any functional presentation is the identified function it serves. Anything else is so much impedimenta.

What you are really seeking, in a nutshell, is your own assurance that any environmental feedback or sensory perception that your audience receives along with your idea, if at all possible, supports and strengthens that idea; that the sights, sounds, odors, or whatever else become as much a functional part of your presentation as you can possibly make them.

The possible environments and locations, of course, may vary greatly. We obviously cannot tell you what would be best in all situations. The only thing we can do is to help you get yourself conditioned to taking a total look at the physical environment of whatever presenting situation you find yourself in . . . and at least consider what the possibilities for physical reinforcement of your ideas are. This consideration alone will place you in a far better position than most of your contemporaries, and most certainly in a far better strategic position.

4 UNDERSTANDING SENSORY COMMUNICATION

Knowing or being reminded of how the human physical drives and senses function also can help you to use the physical dimension more effectively and efficiently. First, there are the basic human drives or what psychologists generally call the primary-motive forces. These revolve around such basic bodily "survival" requirements as hunger, thirst, rest, respiration, sex, evacuation, and so forth.

There is an old saying that, "the head can only absorb as much as the seat of the pants can stand." And this really puts the finger on one of the basic principles involved here. We call it the "point of intolerance," and it is something that unthinking or preoccupied idea presenters often forget. It's simply the fact that:

Any basic human physical need, when it reaches a certain point of discomfort, can interfere with the perceptions and can even cancel out perception completely.

Therefore, as basic as this may seem, and as aware as any presenter might be presumed to be of it, it can be forgotten with dire consequences to the effectiveness of presentation. The practical application is to have a constant awareness of these fundamental needs, and to make sure that they are kept satisified for your audience well above the point of intolerance. The alert instructor will not teach too long without a break. He will be aware of changes in temperature and ventilation, the hour of the day, the hardness of his audience's chairs, and so forth. The way to a human being's heart truly is not only through his stomach but also through his nose, his lungs, his rest and comfort, his bowels, and anything else connected with his instinctive physical being, comfort and survival.

5 BEYOND THE BASIC NEED

The strategic professional communicator goes a step beyond the mere satisfaction of the basic human drives, beyond merely keeping them above the point of intolerance. A drive such as hunger or thirst, for example, once it is primarily satisfied and ceases to function as a barrier to communication, can often then begin to be used as a tool of idea reinforcement. A meal hour, for example, might be used for a presentation, or refreshments might be served at a presentation break, with the planned intention of reinforcing the ideas under discussion. Remember: one of the functions of idea support is to generate or increase a desired mood relating to the idea.

Question D: What is the point of intolerance?

_____

_____

_____

_____

_____

The thinking can be carried yet a step farther. For not only is there a kind of crossover point between tolerance and intolerance, but once you cross this point, some basic human drives exhibit a kind of hierarchy of additional communicative possibilities. Hunger is an excellent example. You can start by making sure it hasn't reached its point of intolerance. You then can use it motivationally, say, by serving coffee for the mere purpose of refreshment. If you serve the coffee in paper cups at the back of the presentation room, you say one thing and have one mood. Move the "break" to a pleasant reception area and you move up the range a little. Appoint the refreshment area with fine furniture, serve the coffee with good Danish pastry and in real china cups and saucers, and you reach yet another level of mood and emotional appeal. Now, dress a waiter in a fine martial uniform, provide cloth napkins, have the coffee served, instead of buffet style, and you move up yet another level.

So, you see, a simple thing like a cup of coffee, whose use emerges out of the basic human hunger or thirst need, actually presents a whole range of idea support possibilities. The human need for pleasurable sensations, sex, rest, and so forth, can be seen in similar spectrums by the astute communicator. The very walls of a presentation room can be made to say, "Listen, we have your best interests at heart." "We know you are a very important audience," "Don't hurry away; stay; let us 'close a deal' with you after the presentation," and so forth.

Answer to Question D: The point of intolerance is that moment or place at which a basic human need or drive such as hunger, thirst, fatigue, evacuation, and so forth will interfere with the sensory or rational perception of an audience member.

Question E: When we say that a basic human need or drive presents a "hierarchy" of communicative support possibilities, what do we mean?

_____

_____

_____

_____

_____

6 USING THE FIVE SENSES

It is well established that ideas very often are better grasped, are more meaningful, and are retained longer, when they are expressed and perceived at purely sensory levels as opposed to through the written or spoken word. It is one thing, for example, to merely be told that a stove is hot and another to be burned by it. Or which makes the greater impression: the taste, odor, and sight of food, or a verbal description of it? As he does with the basic human motive forces just described, the multidimensional-thinking communicator regards all of the human senses as possible tools for stating and reinforcing his ideas.

Answer to Question E: What we mean here is that all human drives emerge from a very primitive physical survival need. But, once this is satisfied, a drive can often be ministered to "above" the point of intolerance in a way that has a motivational connotation, an emotional appeal.

As a strategic idea presenter there are five important phenomena and principles that you should be aware of in order to effectively deal with the human senses. They are:

- *Sensory statement and reinforcement*
- *Sensory distraction*
- *The necessity for simplicity*
- *The importance of duration*
- *The path of least resistance*

7 SENSORY STATEMENT AND REINFORCEMENT

This principle is the foundation for many specialized fields of communication such as the graphic arts, illustration, audio-visual aids, "human engineering," typography, "motivational packaging," merchandising, and management. The premises involved are that:

- *It is possible (and often necessary) to state an idea as a purely sensory experience.*
- *It is possible (and often necessary) to strengthen or intensify the perceptive efficiency of a given human sense avenue or to reinforce it with one or more of the other senses.*

There are two principles that underlie the use of the human sense to state or reinforce an idea. These are:

- *Same-sense reinforcement*
- *Other-sense reinforcement*

Question F: What is "same-sense reinforcement?"

_____

_____

_____

_____

_____

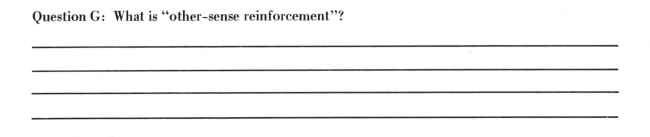

Question G: What is "other-sense reinforcement"?

_____

_____

_____

_____

_____

Normally, in any specific communicative act, one of the senses is used more than the others. This is known as the "primary sense avenue." For example, in reading, sight is the primary sense. In speech or conversation, hearing is the primary avenue with sight playing a secondary, though important, role. "Same-sense reinforcement" is the doing of whatever is necessary to optimize the effectiveness of the primary sense. One of the most common examples can be seen in the showing of movies. Seats and lights are obviously arranged to increase the effectiveness of the viewer's sight sense avenue.

The same would apply if the primary sense were hearing, whatever is done with sound to reinforce the hearing would be same-sense reinforcement (this would include both omission and inclusion of sounds). Visually, same-sense reinforcement is the "first line of defense."

"Other-sense reinforcement" is the intentional use of any combination of the senses to even further enhance the perception process. For example, if an idea is seen (as efficiently as possible) and also is heard—or perhaps felt, or even tasted or smelled— there is an additional strengthening of the intended effect. You actually multiply the perception, making it stronger and more perceivable.

Hearing, for example, can reinforce seeing and vice versa. Touching can reinforce seeing, and so on. And the sequence often will be significant, too. You may want someone to see before touching, to hear before seeing, and so forth. Therefore, what you really have available to you in the realm of the five senses are not five, but a composite of many sense avenues. And you should actually plan when, where, and how you will combine and use them to state or reinforce specific ideas within your presentation.

Answer to Question F: "Same-sense reinforcement" is the inclusion or omission of something in the primary sense avenue being used to perceive an idea. If hearing, for example, were the primary sense avenue, additional sound or the elimination of any sound would be same-sense reinforcement.

Answer to Question G: "Other-sense reinforcement" is the use of an additional sense avenue to support the primary one. A picture, for example, could reinforce hearing about something, as could a taste, a touch, or an odor.

8 SENSORY DISTRACTION

This is the other side of the sensory reinforcement "coin." It means that the human sense can function in a negative way. The effect is similar to that of the point of intolerance when dealing with the basic human drives. For example, it is very difficult to listen to two speeches simultaneously. You cannot read two things at the same time. But, even further, if you are using your eyes to read, anything else that makes you use that sense avenue will interfere with the primary activity. A flashing light, a dirty page, bad type or design, narrow margins, a bright patch of unrelated color near the printed page, movement or activity that tends to draw the eyes away from their main task or make them work harder than necessary, all will tend to diminish the efficient use of your sight. The same applies to listening. If you are listening to a speech, another sound would be the first thing to interfere with the effectiveness of your hearing and so on. The prime concern of the aware communicator, therefore, must always be toward keeping the main channel, (the main sense avenue necessary for his particular attempt), as open and free from interference as possible. The average person admittedly does this to some degree, but the really effective communicator works at it.

Other sense-avenue distraction can be a little more elusive. Frequently, for example, sound can interfere with sight without one really being aware that the interference is taking place. Sight can interfere with sound, even with taste and smell. You can easily test this phenomenon. Try serving someone a glass of milk with a little tasteless, odorless, green or brown vegetable coloring mixed into it. Although the taste of the milk is in no way affected, you will invariably see that the sight can indeed interfere with the taste. In practical application, the professional speaker, for example, knows that the sight of an iridescent necktie or dress can interfere with the listening ability of his audience, that their sense of touch can affect their listening, as can distracting impedimenta or the sight of another person on the platform with him. Similarly, movement other than that of the speaker at a podium might cause an audience to let their eyes interfere with their ears. These things seem obvious, yet most of us ignore all but their most apparent and most pressing effects.

9 THE NECESSITY FOR SIMPLICITY

No matter how advanced our minds might be, at the purely sensory level we are still quite primitive. It is very easy to confuse our senses. Thus, simplicity is an overriding necessity in all sensory communication. Amateurs tend to say too much to the senses at one time. One researcher has estimated that in an average day in the life of a member of modern society, he is assailed with some two thousand individual appeals to his senses. By sheer volume alone, is it any wonder that many of us sometimes become confused as to exactly what our eyes and ears are sensing? The human senses simply are not capable of efficiently perceiving or reacting to highly complex stimuli.

The human senses do not adapt well to abrupt changes either. It is just as important to have a singular, cohesive, homogeneous pattern and pathway in the physical realm as it is to have the same kind of pattern in the intellectual structure of the idea. Sharp shifts in sound, design, color combinations, type styles, and basic formats have an effect of discontinuity that usually is detrimental to the overall flow and movement toward an objective. Kaleidoscopic effects have a certain value when selected intentionally as the best devices for the occasion. But, when inadvertent, they rarely effectively serve the interests of the function-oriented communicator. Variety may be the spice of life, but too much of a condiment at the wrong time and place can also ruin the taste.

Question H: What is the principle of duration?

---

10 THE IMPORTANCE OF DURATION

When you are dealing at the purely sensory level, you also are talking about something that is a momentary or transitory stimulus. That is, something happens and then stops happening. For example, if you see something and then turn your back, you no longer see it. Once a sound is heard, you no longer hear it. When you taste something, you no longer taste it after it has been eaten. Thus, in addition to being loud enough or visible enough to be heard or seen, in order to be comprehended, something must be sensed long enough.

Duration may not seem very important. It is true that you can look at a picture in a book as long as you want in order to comprehend it. But remember, printed matter is only one of many media. And, even there, the length of time that something is in view can be significant. Take, for example, an illustration that appears on a page with perhaps only a line or two of a rather lengthy description of it, with the rest of the description appearing on another page. In effect, the reader is not seeing the illustration long enough. If the book designer does his job right, he will design and lay out the copy and its accompanying graphic support so that both come as close as possible to being exposed together for the most advantageous length of time. There are, of course, some limitations. Sometimes space does not permit what would be the best layout.

When you move into the various areas of live communication, the matter of duration becomes even more significant. For now, whatever is seen, heard, or sensed truly will pass out of range, perhaps never to be sensed again. It is very simple to test the significance. Simply recall or look at a scene or segment of any live audio-visual presentation, and ask yourself the question, "Did I see that long enough for it to register in my mind; did I really comprehend it?"

Answer to Question H: The principle of duration means that any sensory experience must be perceived long enough for it to effectively serve its supportive purpose.

Question I: What is the principle of least resistance?

---

11 THE PATH OF LEAST RESISTANCE

Human beings are among nature's laziest creations. They invariably take the path of least resistance when it comes to using their senses. Thus, any appeal to one of the senses increases its chances of gaining attention and response when that appeal is as easy, convenient, and comfortable to sense and respond to as possible. Perhaps the best example of the application of this fundamental principle can be found in the "impulse buying" techniques of retail stores. Research has proven that items sell better when they are displayed at eye level or where it is convenient to feel or fondle them. But there are other applications. We've already pointed out that a printed page can appear either comfortable or uncomfortable, affecting the reading in much the same way that a certain kind of chair can affect listening. The relationship here with such ideas as simplicity and duration and distraction is quite obvious. In fact, the idea of comfort and convenience is merely a refinement of these ideas. If something is simple and comprehensible and gains the attention of the senses, it probably is comfortable and convenient. Regardless, the planning communicator will always ask himself the fundamental question:

> *How can the sender, the message, and the recipient be placed in the most convenient and appropriately comfortable circumstances?*

But, the fact that he is a multidimensional thinker will automatically lead him to also ask:

> *Would it suit my purposes to make it inconvenient or uncomfortable for my correspondent to sense and respond, perhaps, at this time?*

Answer to Question I: The principle of least resistance is that the human senses are basically lazy and will do what is easiest for them to do first, e.g., listen to a distracting sound as opposed to concentrating on a speaker's words.

12 SUMMARY
Perhaps you have never viewed the physical dimension in quite this way. In fact, the idea of such manipulation might at first seem almost too calculating, even too shifty for your tastes. Such a reaction is not uncommon, especially if these things are taken out of the context of the other things said here. Remember, therefore, that any manipulation in the act of communicating must be based upon, and grow out of, the context of the other things said here. If any part of your perspective is missing, although a given manipulation or device might still accomplish an objective, the net effect will be distorted in some way.

Even many professionals remain oblivious to the fundamental principles of human communication. Consider, for instance, the well-trained salesman who has bad breath or dirty teeth. The truth is that if he has these problems, he is not as well-trained as he might like to think. Few of us like to talk about such things. Yet, suppose that this person is standing very close to you as he explains his product. Can you say that the sight or smell will not have some effect upon the sound? In all probability it will interfere, even if your reaction is at an unconscious level. His logic may be impeccable, but all your instincts can tell you is to get out of the sensory range. In fact, you may even have a negative emotional or intellectual reaction to what you hear. Similarly, you might sit next to a person at a business luncheon, or in an interview, whose logic and intellectual presentation of an idea per se are above reproach. Yet, all you can concentrate on is the gravy spot on his necktie, or the stifling smoke of his cigar, or the noise he makes while eating his soup. Again, you yourself may not be fully aware of why you are not listening to him and, perhaps, why you ultimately make a certain value judgment of his idea.

The main difference between the average, subjective, unaware person and the strategic, functional communicator is simply that the later thinks about and consciously plans for these contingencies. You may not be able to control all of the sense avenues all of the time, but at the very least you can be aware of the possibilities. If nothing else, you can eliminate a great many of the potential sensory distractions, nullify their effects, or make them inert. "Awareness," thus, once again arises as the main watchword.

NOTE . . .
When it comes time for you to prepare so–called visual aids for your presentation, what we have discussed in this segment constitutes the underlying principles of all such material.

Summary Exercise: Here is a two-part flowchart that will graphically summarize this whole segment for you. Based on what you've just read, select the right captions from the list and write them into the flowchart boxes.

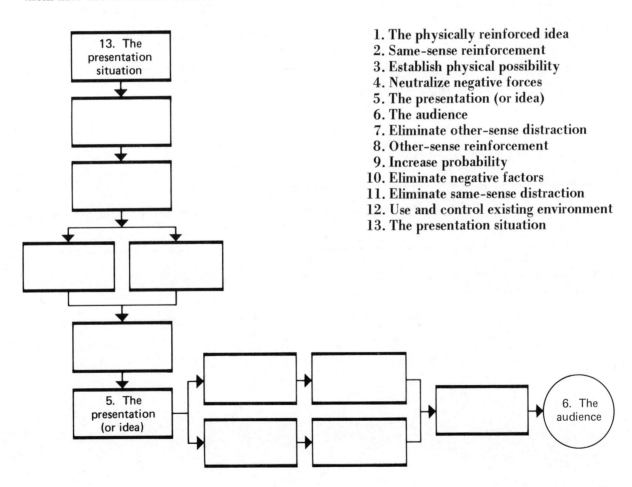

1. The physically reinforced idea
2. Same-sense reinforcement
3. Establish physical possibility
4. Neutralize negative forces
5. The presentation (or idea)
6. The audience
7. Eliminate other-sense distraction
8. Other-sense reinforcement
9. Increase probability
10. Eliminate negative factors
11. Eliminate same-sense distraction
12. Use and control existing environment
13. The presentation situation

Scorable Quiz: Give the term used in the text to denote each of the following.

1. The principle that ideas can be stated or strengthened through use of the physical senses.

   _____

2. The principle that the human senses are basically lazy and will normally do what it is easiest for them to do.

   _____

3. The process of doing something that will nullify the negative effects of something in the physical dimension.

   _____

4. Making sure at the outset that it is fundamentaliy possible for a presentation to be seen or heard.

   _____

5. Interference with the functioning of one sense by another sense.

   _____

6. Interference with the functioning of a sense by something else affecting that sense.

   _____

7. Making sure that something is perceived long enough.

   _____

8. Speaking and showing something simultaneously.

   _____

9. Arranging the presentation situation for maximum effectiveness of the primary sense in use.

   _____

10. Taking something that may interfere with communication and using it as a tool or channel of communication.

    _____

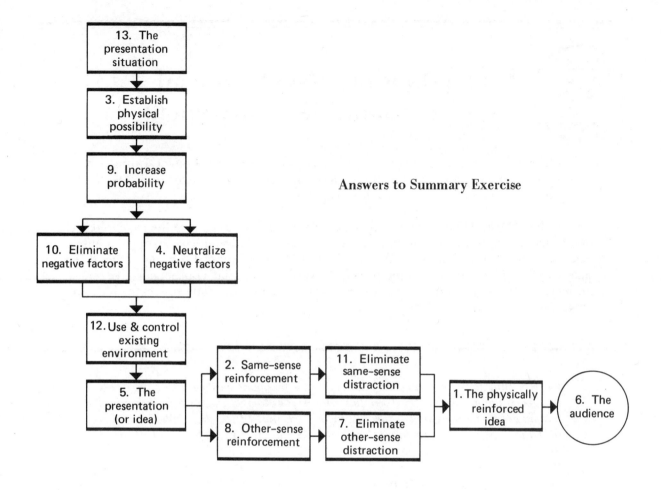

Answers to Summary Exercise

Answers to Scorable Quiz: (Each correct answer = 10%.) (1) Sensory statement or reinforcement; (2) The path of least resistance; (3) Neutralizing, equalizing, or compensating; (4) Establishing possibility; (5) Other-sense distraction; (6) Same-sense distraction; (7) Duration; (8) Other-sense reinforcement; (9) Same-sense reinforcement; (10) Converting barriers to channels.

Understanding Psychological And Emotional Reinforcement

PREMISE: That all presentations have an emotional/psychological dimension, whether ignored or taken into account, and that this ought to be taken into account and used as idea reinforcement.

SEGMENT OBJECTIVE: That your sensitivity to and awareness of the psychological emotional dimension of communicating be increased. That you have an open-minded, eclectic view of this dimension; that you will be better equipped to avoid some of the major pitfalls involved in working in this dimension; and that you be able to exercise an increased personal control over its various aspects as they relate to making idea presentations.

We feel that it is necessary to issue you a warning as we begin this segment. It is very dangerous to try to reduce the psychological makeup of individual human beings to a single interpretation or "school of thought." We warn you that there is, in fact, no one school of psychological thought or set of interpretations that has the whole answer to how the total human psyche functions. Be cautioned that you do not become a disciple of one psychologist or another. Rather, gather what information is available, keep your mind open for more data. Say not, "I have found the only truth about a human being," say rather, "I have found one truth."

1 CONSTANTS

As we said in Segment 4, there do seem to be some things that remain relatively constant in the human communication situation, and therefore, in the presentation situation. We can at least begin with this as a base for further understanding.

Question A: What did we say were the "constants," that is, those factors that can pretty much be assumed to be always present in the communicative (presentation) situation?

1. _____

2. _____

3. _____

4. _____

5. _____

24

Answers to Question A:

1. There are always only "two" people in your attempt to communicate: you and the "other person" (no matter how many other people there are).
2. You can almost invariably assume that the other person is self- or egocentered; that is, that he is interpreting the world and all of its happenings in terms of self.
3. You can almost always assume that the other person not only interprets in terms of self but will act, consciously or unconsciously, to defend or protect that self. Such a person is ego-defensive.
4. You'll usually be able to assume that the other person is basically unaware of the complete range of his own reactions at the moment, although he may very well be able to give a pretty good objective evaluation of his own actions if asked to do so after completing those actions.
5. And, of course, the three dimensions always are present.

2 PSYCHOLOGICAL SUPPORT

At this point in our course you grasp the concept of idea support; you know how the concepts of rational support and physical/sensory support grow out of it. The next logical step—the third dimension—is the one for which we use the terms "psychological" and "emotional" as interchangeable descriptives. You already should have a good idea of how psychological reinforcement functions. The basic principle is that:

> *It is possible (and usually necessary) to clarify, strengthen, or support ideas through the human emotions. By discovering what particular emotional forces motivate a given person at a given time, and linking your idea to those forces, you in effect give that idea added momentum and effectiveness.*

Supportively speaking, the emotional, or psychological, is parallel to the rational and physical in both tenet and application. The building of emotional appeal into your message must be measured against the same criterion of functionalism. The emotional also exhibits a point of intolerance, similar to the physical. And, of course, sound and thorough analysis forms the base for any really effective use of emotional or psychological appeal.

It should be pointed out here that some teachers and writers urge that an emotional approach to communication be totally eschewed, which may be all well and good in the classroom or on the pages of a textbook. But, when you become involved in a real situation, it just doesn't work that way. This course does not espouse a purely emotional approach. Such would be as erroneous as a purely rational or physical one.

The wiser approach is to allow for how people feel—what they hate, love, need, believe, do or don't do—on the psychological level. It is infinitely more prudent to contend with these feelings as an existing part of the communicative milieu and, like anything else in that milieu, to attempt to structure and control them as much as possible. For, perhaps even more than the physical, there are very few instances where the emotional will not work against you if you do not take it into account. Your first step is to become aware of and view the psychological forces present within all persons as a potential addition to your repertoire of idea support tools. The second is to remain aware that the use of these tools must conform to the same basic rules that apply to the use of any form of idea support.

Question B: What watchwords are to be used in dealing with the psychological dimension?

_____   _____   _____

We caution you also that it takes considerable skill and maturity to arrive at a valid evaluation of what motivates a person emotionally. It takes even more skill and maturity to effectively build an emotional appeal into your attempt to communicate. Nevertheless, if you can show or tell a person how believing, learning, accepting, or acting upon your idea can fulfill his psychological needs, your chances of success will greatly increase. And, most of the time you will have to show or tell him without letting him know that you are showing or telling him. Thus, "subtlety" always will be a watchword.

In reality, as with the idea structures and forms of idea support, the basic aspects of the human psyche haven't changed much in thousands of years. The fact is, man probably hasn't evolved much further psychologically than where he was at the end of the paleolithic era, or even earlier, although there is no record before then (roughly 13–14,000 years ago). You'll find much of what modern psychologists call by new names expressed in religious or philosophical terms back as far as man has kept records. But we'll stick pretty much to the modern terminology. Again, we should warn you that just about anything we, or any other psychologists, say about the human psyche will find dispute or debate somewhere, from some school of thought or other. So, start with what you already know about your own and other people's psyches, add this material, and continue to eclectically gather new knowledge.

Let's begin by studying the following chart. It shows one way of looking at the psychological dimension. We know that human beings have many instinctive and socially acquired psychological drives, motives, and forces which govern their behavior and their responses to attempts to communicate with them. Further, very few people are completely governed by a single psychological drive or motive. Most of us have a multiplicity of psychological forces working within us at any given time, and the "mix" changes with the situations we find ourselves in.

You have probably already observed that in life in general, and in the actual presentation situation in particular, it is difficult to determine exactly where the emotional leaves off and the physical and rational begin. Sometimes these dimensions actually will appear indistinguishable from one another.

Nevertheless, when it comes time for you to analyze a specific audience in order to plan and prepare a presentation of an idea to them for the accomplishment of a specifically stated objective, you will want to bring all of your knowledge of human nature to bear in order to come up with the most reasonable possible assumption of what is the best form of psychological support that you can give your idea.

Question C: Indicate true (T) or false (F).

1. Each individual is governed by a very specific motivating force. _____

2. Because of the accelerated pressures of our modern times, the human psyche has been forced to evolve faster. _____

3. It is very easy to differentiate between the physical, rational, and psychological contents of a situation. _____

Answers to Question B: (1) awareness, (2) maturity, (3) subtlety.

26

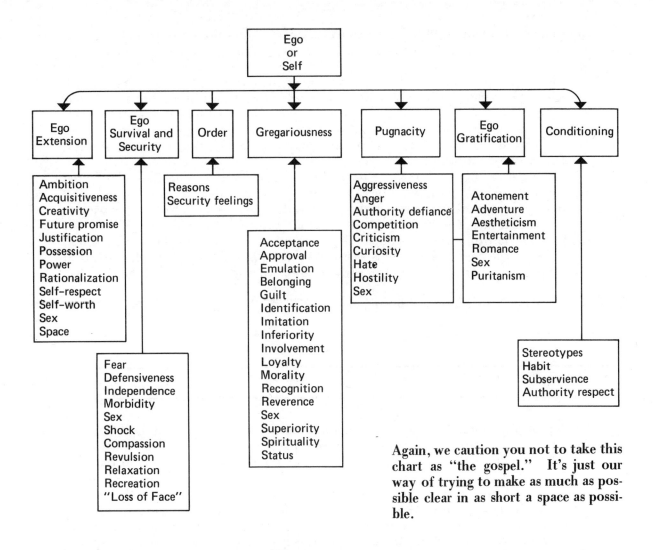

Again, we caution you not to take this chart as "the gospel." It's just our way of trying to make as much as possible clear in as short a space as possible.

Answers to Question C: (1) F, (2) F, (3) F.

Question D: What is the difference between the "herding instinct" and "gregariousness"?

_____

_____

_____

3 GREGARIOUSNESS

What we've done in the preceding chart is to try to come up with some general categories that describe the major aspects of human behavior and reaction in terms of basic psychological drives and needs. It's pretty safe to begin with the general concept of ego, or self, and build upon this. "Self" is the person in the total sense. The next question is: What does the self do and feel as a being—how does it respond to its environment, the people and stimuli in that environment, and attempts to communicate with it?

We know that almost all human beings have some form of this basic drive, which is really a grouping of drives, impulses, and needs as we view it here. Some psychologists call it the "herding instinct." What it really means is that humans most definitely exhibit some kind of need to seek the company and acceptance of other humans, to have a sense of involvement. This instinct may manifest itself in a variety of ways, some of which we've listed.

It is, for example, the rare person who is not influenced by a need to be accepted by someone, to seek, as it were, the approval of other members of a real or imagined group. Some psychologists also call this the "need for belonging." Notice that we say, too, a "real or imagined group." That is, it isn't necessary to think only in terms of organized or institutionalized groups. A person might very well be the only person in his "group" and merely be seeking acceptance or approval from other hypothetical members; e.g., what is "moral," or perhaps even what is acceptable to the Divinity.

Question E: What is the source of human guilt?

_____

_____

_____

Guilt probably falls best under this general heading for the simple reason that it is a form of self-measurement against which one might measure one's own behavior in order to become acceptable. (Acceptable to whom?) It could be a clearly distinguishable institution such as a spiritual concept or religion; it could be the group of "all the good and righteous people who ever existed." A person may need to feel that he is a-toning for his guilt. Sometimes he may need to feel less guilty. Usually, if a message helps him to fulfill such needs, that message gains in strength. Sometimes, an idea presenter actually can establish guilt in the idea recipient's mind and then also give him the means to eliminate, or atone for, that guilt. The classic example of this is the free merchandise that arrives in the mail. You are supposed to feel guilty if you then don't do what you're asked in return.

The status seeker, too, for example, is seeking approval of his "herd," as is the person who identifies with, imitates, or emulates others whom he presumes are more acceptable in some way than he is. Thus, we also have the classic "inferiority complex" or its other version, the "superiority complex." There are few more effective ways to gain affinity and action than to let a person know that he is not inferior, that he counts, and that he is important and worth something. On the other hand, there may be times when you would want to intimidate him.

Usually, the older a person gets the less likely is he to seek overt forms of belonging and group acceptance. He is more likely to play to an image or hypothetical "accepter within his own mind."

Generally speaking, if you can find out by whom or by what a person needs to be accepted or to whom or what he is loyal, or from what group he is seeking approval or a sense of belonging—and then show him how accepting or acting upon your idea will gain him this approval or acceptance—your idea will gain considerably in strength and acceptability.

Answer to Question D: There is little if any difference between the "herding instinct" and "gregariousness." They both describe the basic need of humans to be in the company of other humans.

Answer to Question E: Probably the major cause of guilt is a sense of failure to comply with the standards of approval or acceptance by the group, or "herd," whether that group is formally institutionalized with a stated code of behavior, or whether it is merely a mental image or imagined group.

4 PUGNACITY

It certainly should come as no surprise to you that human beings also exhibit a certain paradoxical or enigmatic nature. They are drawn to group themselves together. What do they frequently do as soon as they do get together? Right! They fight! They become aggressive and pugnacious toward each other. They compete. They try to seem better than one another. They hate each other. They become angry and hostile toward each other (which, incidentally, usually emerges from a fear of one another).

Look at the sublist under this heading on the chart. Hate, anger, or any other form of hostility can be directed by the skilled communicator. If you can just find out what a person hates or is hostile toward (e.g., inefficiency, disorder), or, give him something to be hostile toward, then show him (very subtly, of course) how to vent that hostility by accepting your idea, your idea's impact and chance for acceptance increases. Sometimes, by showing someone how he can defy authority or "beat the system," you can reinforce your idea.

So, pugnacity is that group of human drives and instincts that makes people aggressive or hostile toward each other, toward "outsiders," toward nature and being. And audiences can be caused to believe, learn, and accept by appeals to this pugnacious drive. The significant thing is that human pugnacity (in most of its forms) need not always be negative. A skillful communicator can direct this drive toward the elements, confusion, disease, evil, social injustice, inefficiency, disorder, and similar deleterious influences. Directed and controlled anger also is a powerful force. Give someone something to fight for that is meaningful to him, and you'll persuade, convince, prove, sell, and teach/present more effectively.

Question F: What is a "hypothetical" or "image" group?

_____

_____

_____

Answer to Question F: There need not be a group of actual people from which someone is seeking approval or acceptance. One can be seeking the acceptance in terms of some ideal or morality. In this case, the ideal represents what the "ideal" people would do.

5 EGO SURVIVAL

The need to survive merges almost indistinguishably from the physical to the psychological. We not only instinctively seek to survive physically by breathing and so forth, but each of us also must survive as a "self." Each of us has a concept of his own self which must survive and be defended. "Loss of face," for example, can be as serious to the psyche as loss of life itself. The need for a sense of independence is present in all of us, which is in effect a strengthening of the chances of survival for self. You can see connection to the survival drive in such life activities as selection of certain brands of food or cigarettes or going to church. Survival includes living longer and having thoughts and ideas live on after death; it includes health, children, safety, financial security, and fear. It ties directly into such mundane business motives as saving time and effort, automation, safety devices, coffee breaks, or letting audiences out early because what these things really do is afford more "life" time. This is what recreation and relaxation also do. They give more "self" time.

Similarly, when you shock a person, you in effect cause him to identify with the possibility that the same thing could happen to him and his chances for survival. The same effect is gotten through "morbid curiosity" and appeals to compassion. They give a person a chance to identify with his own survival needs in the feeling that "there, but for the grace of God, go I."

Everyone, of course, doesn't go around consciously planning within himself how to survive. Actually most of the drives reside within the unconscious mind. As we've said, most people are unaware, most of the time, of their own true attitudes and feelings. They not only wouldn't admit them to someone else; they rarely admit them to themselves. An excellent example is the commercial airline, which stresses—not the safety features of its aircraft and services—but the comfort and status that one gains by going first-class; the food, the sophisticated people who use the airline, etc. Nevertheless, the real thing that everyone is concerned with is: "Will it get me up there, stay up there, get me where I'm going, and get me back to the ground safely?" The public is quite willing to work along with the airline advertisers and push their fears as far back into the recesses of their minds as they can. What the advertisers really are saying is, "Safety is such a foregone conclusion that we concentrate on the comforts, the conveniences, and the status that air travel affords you." So in a real way, they are subtly using the survival drive by *not* stating it. This is an example of how subtle the presenter's use of all these drives should be. If a message can effectively build in an undertone of real physical, or ego, survival the presenter can be reasonably sure of not only getting a hearing for it but of retaining attention throughout his presentation—and come that much closer to obtaining the audience response he is aiming for.

Question G: How can a coffee break be connected to the "survival" drive?

_____

_____

_____

Question H: How might an appeal to a person's compassion be connected to the survival drive?

_____

_____

_____

6 EGO EXTENSION

We've said that all humans are egocentric and that they'll usually go a step farther and be ego-defensive. We can go even a step farther. For, most of them also have an almost instinctive need to extend themselves, which also manifests itself in a variety of ways. Ambition and getting ahead are forms of ego extension. You should also be able to see the relationship here to certain forms of the need for approval, to belong, and so forth. Acquisitiveness, the need to possess goods, material, and property, are frequently forms of ego extension, as is the seeking of personal power.

One psychologist has referred to this kind of need as the "territorial imperative," meaning that we all have some kind of need for additional "ego space." We create things in order to extend ourselves. We do a great variety of things in order to increase our own senses of self worth—often also because of our belonging needs.

We may even extend our needs to possess and extend our egos in terms of "possessing" other people by making them extensions of ourselves. We often want to feel that our ideas are our exclusive property—parts of ourselves. Few of us do not fear, hope for, or desire what the future will bring, for this, too, is a promised extension of self, as well as a promise of survival!

It probably is the ego extension drive to acquire and possess space, goods, property, possessions, and knowledge (including the fear of loss of same) that propels millions of people into debt. It drives men away from their families to "moonlighting" jobs. It drives us up the ladder of success and sometimes down the road to ulcers. It is a measure of a person's worth among his neighbors, his friends and associates—and often even a measure of his value to his god. He also measures himself by what he possesses. Money is by far the most potent aspect of the possession drive, mainly because of its universal capability to bring other possessions and power. Any message couched in terms of money saving, acquisition, or protection almost automatically gains a hearing, and almost certainly will evoke action.

Question I: What is the probable relationship between the need for ego extension and the need for belonging?

_____

_____

_____

_____

_____

Question J: How can ownership of a car or home be construed as a form of ego extension?

_____

_____

_____

Answer to Question G: A coffee break gives more "life" time, thus allowing a little longer time for the ego to live or survive under its own control. Recreation and entertainment could do the same sort of thing.

Answer to Question H: Most of us identify with the less fortunate, the suffering, and so forth. We're all involved with mankind. It's partially the "there, but for the grace of God, go I" sort of thing. A message appealing to compassion frequently gains strength because it calls attention to that involvement, and we, at least in part, assure ourselves that we're helping ourselves or perhaps preventing the same misfortune from befalling us.

Answer to Question I: Approval from someone else tells us that we "belong," too. It thus enlarges our own sense of self.

Answer to Question J: Possessions often are expressions of the self-concept; not only autos and homes, but clothing, titles, status, big offices, college degrees, *ad infinitum*. The more self-owned things, the more self there is.

Question K: What is ego gratification?

_____

_____

_____

7 EGO GRATIFICATION

You ought to be seeing the interrelationships of almost everything listed in our chart. You could say, for example, that everything in it is a form of ego gratification—ego extension, ego survival, and so forth. We're just trying to give some comprehensible order to the discussion. So, there is a category of drives, or urges, under this heading. Everyone seems to have a need for pleasant sensation. For example, one of the beauties of being human beings is that we can appreciate beauty. Dig deeper, and you'll find this drive directly related to a basic need for pleasurable sensations. This, in turn, is connected to the basic survival drive. For, what pleasurable sensation says to a person is that he is "getting more life for the money." It thus often will make sense to support an idea with some form of beauty or possibility for pleasurable sensation. Some practical examples include interior decoration, architecture, automobile design, and clothing manufacture.

Similarly, everyone enjoys comfort, entertainment, luxury, simply as relief from the restraints and serious matters of life. This is why occasional tasteful humor, refreshments, breaks, and pleasant environments make presentations turn out better. It is one of the prime reasons why it is a good idea to end a presentation sooner than scheduled. No audience ever rejected a presenter on the basis of being released a little earlier than they had expected. On the other hand, there usually will be a slight tinge of resentment at being held later than planned—unless of course, they themselves demand an "encore."

To our knowledge, folly has never before been listed as a communicative tool, but indeed it can be one. A clown, for example, has no difficulty in communicating with a child. Sometimes, sheer nonsense furnishes pleasurable sensations that can bring the other person to a point where the serious business can begin, or the serious business can be conducted under the guise of folly. And, after the business is over, there may be no better way than to revert to nonsense—perhaps for no other reason than to take his attention away from something at the right time.

"Scratch the surface" of this ego-gratification instinct, and you'll find yet other possibilities. There is, for example, an apparent connection between enjoyment and guilt and atonement. Some people actually like to suffer. Sometimes helping them to suffer, or to feel a sense of joint suffering, may be an excellent way of getting them to accept an idea.

Anyone who has studied American history is familiar with the Puritan ethic, which essentially says that a thing or accomplishment is not worthwhile unless it is the result of hard work. Puritanism is not an instinctive social drive. However, in Western culture, through social conditioning it has acquired many of the qualities of the instinctive motivating force. It is not as widespread as it was a decade or two ago. More and more people are espousing the "work smarter, not harder" theory of the pragmatist. Yet, even today, the practical communicator can do worse than convince his hearer that the idea is not the result of superficial thought or effort but of a pronounced struggle—thus, making it worthwhile.

Answer to Question K: The human ego has a voracious appetite for indulgences and pleasurable sensations. It is basically selfish and self-satisfying. Messages that minister to this ego-appetite usually have great appeal. Ego-gratification also is undoubtedly very closely related to survival itself. The more surfeited the ego, the more secure it feels.

8 THE NEED FOR ORDER

We don't have to say very much about this, because we've already devoted several learning segments to the approaches and techniques that emerge out of it. That is, you can view the need for rational idea structure as emerging at least partially out of a human emotional, as well as practical, need. Human beings do have a psychological need for order. They need to arrange things. They resent chaotic or random conditions or ideas. They actually seem to prefer believing and accepting well-ordered lies than chaotic truths. So make sure that even your lies are well structured, and you'll stand a better chance of having them believed.

9 CONDITIONING

In all of this, we're also still creatures of habit. We can actually be made to believe, do, or act solely on the basis of the fact that we've been habituated in a certain way. We are, for example, inherently submissive (as well as pugnacious) by nature. A communicator usually is automatically a leader or authority figure or can establish himself as one. The skillful one takes advantage of this, but in such a way that he does not go against other strong drives such as anti-authority feelings. Appeals to laws, morals, rules, mores, governmental authority, policy, and the like fall within the scope of the basic human need to obey someone or something. Sometimes a stern, parental tone is all it takes to get someone to act on an idea. Perhaps, all you have to do is give an order.

Then there are our stereotypes. "Stereotype" refers to any fixed image, impression, idea, response, or way of thinking. It reflects a form of conditioning. Usually, a stereotype evolves as a result of exposure to or association with an idea or way of thinking over a period of time. A stereotype can be either negative or positive. A good example can be found in the attitude of some people toward the drinking of beer as "cheap." More serious examples can be seen in such things as racism and attitude toward women or minority groups. One of the classic examples of stereotype development is the way in which movie stars and other celebrities generate fashion styles and fads. Whole industries have risen and fallen almost solely on the basis of stereotypes. The objective communicator should regard them as unreliable, preferring to reach his own conclusions on the basis of clinical evaluation. Yet, they remain a valuable tool for reaching people. Find a person's stereotypes, identify your idea with one or more of them, and you, in effect, speak his language.

Question L: What is the personal unconscious?

_____

_____

_____

10 THE CONSCIOUS/UNCONSCIOUS IDEA

The total human psyche (self or ego) also can be viewed as a composite entity consisting of the "conscious" and the "unconscious," with the various drives, instincts, and needs (that is, the psychological dimension) arising out of both the action of each and the interaction of both.

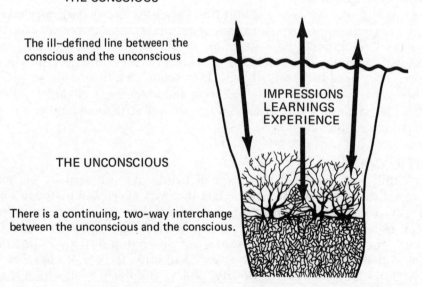

THE CONSCIOUS

The ill-defined line between the conscious and the unconscious

IMPRESSIONS LEARNINGS EXPERIENCE

THE UNCONSCIOUS

There is a continuing, two-way interchange between the unconscious and the conscious.

The human unconscious is very much like a deep well. Many experiences, impressions and learnings, both recent and past, are stored in it. Almost all of its contents are accessible and frequently come forward, regardless of how old they are. In addition, the unconscious continually exerts an influence upon conscious behavior. There is evidence that the unconscious is even more expansive and inclusive than the conscious. Tests in hypnotic regression, for example, indicate that the details of incidents in a person's past life, from earliest childhood to the present, are stored somewhere beneath the conscious surface of the mind.

Somewhere within the psyche of the individual person there seems to be an almost limitless repository of remembered information and experiences. This we call the "personal unconscious."

Labeling the unconscious as a "subconscious," as some psychologists do, implies that it is "under" or separate and apart from something; that is, from the conscious. The evidence is much stronger that it works with the conscious—that it exists and functions during consciousness and wakefulness, as well as during sleep, dreaming, the hypnotic state, or any other psychic suspension of conscious activity. One might say that the unconscious never sleeps or lies dormant. It is more accurate, perhaps, to say that it lies in wait.

Generally speaking, more recent experiences seem to be stored in the ranges nearer to the conscious level, and older experiences seem to seep to the deeper reaches of the psyche. There also seems to be a rather ill-defined area between the unconscious and conscious where various thoughts, feelings, impulses, and responses bounce into and out of the conscious and the unconscious. Nearly everyone has had the "on the tip of my tongue" experience. Some thought or idea momentarily flits through the consciousness, almost penetrates to the brain's speech center and then is forgotten. Where did this thought come from? Where did it go? It was already in the mind or it would not have evidenced itself. Did it then somehow leave the mind? No, it probably came out of and receded·back into the unconscious.

All of the things that a person knows or has experienced (through the senses, intuitively, rationally, or emotionally), but of which he is not aware at the moment, are contained somewhere in his unconscious. This may even include things which may have been perceived without one's realizing that he has perceived them. For example, one might consciously remember having been in a certain room. Suppose that room had a clock in it that was not even consciously noticed. If the eyes had seen the clock, the unconscious has a record of the time, and under the proper conditions that time is retrievable. This has been proven with subjects under hypnosis.

The unconscious exerts a continuing influence upon the conscious. Its contents frequently behave as if they were conscious. Its host of obscured experience, impressions, feelings, images, and thoughts (despite the fact that we do not consciously "know" them) are nevertheless present and influence both our thinking and behavior. Take the person, for example, who starts to do something or go somewhere. Suddenly, he has forgotten what it is that he has intended to do. Yet, he continues in the direction of doing it. He is guided by his unconscious mind. Then he remembers what he had set out to do. It is his unconscious that has prompted him.

It is possible to see the unconscious at work, particularly in the observation of neurotic behavior. Often, this is the only way to explain the frequently totally irrational and disconnected behavior of patients in terms of both speech and action. The unconscious actually takes over and supersedes the conscious.

The simple truth is that the conscious mind exercises, at best, a tenuous control over the total psyche. Most people do not realize just how weak so-called will power really is.

Answer to Question L: The personal unconscious is that composite mental storehouse of experiences, impressions, and learnings stretching back over a person's whole lifetime and retained within the deeper reaches of the mind not normally in a state of awareness, although triggerable and recallable almost at any time.

Question M: When does the unconscious mind function?

_____

_____

_____

Probably the most significant aspect of the influence of the unconscious to the analytical idea presenter, is that he ought to be able to recognize when certain behavior in his audience may actually be under the control of that person's unconscious mind. "Trigger" events can spontaneously focus the contents of the unconscious into the overt behavior. Frequently, such events are caused by the senses. For example, a certain odor recalls a whole series of events which a moment before was not present in the conscious. One enters a room for the first time and senses that he has been there before. The sight of, perhaps, a certain chair, or wallpaper, a forgotten tune, the ticking of a clock, or the velvety feeling of a drapery suddenly recalls a whole chain of "subliminal" (below the level of usual arousal) experiences and impressions hitherto "forgotten," but not really forgotten, merely sorted; for the unconscious forgets nothing. Actually, it is a quite normal function of the conscious to store information in this manner. Because its job, as the modern computer operator would say, is to remain "online," in a "real-time" mode, and processing current incoming data. If this did not happen, the conscious mind would become a hopelessly confused and jumbled clutter and would not be able to perform its primary waking tasks.

This concealed recollection can have several important functions in waking life, and can actually be controlled and directed by the idea presenter towards specific objectives.

The unconscious also is the source of "body language," kinetics and proxemics, which are quite important to the presenter who is interested in interpreting audience feedback, which we'll discuss in detail in a later segment.

It should be obvious that we could go into much more detail and depth in talking about the psychological dimension of making a presentation. But what we've said here ought to give you a good start in developing your awareness of its importance. Make no mistake, too, what we're talking about here is rarely effectively built into an idea presentation on a very overt, obvious level.

Psychological reinforcement cannot be used lightly or capriciously. Its effective use requires great subtlety, finesse, empathy, and understanding of the complexity of human nature. The successful use of emotional appeal often actually will require the omission of certain things. For example, the speaker who comes across as pompous to his audience is almost lost before he begins. The presentation filled with first person pronouns tells the other person, in effect, "You don't count . . . I am the one who is important . . . you must look at this situation from my point of view." An aura of condescension is equally deleterious, as are insincere compliments or praise, jokes about special-interest or minority groups, and anything else that in any way thwarts or opposes any of the basic motivating forces present in the audience.

Answer to Question M: The unconscious mind is always awake, functioning, and influencing a person's behavior and reactions. It's even awake while the conscious mind is sleeping.

11 SUMMARY

It should be fairly obvious that we could have said much more about the psychological dimension here than we have. But if we've gotten you thinking about it and more aware of its presence in any presentation situation, this is a good start. We recommend that you become more of a student of human nature by becoming aware of of the psychological makeup of the people who compose your audiences.

Summary Exercise: Following is a list of devices and ideas that you might find included in a presentation of one kind or another. Refer to the chart given earlier in this segment as necessary, and see if you can identify which psychological or emotional needs they would be most likely to appeal to or fulfill.

Item	Emotional Need or Drive
1. A cigarette with less tar	
2. A "top salesman" award	
3. An order to "please be seated"	
4. Possession of privileged or "secret" information	
5. A product used by a top sports figure	
6. A paid vacation for two	
7. A promotion to manager	
8. A "free" sample in the mail along with a request for a contribution	
9. A sales contest	
10. An appeal for 100% participation in the United Givers' Fund	
11. Why you purchased this Professional Development Program	

Scorable Quiz: Circle the correct answer or answers.

1. A company that mails free merchandise to you and requests you to do, buy, or send something to them is probably playing on your need for or sense of
   a. power
   b. possession
   c. guilt

2. The personal unconscious is
   a. your basic need to belong
   b. a repository of almost everything that has happened to you
   c. always functioning simultaneously with your conscious

3. The ownership of property and artifacts probably comes under the heading of
   a. ego extension
   b. ego defense
   c. pugnacity

4. A fixed image or habituated way of responding to something comes best under the heading of
   a. gregariousness
   b. conditioning
   c. ego extension

5. Arousing an audience's curiosity probably is an appeal to their
   a. need for order
   b. gregariousness
   c. pugnacity

6. Sexuality or appeals to the sex drive comes best under the heading of
   a. ego gratification
   b. ego extension
   c. pleasurable sensation

7. All humans
   a. will exhibit most of the psychological needs and drives
   b. will vary greatly in the kinds and intensity of the various needs and drives that they exhibit
   c. when grouped together, will tend to subvert their own needs and drives in favor of the common needs and drives of the group

Answers to Summary Exercise: These are only a few of the many possible questions we could ask here. And, there are undoubtedly answers other than these that could be given, simply because there is so much overlap among the human emotions and psychological drives. The main purpose here is not to be exhaustive, but to help you get into the habit of thinking in the psychological dimension as you plan and make your presentations.

1. Most likely, this would come under the general heading of the need to survive and feel secure (and, of course, fear connected with same).

2. This could be an appeal to the basic pugnacious impulse, particularly competitiveness. But it also has a pretty obvious connection to the need for recognition and ego extension.

3. This would almost definitely be an appeal to conditioned behavior. Politeness often is a form of conditioned behavior, but may also be a form of ego defense in the sense that one might obey rather than take the chance of standing out and being called to task to defend oneself.

4. If you're let in on a secret, you're obviously in the "in" group. You really belong and are accepted. Also, the possession of privileged information is a form of power and thus extends the ego.

5. Advertisers call this "transfer." That is, if a person already popular and accepted by many people uses something, it could be thought that anyone else who uses it will have the same acceptance. It's a form of identification, also.

6. This may be ego gratification, but could also connect to survival as any recreation does. If it's a prize, you've got all of the pugnacious and gregarious aspects of it, too.

7. A promotion, with or without pay increase, is definitely an extension of the ego, also clearly a form of acceptance and approval.

8. As pointed out in the text, this is basically an attempt to establish guilt in you if you don't do what's requested in return for the free gift.

9. Clearly an appeal to the aggressiveness drive, with a little acquisitiveness thrown in for good measure (for there'll surely be a prize for the winner).

10. An appeal to the need to belong with a little guilt for icing, since you don't want to be the one who caused your office or shop not to have 100% participation.

11. We'll never tell!

Answers to Scorable Quiz: (Each correct answer = 10%.) (1) c, (2) b and c, (3) a, (4) b, (5) c, (6) a, b, and c, (7) b.

Analyzing The Specific Audience/Situation

PREMISE: That it is necessary for an idea presenter, based on his general knowledge of the three–dimensional aspects of any audience or situation, to perform a detailed analysis of the specific audience/situation for a given presentation.

SEGMENT OBJECTIVE: That you become able to meaningfully and purposefully gather sufficient information about a specific audience/situation to formulate a realistic and accomplishable presentation objective.

Question A: What will the following items of information about a person be most likely to tell you about him as an audience for your presentation?

1. Age _____

2. Sex _____

3. Education level _____

4. Occupation _____

1 INTRODUCTION

A successful idea presenter invariably exhibits audience awareness, an understanding of human nature, empathy, or some other way of denoting that he really takes the time to try to understand each of his audiences. To be effective, you must have a clear picture of the actual people to whom you are addressing yourself, and the actual conditions under which you will do so. As we've tried to show you, this analysis has deeper roots in a basic awareness of the genesis of human behavior, drives, needs, and so forth. For, you must not only be aware of these constants, but you must be aware of and be able to establish a rapport with the specific interests and motives of each particular audience. Further, as a sensitive and aware presenter, you also will be receptive to on–the–spot feedback from both your live audience and the conditions and environment in "real time."

To establish this analytical base, there are some very specific questions that you can ask about an audience/situation. You can think of this segment as your presentation audience/situation checklist. What do you do with the information after you get it? Hopefully, you use it, first as a foundation for the formulation of your stated presentation objective. Then, you continue to use it as an operating base for your actual interchange with your audience.

40

We can divide our checklist questions into the following categories:

- *The Audience*
- *The Situation*

Answers to Question A:

1. A person's age, treated as an item of analytical data, can tell you many things about him; for example, his level of comprehension, the experience base that he brings to your presentation, the kind of vocabulary he might understand, and what he relates to.
2. Men and women differ in their interests, motives, and responses. Some drives and reactions overlap; yet, an alert presenter consciously considers what the sex of his audience might tell.
3. A person's education can tell you many of the same things his age will tell you. It also will tell you what ideas he may already be familiar with, what he can comprehend, what thinking methods he employs, or how he is likely to evaluate your idea.
4. Occupation, like education, tells you much about a person's experience base, his interests, motives, style of thinking, and so forth.

Question B: As you analyze the specific audience/situation, you will always be looking for that single motivating drive, or force, that binds this group together as your audience on this occasion. True _____ False _____

2 THE AUDIENCE: WHO?

The simple, three-lettered word "who" takes in a great deal of territory and provides much information when asked analytically and exhaustively about a given person or persons. Following are some useful applications of this word:

- *Who does he appear to be?*
- *Who does he think he is?*
- *Who does he say he is?*
- *Who do you think he is?*
- *Who is he in reality?*

Face the fact that people rarely are what they appear to be on the surface. What they appear, think, say, and really are usually all are different matters. Egocentricity is considerably more refined than merely interpreting or reacting at the more or less instinctive levels described. Consciously or unconsciously, people usually have formed rather elaborate images of themselves, which they try to build and uphold both in their own and in others' eyes. Some do not realize that they have these self-images. Some are afraid to reveal themselves. Others are intentionally devious. In any case, it behooves the potential communicator to determine as accurately as possible exactly what each person in his audience thinks of himself.

Question C: Most of the people in an audience will have a quite clearly defined self-image and be quite aware of it. True _____ False _____

There is no particular reason why you should try to dispel a person's self-image, or "put him down." You probably, in fact, will want to help him maintain his view of himself throughout the course of your interchange with him. For, remember, if you become a threat to him, he is quite likely to "turn you off." But you yourself are un-realistic if you do not try to see through to the real person. Allow your first impressions to prevail, if you like. But form them as objectively and realistically as you can, always including the possibility that you could be partially or totally wrong. Then begin to probe, subtly, carefully, tenderly, to see if the evidence matches the first impression. Generally speaking, a good audience analyst will exhibit a fair degree of suspicion and skepticism—even toward his own senses.

Answer to Question B: True. This sounds a little like our earlier statement about people being too complex to be thought of as having a single motivating drive. But, in the case of a group of poeple, they very well could have a psychological, rational, or physical need in common.

Answer to Question C: False. You can usually assume the opposite. Not only are most self-images complex, but usually the individual doesn't consciously know what his own concept or image of his self is (or at least he doesn't have it clearly defined, or think about it very often).

Question D: Generally speaking, a good presenter will do whatever he can to dispel his audience's self-image in favor of what he, the presenter, has to say. True _____ False _____

3 WHAT DOES THE AUDIENCE EXPECT FROM YOU?

What does he say or think he wants or needs, as opposed to what he really wants or needs? There is an old saying that the majority of people are walking around with needs and desires that they don't even know they have—just waiting for a good idea presenter to come along and help them discover those requirements.

What powers does he have? Can he do what he says or thinks he can do? Most important does he or can he have the decision-making power to do what you are trying to get him to do?

What groups does he belong to? If, for example, he belongs to an organized group with announced tenets or premises, your best assumption will be that he, too, espouses those same principles and cannot be made to go directly against them, (unless, of course, your objective is to get him to do so).

What are his vested interests? If a man holds property in a residential section, it may be hard to convince him that a factory should be built next door to him, (unless, of course, he happens to hold stock in the factory).

What are his prejudices, preconceived ideas, and basic attitudes? It is rare that your communicative interests can be served positively by a frontal attack on something like racial prejudice or some other form of emotionally based or socially conditioned bigotry. People must be very subtly led to discover and correct such things within their own minds.

What are the other limitations in communicating with this person? Are there, for example, any physical restrictions or hindrances such as distance, his tiredness, where he is sitting or standing, and so forth? Similarly, are there any special emotional limitations?

The most basic guideline for each situation is to never exceed its inherent limitations (those borders beyond which you cannot go and still retain contact with the person). At least, do not exceed them without first gradually and subtly extending them. For example, it could gravely injure your cause to ask a husband to go against his wife. Similarly, if you are speaking to your own management, there are certain obvious lines beyond which you cannot go. Use common sense!

42

What is his objective? Never disallow the fact that the other person is not sitting still while you are planning and executing your attempt to communicate with him. While it is doubtful that he will be proceeding as strategically as you are (if you are following the advice in this course), in all likelihood he will be proceeding, and he may have an objective just as clearly defined as yours is. Many times your objectives may be complementary. By all means, if you can help him get what he wants while you are accomplishing your own goal, do so. You will, in fact, usually diminish your own chances if you thwart his goals in trying to obtain yours. Usually, knowing the other person's objectives also can give you a clearer idea of how reasonable and accomplishable your own objective is. In any case, part of your sound and realistic base must be a knowledge of what the other person is seeking.

What is he or will he be doing, feeling, and thinking when he first encounters you and your idea? Can you control this?

What are his "hot spots"? With many people, certain words, images, ideas, and impressions almost consistently can be counted on to "set them off," either positively or negatively. "Hot spots" or "buzz words," of course, work both ways. Take, for example, the man who believes himself to be quite objective and claims that he bases his decisions on facts. It stands to reason that, if you bring this man facts for his "objective" decisions, you'll have a much better chance of leading him where you want him to go. On the other hand, you could hardly serve your cause by using profanity in a meeting of ministers, or telling a temperance group a drinking story.

What does he know about the specific idea that you are trying to communicate to him? In professional communicators' jargon, this is known as "level of awareness." Many amateurs almost totally ignore their audiences' previous exposure (or lack of it) to a subject at hand, and hence injure their efforts to communicate by boring their audiences, talking over their heads, or ignoring prejudices or existing attitudes toward a particular idea. Thus, always ask yourself, "What does this person know and how does he think or feel about my idea before I even begin telling him about it?"

What is your basic relationship with this person? For example, is he your superior at work, your subordinate, or do you approach him essentially as a peer? Are you the expert, or is he? Are you strangers or fairly well acquainted? Most relationships carry with them certain limitations and, on occasion, certain prerogatives or privileges. More important, from an analytical point of view, what are the communicative limitations that a given relationship might place upon you and of which you should be aware during an interchange? Perhaps the best example of this can be found in your job. It can, for example, rarely serve your interests to become subjective and forget the inherent limitations in your relationships with your superior. For when it comes time for him to appraise you, you can bet he won't forget any negative encounters with you!

Answer to Question D: False. How could anyone be so insensitive? The opposite is true, of course. The more you affirm a person's self image, the greater your chances of winning him to anything.

4 THE SITUATION

There is an obvious overlap in analyzing the presentation situation as opposed to the people in the audience. There are no rigid rules of analysis. The important thing is that as many questions as possible be asked and answered. Allowing for his overlapping, the following questions outline what a presenter should ask about the presentation occasion.

- *Why is the presentation being given?*
- *Where will the presentation be given?*
- *How long is the presentation?*
- *What is the presentation a part of?*
- *What time will the presentation be given?*
- *What facilities are available?*
- *What is the audience's authority?*

Question E: List five "who" questions that you can ask about an audience member.

1. _____
2. _____
3. _____
4. _____
5. _____

Question F: List five "what" questions that you can ask about an audience member.

1. _____
2. _____
3. _____
4. _____
5. _____

5 WHY IS THE PRESENTATION BEING GIVEN?

Those who decided to include this presentation in a program or series of events presumably have an inherent purpose; more specifically, what do they expect of the presenter; what is their objective? A good presenter will ask these questions, taking careful note of what they say. Many times he will find that they themselves are not sure. Nevertheless, before he accepts the assignment or invitation, the person who is going to do the presenting must have a clear understanding with his host of why this presentation is being made. And it must be articulated, written down, and approved, if at all possible. There are far too many presentations given just because someone thought the subject ought to be included in the program. If the reason for a presentation cannot be stated and written down in terms of a desired audience response, there can be no deliberate act.

If the host does not or cannot state the reason for the presentation, the presenter, knowing what he is about and that he is in business to accomplish specific objectives, should articulate his objectives and respectfully submit them to his host for formal concurrence.

Answers to Question E:
1. Who does he appear to be?
2. Who does he think he is?
3. Who does he say he is?
4. Who do you think he is?
5. Who is he in reality?

Answers to Question F: (Choose any five.)
- His age?
- His education?
- What does he say he needs or wants?
- What are his powers?
- What are his prejudices?
- What does he know?
- What are the other limitations?

- What is the person's gender?
- His occupation?
- What does he really need or want?
- What are his vested interests?
- What groups does he belong to?
- What is your relationship with him?
- What is his objective?

6 HOW LARGE IS THE AUDIENCE?

Audience size dictates many things to the presenter. For example, if a microphone is needed, does he know microphone technique? Audience size dictates the types of visual aids to be used, the number of handouts to prepare, whether or not a question period can be allowed, and similar matters. Knowing audience size also helps the presenter to set himself mentally for his delivery. Any experienced speaker knows that it takes a different, perhaps more style-conscious, disposition to face a large audience than a small one.

7 WHERE WILL THE PRESENTATION BE GIVEN?

Many a speaker has spent anxious moments just before his presentation hunting for the address or room number, only to arrive breathless and with a little extra nervousness to add to his regular portion of prepresentation jitters. Experienced presenters never ignore such details; as experienced planners they assemble all pertinent logistic information well in advance. They also arrive early whenever possible—for a number of reasons. If the presentation is out of town, there are problems of transportation and housing, which should be seen to well in advance, with arrival times, connections, and reservations all fully verified. It is true that many of these details are automatically taken care of by committees and secretaries, but a professional makes sure for himself.

8 HOW LONG IS THE PRESENTATION?

This is a seemingly inconsequential fact, but it actually has a major influence on the presentation. Most presenters try to cover far too much material in the time allotted, mainly because their selection of topic is too broad or general. Can the desired objective be accomplished in the allotted time? How much detail must be included to adequately prove the main point of the presentation? The emphasis here is on restricting and narrowing the presentation objective because rarely can a presentation be too narrow in terms of subject matter. The average presentation will seldom be more than an hour and a half long. From the presenter's point of view this may seem extremely short. As he begins to gather information he will find that there almost always will be far more material than he can possibly cover. Therefore, he must restrict and narrow his subject to a point where what he does cover will be treated in sufficient depth. This is also part of the reason for choosing a specific objective. The time limitation will bear directly on what that goal is to be, with a single main thought sequence pattern to guide both presenter and audience to its accomplishment. By fitting his objective to the time limit imposed upon him, the presenter is drawn closer to making his presentation a deliberate act.

Question G: What will audience size tell you?

_____

_____

_____

Question H: How will the length of your presentation affect your objective?

_____

_____

_____

Answer to Question G: It will dictate many important logistical considerations such as types of visual aids, need for amplification, and your mobility on stage. It also will be important to your mental state, for you may have to "psych yourself up" for addressing large groups.

Answer to Question H: Presentation length relates directly to the scope and narrowness of your objective.

9 WHAT IS THE PRESENTATION A PART OF?

A symposium? A workshop? A sales proposal? Whom does the presenter follow? Who comes after him? What is the main theme of the program? Answering such questions guarantees that the presentation will fit, that it will not represent an embarrassing departure from what other presenters have been doing and saying. If his presentation is to complement, elaborate upon, or contrast with other presentations, it is necessary to know what they will cover. It is often wise to obtain a copy of the program in advance, contact the other program participants, or even call a general meeting or rehearsal.

10 WHAT TIME WILL THE PRESENTATION BE GIVEN?

Both the time of day and place in the total program should be considered. The earlier in the program that he appears, the more latitude the presenter will have in use of information commonly known by or available to the other presenters. The earlier in the day and in the program, the more alert and interested the audience will be. Conversely, lateness in the proceedings will govern delivery technique to maintain attention. It will restrict the new information available, but it can also provide valuable grist for the presenter in terms of reference material to relate and integrate his presentation with the others. Some of his points may be preproved or refuted before he gets a chance to make them. Consulting the participants who precede him can therefore be advantageous. If he cannot get their material beforehand, the next best thing to do is to listen to them as they speak, making appropriate notes or comments in his own script or outline.

11 WHAT FACILITIES ARE AVAILABLE?

It is most disconcerting to have notes and no lectern to set them on, slides and no projector, chalkboard notations and no board to write them on, a board but no chalk, easel charts and no easel. These things happen! Again, a true professional takes no chances. Even if he delegates others to see to these things, he checks on them himself. Early arrival will afford him the opportunity he needs to do so.

12 WHAT IS THE AUDIENCE'S AUTHORITY?

Trainees cannot make purchasing decisions. Normally, laboratory technicians do not decide upon budget matters. Executive committees do. It makes little sense to lead an audience to a decision which it has no power to make. Many a technical sales presentation has been wasted on minor company functionaries, when the decision maker was not even present in the audience. Thus, the experienced presenter fits what he is asking an audience to do to what they are authorized to do. He establishes an attainable objective—not only in terms of the conditions and limitations within which he must work, but in terms of the people with whom he is dealing. And once again, the objective is the key element in making the presentation a deliberate, finite, accomplishable act.

Question I: Why is it important to know what the audience's authority is?

_____

_____

_____

13 ANALYZING AN AUDIENCE AS A GROUP

We've stressed the importance of remembering that you are always dealing with individual people in making presentations. And most of the analytical questions are asked in the singular. But it's a good idea to back off a little and also analyze your audience as a group.

What you will usually be looking for is an image of a typical member of the audience to whom you are speaking, or a cross section of that group. For example, in analyzing the ages of the people, you would think in terms of both average age and the span of ages within the group, and gear your approach accordingly. The same would apply to occupations, education, prejudices, and so forth. Sometimes, when dealing with a group (or an organization), depending on your goals, it might pay you to expand your analysis of that group a little more by asking further strategic questions such as the following:

- *Who can be pushed or led?*
- *Who is weak or can be discounted*

- *Who has the real authority, money, power, or control?*

- *Whom do I fear? Why?*
- *Who has the psychological and physical advantage? Can I get it?*
- *Who reveals the least? Why?*
- *To whom do I represent a threat?*
- *Why? How?*
- *Who talks the most? Why? Is he a leader, a follower, a spokesman?*

Divide the group first into major categories in your mind:

- *Factions and "sides"*
- *Points of view*
- *Personalities*

Then ask:

- *Who knows what about me? about the subject? about the situation? about the people?*
- *Who is on my side?*
- *Who is against me?*
- *Who is subjective?*
- *Who is the humorist? Why?*
- *Who trusts and respects me?*
- *Whom do I trust and respect?*
- *Whom do I know? How well?*
- *What are the assumed and real relationships?*
- *Who is a positive or negative leader, follower, or spokesman?*
- *Who has the real decision–making power?*

Answer to Question I: Knowing audience authority relates directly to your objective in terms of its accomplishability.

Summary Exercise: This exercise is for practice in thinking about audiences from a strategic point of view. As we've said, the average person doesn't think about audiences in a very objective or strategic way. For many novice presenters, the audience just exists. No attempt is made to stay in touch with reality in order to establish a realistic base for dealing with the audience. This exercise is for generalized practice in thinking about audiences. Following are a series of audience descriptions and a list of possible general audience attitudes.

1. Read each audience description.
2. From the list of possible attitudes, select one or more terms that are likely to describe that particular audience and write your answer in the space provided next to the audience description.

LIST OF ATTITUDES			
Apathetic	Unfriendly	Receptive	Unfavorable
Hostile	Apprehensive	Relaxed	Sympathetic
Interested	Enthusiastic	Happy	Condescending
Curious	Resentful	Unhappy	Prejudiced
Friendly	Lively	Favorable	Distrustful
	Capricious		

AUDIENCE	ATTITUDE
1. A group of employees gathered to be given the details of a major reorganization of the company they work for	
2. A group of busy professional technicians ordered by their management to attend a training session to learn how to fill out a series of work–study forms being used by an outside firm to study their efficiency	
3. A group of factory workers gathered by management to hear how new machinery is going to automate their jobs	
4. An annual "outstanding achievements" convention	
5. A presentation given by a Democratic committee to a Republican City Council	
6. A group of citizens to hear the details of an increased tax assessment program	
7. A group of high school students touring a manufacturing plant	
8. A group of salesmen gathered to hear a new product announcement	

49

AUDIENCE	ATTITUDE
9. A group of professional communicators to review the work of some amateurs	
10. A group of engineers and technicians ordered by their management to attend a night class in effective communication without overtime pay	

Scorable Quiz: Indicate true (T) or false (F).

1. If you have adequately given advance notice of the title of your presentation, most members of your audience will arrive with a very clear picture in their minds of exactly what they want to hear. _____

2. If you can get a person to state in words what he needs or wants, you will have a very good foundation for dealing with him. _____

3. From a single item of information such as a person's age, sex, or occupation, it is possible to discern a great many other fairly accurate items of information about him. _____

4. It is not necessary to affirm people in their preconceived ideas, so long as you accomplish your objective of reaching them. _____

5. One of the best ways to be sure that your presentation will reach its mark is, during your preparation of it, to keep a mental image of the expected audience members in your mind. _____

6. It is not important to know the size of your audience in advance, since they are all human beings and the important thing is to be thinking about and talking to real people. _____

7. Knowing what a person's vested interests are, (what groups he belongs to, for example), will be an important indicator of possible "touchy" subjects or "sore spots" that you might want to avoid. _____

8. It is not necessary to know anything about any larger program your presentation may be a part of, because your own presentation will have been constructed as a stand-alone entity and will speak for itself. _____

9. Usually, any factions or "sides" that might exist within a given audience won't have any effect on your presentation. _____

10. It is always extremely important to analyze your audience members at the individual level, since each person is different; as we've said, there are always only "two" persons in any presentation situation—you and the other person (no matter how many "other" persons there are). ———

Answers to Summary Exercise:

1. Apprehensive, perhaps resentful or distrustful.
2. Probably hostile, unfriendly, resentful—at least generally unfavorable.
3. Also probably fairly hostile—who wants a machine to put him out of work?
4. A good, probably happy and friendly audience, interested, curious, receptive.
5. Hostile, distrustful, curious.
6. Not very happy.
7. Curious, capricious, lively.
8. Happy, curious, receptive.
9. Condescending, probably.
10. We've had this one. They'll take a bit of motivating.

Answers to Scorable Quiz: (Each correct answer = 10%.) (1) F, (2) F, (3) T, (4) F, (5) T, (6) F, (7) T, (8) F, (9) F, (10) F.

ISBN 0-471-01631-4

EFFECTIVE PRESENTATION
Outlining And Data Gathering

UNIT

VI

W. A. Mambert

Executive Director

National Communication and Education Association

Wiley Professional Development Programs

Advisory Editor

Steven C. Wheelwright

Harvard Business School

John Wiley & Sons Inc.
New York • London • Sydney • Toronto

Center for
Professional Development
University of Dayton
Dayton, Ohio

Library of Congress Catalogue Card Number: 75-39750

ISBN 0-471-01632-2

Printed in the United States of America.

10 9 8 7 6 5 4 3 2 1

Making A Workable Outline

PREMISE: That it is next to impossible to prepare an effective presentation without first preparing a written outline.

SEGMENT OBJECTIVE: That you become able to bring to bear the information discussed in all preceding segments and to prepare a functional outline that will be a true and meaningful representation of the contents of your actual presentation.

NOTE ...
This segment and the next are integrally related and should be studied as closely together as possible.

Question A: As the above objective states, this is where you bring to bear almost all of the things we've been talking about thus far, particularly your knowledge of objective development and idea structure. For this reason, let's review for a moment:

1. What are the characteristics of a good objective?

_____

_____

_____

_____

_____

2. What are the main structures available to you in preparing your outline?

_____

_____

_____

Answers to Question A:
1. Characteristics of a good objective: narrowness and specificity, "the end is the beginning," must be accomplishable, stated in terms of audience behavior, must be written.

2. Types of structure: spatial or chronological; inductive or deductive; causal; state, condition, quality, or degree; two-sided; any combination.

1 OUTLINING CONVENTIONS

There are no rules as such for the format of outlines. The only important conventions are those that are truly functional for you, those that suit your needs and provide you with the planning devices that actually will give you and enable you to present a clear understanding of your whole presentation idea. You are not preparing an outline for a college professor to grade, but a working tool. It is, however, difficult to improve upon the traditional method of using Roman numerals, capital letters, arabic numerals, small letters, and so forth. An example is:

> *INTRODUCTION*
> *1. Main subject division*
> *A. Main subject division*
> *1. Further subdivision or supporting detail*
> *a. Detail*
> *(1) Detail*
> *(a) Detail*
> *II. _ _ _ _ _ _ _ _ _ _ _ _ _*
> *A _ _ _ _ _ _ _ _ _ _ _ _*
> *1. _ _ _ _ _ _ _ _ _ _ _ _*
> *a. _ _ _ _ _ _ _ _ _ _ _ _*
> *(1) _ _ _ _ _ _ _ _ _ _ _*
> *(a) _ _ _ _ _ _ _ _ _ _ _*
> *CONCLUSION*

Question B: Why is the traditional outline method probably still the best one?

The main advantage of this method is that it clearly distinguishes between main ideas and their supportive parts and effectively displays subordination in a clear visual way.

Notice particularly in the sample outline format just given that the introduction and conclusion are shown as separate parts of the outline. Many people have misconceptions about what the functions of introductions and conclusions really are. We'll clear these up in later segments, when we talk about how to make good introductions and conclusions. For the moment, it's sufficient for you to remember that in looking at the actual detailed anatomy of a presentation outline, the introduction and conclusion are properly treated as separate parts.

2

Answer to Question B: Because it is the best way to quickly show main and subordinate ideas in relationship to each other.

2 WHAT SHOULD YOUR OUTLINE CONTAIN?

A complete presentation outline should contain the following:

- *Title*
- *Audience description*
- *Statement of objective*
- *Thesis statement*
- *Introduction*
- *Outline of body of presentation*
- *Conclusion*

Question C: Give three functions of a presentation title.

_____

_____

_____

3 THE TITLE

Give proper attention to this important task. After all, the title is the first thing that almost everyone is going to see respecting your presentation. A well-stated title will do as much for you as for your audience, because it also will isolate the idea in your thinking. The title integrates the presentation as an "idea package." It is a major attention–gaining mechanism. It establishes an initial presenter–audience relationship. It also should give meaningful information. It is, in reality, a miniature introduction to your presentation. Frequently, if the title is not stated effectively, you won't even get a chance to give your presentation.

Both your title and your introduction, in final form, will grow out of your whole presentation; they won't precede it in the preparation. Often, selection of a title will be one of the last things you do; for only after your presentation is completed can you truly reflect on the content, temper, and aim of it as an integrated functional unit.

Some guidelines for selecting a title are:

1. *Make it a deliberate act. The title is important.*
2. *Leave it until very late in the composition process. Use a working title if necessary, but do not make the mistake of unconsciously building the presentation to meet the demands of a preselected title.*
3. *Good titles usually are brief. Many technical presenters try to write a complete introduction in the title.*
4. *Use the basic motive appeals and all of the other devices.*
5. *Make it actually give meaningful information, unless the main aim is to pique curiosity. Even here, it should be meaningful.*

3

6. *Remember its real objectives, which are to:*
   a. *Stand alone as a message to a potential audience.*
   b. *Help integrate the presentation.*
   c. *Arouse interest.*
   d. *Establish a relationship.*
   e. *Tell something about what the presentation contains.*
7. *Relate it to the objective and thesis if possible. Sometimes it actually can be a miniature thesis statement.*
8. *Consider borrowing a significant phrase from the presentation.*

In short, title selection should be a deliberate act. A thinking communicator can make it do many things, even give his presentation outline. For example:

A presentation outline in a title	"Input, Store, Process, Output"
A thesis in a title	"Convert Now"
A question	"Why Buy Cryoflex?"
Curiosity and information	"Cryoflex Goes to Sea"
The first half of a two–sided structure	"Competition Advances"
Both halves	"Competition Advances—Sell and Service"

Answer to Question C: Here are five answers, although we only asked you for three. (1) It helps you to isolate the idea you're dealing with, as well as doing it for your audience. (2) It integrates the idea as a presentation package, or single, homogeneous unit. (3) It is an attention-gaining mechanism. (4) It establishes a presenter-audience relationship. (5) It is a miniature introduction.

4 **AUDIENCE DESCRIPTION**
This also is appropriately a part of a presentation outline, because it is the basis for the outline. It is the basis of the logic for your objective statement and your thesis, which, in turn, is what the whole presentation outline is supporting. So, by including an audience description right in your outline (which, don't forget, is your private plan—not for public consumption, unless that's functional, too), you "close the loop," as it were; you make your outline a complete, predicated plan of action.

Remember all of the rules for formulating a good statement of objective, which we've just reviewed at the beginning of this segment. Let's do an exercise to be sure that you'll know when your objective actually does meet the criteria of functionalism.

4

Question D: Identify which of the statements below represent functional statements of objective, and which do not. Then indicate the reason for your evaluation in the righthand column.

STATEMENT	MEETS CRITERIA YES/NO	REASON
1. To teach physics		
2. To enable trainee to type 40 WPM		
3. To inform audience of benefits of product X		
4. For audience to know the elements of effective presentation		
5. To get a sales appointment		

Answer to Question D:

STATEMENT	MEETS CRITERIA YES/NO	REASON
1. To teach physics	no	Because it's stated from teacher's viewpoint, not from audience's; thus there is no audience action or behavior included, and it's not measurable.
2. To enable trainee to type 40WPM	yes	Because it does tell what the audience is expected to be able to do. It describes an actual, measurable audience response.
3. To inform audience of benefits of product X	no	For the same reasons as 1. There is no measurable audience response.
4. For audience to know the elements of effective presentation	yes	Because it does describe something that the audience will have, know, or be able to do. True, you'll have to devise the right test to be sure that they actually do know.
5. To get a sales appointment	yes	Because the audience action is inherent; that is, there is a definite assumption that he will say, "Yes, you have an appointment." The actual objective would be "to get him to say this."

5

The best way to find out if your statement of objective is a true statement of objective is to actually put it to the test against the following checklist:

1. *Is it sufficiently narrow to be accomplished within the time, space, and audience limitations?*
2. *Is it, in fact, accomplishable? Does the audience actually have the decision-making or other power to do, know, be able to, and so forth?*
3. *Is it stated in terms of very specific audience behavior, possession, or ability?*
4. *Is it written down?*

If you can answer yes to these questions, you'll have a very good start toward making your presentation actually do and accomplish some specific thing.

5 **THESIS STATEMENT**
Take this opportunity to review what you know about theses.

Question E: A thesis is a private _____ converted for

_____ . Convert the following objectives to theses.

OBJECTIVE	CONVERTED TO THESIS
1. To enable trainee to type 40 WPM	
2. For student to be able to formulate a meaningful functional objective	
3. To sell product X	
4. To get a sales appointment	
5. For the student to be able to balance a chemical equation	

Answer to Question E: It would be difficult for your words and ours to match exactly. Simply match your statements with ours. The key is, have you now stated what you want to do in a way that gives the audience a reason or a motivation (from his or her point of view) for learning, doing, not doing, changing belief, or attitude?

OBJECTIVE	CONVERTED TO A THESIS
1. To enable trainee to type 40 WPM	"To be able to type 40 WPM is the first requisite for obtaining the kind of job you want."
2. For a student to formulate a meaningful functional objective	"If you really want to give a good presentation, you must be able to formulate a meaningful functional objective."
3. To sell product X	"Sir, we know that for some time now you have been having a problem with Y. We believe, sir, that product X is the solution to your problem."
4. To get a sales appointment	"Mr. Smith, I believe that I have the solution to a problem that I know has been troubling you for some time."
5. For the student to be able to balance a chemical equation	"Being a pharmacist is a very lucrative profession. You'll have great difficulty in getting into it if you don't know how to balance a chemical equation."

Hopefully, you now see clearly the difference between an objective and how that objective is phrased as a thesis, to give your audience predication for what you have to say to them. May we suggest our thesis here that, "If you don't understand the difference between an objective and a thesis, you could very well make a fool out of yourself in front of an audience before you even get into your presentation." Enough said!

Question F: Bet you thought you could just slip by the word "predication." What does it mean?

_____

_____

_____

NOTE . . .
Remember now: Don't look at our answer until you've written in your own.

Answer to Question F: Many people misuse this term by saying that something is predicated upon something else. Actually, it's the opposite. Something predicates something else. In logic, the predication is the basis or reason for something. It literally means, "to be caused to be based upon."

6 THE PRESENTATION INTRODUCTION

We're going to cover this important matter in a separate segment. For the moment, be content with seeing where it fits in the total presentation outline.

7 SENTENCE OUTLINE OF THE BODY OF THE PRESENTATION

If at least one sentence cannot be written about every point in the outline, how can anything be said about it in the presentation? It means that this is an invalid point and does not belong in the presentation at all. But there are other important reasons for writing a sentence outline (which most presenters do not do).

1. *Writing a sentence for each point forces you to think out the idea. It makes you decide step by step precisely the thought that you want to cover.*
2. *It will show immediately whether or not the whole presentation will flow logically and what its basic pattern is.*
3. *It clarifies the relationship of each idea and supporting idea to the thesis, hence to the objective, and therefore to the function of the presentation itself. The sentence outline, therefore, becomes an automatic test of whether or not everything in the presentation is objective-oriented.*
4. *The sentence outline is a means of communication itself. Written in paragraph form it is as meaningful an abstract as anyone could prepare from a given text. It also is immediately understandable to anyone else, even if the supporting details and evidence for the ideas are missing.*
5. *It divides preparation of the body of the presentation into workable tasks. It tells you exactly how much you have to do. You need not prepare the whole presentation at a single sitting for fear of losing one of your ideas or thoughts. Your thoughts will be there, articulated, no matter how often you interrupt your work.*
6. *The sentence outline often furnishes you excellent material for your presentation introduction.*
7. *The actual statements used for each point often will provide the* topic sentence *for each section of the presentation.*
8. *Using the topic sentence as a guide, you will be better able to provide transition from point to point for the audience—giving what you say the valuable quality of unity and cohesiveness for its hearer.*
9. *These same sentences will provide a means of intermediate and final summary of important points.*

These advantages should be sufficient evidence that preparing a sentence outline is an essential part of presentation planning. It is not necessarily an easy task, but it makes the rest of the presenting job easier in so many ways that it is well worthwhile. Aside from the fact that it is difficult to see how anyone can do any logical or meaningful thinking on his feet without having done some thinking beforehand, sentence outlining is just plain good planning.

8 SAMPLE SENTENCE OUTLINE

The objective of the following outline is to obtain permission to run a thirty-day test of a new system for fully controlled, automatic, precision drilling. The thesis is this: The present methods of hand or partially automated machine drilling are slow, dangerous, inaccurate, costly, and wasteful of both material and manpower—all of which can be alleviated with the installation of the new system.

    I. *The part must be moved to the work table and secured.*
        A. *Movement and securing are done manually.*
        B. *Control of the work table is semi–automatic.*
        C. *The part is manually tested with calipers and templates.*
        D. *The part is manually removed and carried to storage.*
    II. *The present methods are wholly unsatisfactory.*
        A. *A worker averages five minutes of handling per part.*
        B. *Workers are frequently injured.*
        C. *Errors in testing frequently occur.*
        D. *Present automated control allows for only one- and two–axis movement.*
            1. *Material is wasted.*
            2. *Operators are idle one third of the time.*
   III. *The new method combines all basic phases.*
        A. *The automatic conveyer moves and secures the part.*
        B. *A special new feature also secures the work table.*
        C. *Depth and diameter are preset and cannot change.*
        D. *Removal and storage are fully automated.*
   IV. *The new method provides several specific benefits.*
        A.
        B.
        C.
        D.
    V. *I therefore suggest that a thirty-day test be run, beginning on May 15.*
       Do you agree (Action Step)? (We'll talk about this later, too.)

This is a simplified outline, but illustrates many of the benefits of sentence outlining. In this particular case, the thesis statement can serve as an actual introductory comment when the presentation is delivered—unless the presenter decides to show some pictures of fingerless hands which he has selected as an effective and appropriate motive appeal and attention getter. Note also the difference between the objective and thesis. Note also the narrowness of the objective, probably selected in this case because conditions indicated that a full sale could not be closed at this time. Most of the points would be supported by statistics, charts, and other forms of evidence. An action step has been added to round out the example.

9 OUTLINING BY FLOW CHART

We've seen the use of flow charts (or flow diagrams) throughout this course. This is a method of preliminary outlining which has considerable merit. Some presenters even deliver their presentations by using such charts as scripts. A flow chart can serve in some cases as a preliminary planning aid or even as a final outline, depending on the nature and complexity of the presentation. One of its main advantages is that it affords another dimension for visualizing the relationships between or among subject divisions, especially where procedures, motion, flow, or dependency are involved. Some examples of where it might be used are:

- *Plant description*
- *Process description*

- *Design procedures*
- *Equipment functions*
- *Operating procedures*
- *Techniques*

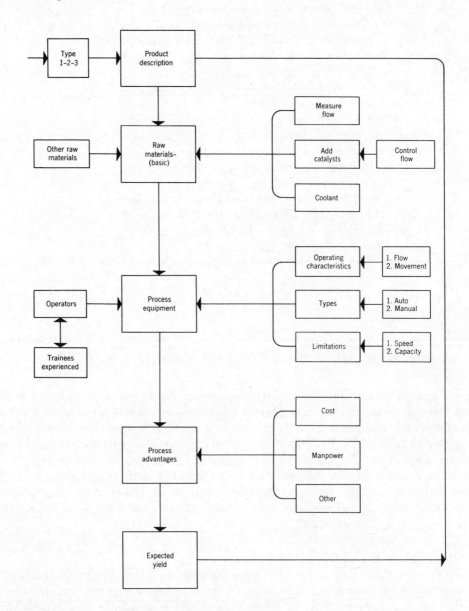

10 THE PRESENTATION CONCLUSION

As with the introduction, we want to get into this in some depth in a later segment, but you ought to see where it should fit in your outline.

11 SUMMARY

The important thing to remember about outlining is that it is a means to an end. As has been pointed out, a well-prepared outline also can serve the presenter for purposes other than those directly concerned with developing his idea. For example, the outline can be used for the following purposes:

- *As a guide to research.*
- *As a complete communication, such as an abstract or a summary.*
- *As a test of idea validity, cohesiveness, and unity.*
- *As a test for omissions or inclusion of specific data.*
- *To prevent omission of important points or information.*
- *To divide the presentation into workable parts.*

Summary Exercise: Following are the elements of an outline in topical form, including an objective and a thesis statement. There is no introductory or concluding material included here, only material for the body of a presentation and its subdivisions. Therefore, do not worry about putting these in your outline at this time. The information is not jumbled or disarranged in any way. Your task is to convert this topical outline into a sentence outline.

Title:

Objective: To convince the city council of Anywhere, USA, that your firm should be hired to develop a "Year–2000 Plan" for urban development of their city.

Thesis: You furnish this from the above objective.

Introduction: (Not to be developed at this time.)

Outline of Body of Presentation:

    I. Present Problems
      A. Traffic congestion
      B. Urban blight
      C. Unbalance of industry, parks, and residential

    II. Future Needs
      A. Planned growth
      B. Planned street development
      C. Funding

    III. Year–2000 Plan
      A. Future land use
      B. Future municipal funds
      C. Accurate forecasts

Title: _____

          _____

Objective: _____

          _____

Introduction: _____

_____

Outline of Body of Presentation:

_____

Scorable Quiz: Fill in the missing word or words.

1. List below the seven major elements that every well-constructed presentation outline should contain:

   a. _____

   b. _____

   c. _____

   d. _____

   e. _____

   f. _____

   g. _____

2. The text indicates that you should usually develop your outline a step beyond the mere listing of main subjects and their divisions. What type of outline does it suggest very strongly that you make in most cases?

   _____

3. What is the alternative method of outlining given in the text?

   _____

4. What is the term that describes the establishment of a basis or reason for something?

   _____

Title: Anytown, USA's Need for a Year-2000 Plan

Objective: As stated

Introduction: Not required

Outline of Body of Presentation:

I. There are at least three present problems that must be overcome.
    A. Present traffic problems alone indicate that something must be done.
    B. Vast areas of the inner city already have fallen victim to urban blight.
    C. There is a present unbalance of industry, parkland, and residential land which adds to the undesirable situation.

II. Future needs must be considered in any attempt to solve present problems.
    A. Only planned growth can keep problems from getting out of hand.
    B. Planned street development will alleviate much of the problem.
    C. We must also have a reasonable and feasible plan for raising funds.

III. A good year-2000 plan is the obvious answer.
    A. It will take into consideration future land use.
    B. It will provide a means for raising municipal funds.
    C. It will provide for accurate forecast of population and other growth.

> *Note . . .*
> *Remember—This is only one possible way of doing it.*

Answer to Summary Exercise: Here again, your wording may differ slightly from ours. Our sentences are not the only ones that would fit. Compare yours with ours. If each of your sentences expresses a complete thought similar to ours, you've come close enough to what it takes to make a good sentence outline.

Answers to Scorable Quiz: (Each correct answer = 10%.) 1. (a) title, (b) audience description, (c) statement of objective, (d) thesis statement, (e) introduction, (f) outline of main discussion, (g) conclusion. 2. sentence outline, 3. flow chart outline, 4. predication.

LEARNING 18 SEGMENT

Gathering Data And Taking Notes

PREMISE: That once you have the kind of underlying background we've attempted to describe in the foregoing segments, this must be brought to bear in the actual process of gathering information and composing the presentation.

SEGMENT OBJECTIVE: That you have a convenient, efficient, and workable method for dealing with the mechanics of choosing and composing the right kinds and amounts of actual information and devices within your presentation.

Question A: In Segment 13, we listed the main functions of idea support. There were five. Without looking back, see if you can list them here.

_____   _____

_____   _____

_____

Question B: What two things are likely to emerge from the data–gathering process?

_____   _____

1 **WHAT ARE YOU LOOKING FOR?**
From the moment that you know you're going to have to give a presentation on a certain subject, you ought to begin gathering the data for that presentation. As you begin to sort and arrange the details you gather, at least two things will begin to emerge:

  1. *Usually, very early in your accumulation of information the inherent structure of the information will present itself.*
  2. *Usually, too, the best strategic structure will emerge almost spontaneously.*

As you sort the individual details and items of information that come to you, you'll thus find that much of your so-called outlining process will take care of itself. Then, the building blocks of the presentation also will almost automatically fall within the proper categories.

As your outline establishes itself, what are you really looking for? If you've studied the foregoing segments on idea structure and rational, physical, and psychological support, you have your answer. You are looking for material that will:

1. *Define or identify the individual segments of your presentation idea*
2. *Clarify the individual segments of your presentation idea*
3. *Strengthen or reinforce*
4. *Prove or substantiate*
5. *Generate or influence mood or flavor of any idea or part of an idea*

Answers to Question A: (You'll find them in the above list.)

Answers to Question B: It is very likely that, as you gather data, the inherent structure of the material will automatically make itself evident. You also will get plenty of hints as to what the best structure to suit your particular presentation objective will be.

2 THE MINIMUM CRITERIA

Only you, of course, can be the final judge of whether your message includes the right amounts and kinds of evidence, persuasion, detail, reinforcement, and so forth. There are, however, certain minimum criteria by which any form of idea support or reinforcement should be judged and which should greatly improve your capability to select these presentation building blocks.

Some tests for determining the effectiveness of idea support appear in the following list. As you examine individual items of information, subideas, possible illustrative material, and other supportive devices, put each to the following tests:

1. The functional test. *Does it have an actual objective within the progression of your idea toward your final objective?*
2. The relevancy test. *Does it have a real relationship or applicability to your main idea?*
3. The clarity test. *Is it actually perceivable and comprehensible? If it isn't, no matter how relevant it is nobody will know it.*
4. The validity test. *To be used especially with evidence, testimony, and so forth. Don't unquestioningly accept anything as true or a fact without checking it out.*
5. The appropriateness test. *Does it fit the occasion, overall mood, level of formality, and so forth? To be used especially with humor.*
6. The efficiency test. *Does it prove, reinforce, and substantiate in as quick, concise, and concrete way as possible, or is wasteful of time or space?*
7. The proportion and place test. *Is it in the right place, position and time?*
8. The accuracy test. *For use especially with facts, statistics, and so forth. Is it accurate and reliable?*
9. The subjectivity test. *Is it objective or subjective? Either is valid, but you should know which it is.*
10. The alternatives test. *E.g., is an analogy better than an example or anecdote? Is a picture better than a list of figures? Is a rhetorical question better than a statement?*

We can guarantee that if your idea support meets these tests, you can be sure that the actual detailed content of your message will be quite "tight" and "meaty."

Question C: Put the following statement to the tests listed above. Which test does it *not* meet?

"The very nature of our times demands sophisticated communication systems for the control and effective operation of the equally sophisticated logistic and production systems which they serve."

Note . . .
Be sure you write down your own answer before looking at ours.

Answer to Question C: This statement basically fails to meet the *validity test*. Statements such as this actually are made in presentations every day. This one is an actual quotation. Yet, is it valid? The answer is no. It is nothing more than an attempt to appear sophisticated. Upon analysis, it breaks down completely. It is faulty analogous reasoning. Just because production systems are "sophisticated" (which itself is a misuse of the term), is no reason why the communication systems which serve them should also be sophisticated. A sharp-thinker will see immediately that simplicity, and not so-called sophistication, probably is the key word.

Many times invalidity is more subtly masked, as in certain forms of advertising. The applicability of impressive statistics in one field is often transferred to another, "authoritative" opinions are used, generalizations are applied erroneously to specific instances, "red herrings" are excavated, and side issues are made to appear relevant to the question under discussion. Take, for example, the almost inherent assumption in many presentations that automation is innately good, regardless of the requirements; that modernization is desirable, that obsolescence is undesirable, regardless of how well the "obsolete" equipment is functioning; that upgrading and growth are to be desired, and the unspoken premise that needs must rise to meet the demands of technology instead of the reverse. This is precisely what some presenters often inadvertently do by unquestioning acceptance of the validity of the existence of any idea in the first place.

Question D: What do you think are some of the pitfalls in data gathering? List six here.

16

_____   _____

_____   _____

Question E: What might be some advantages of taking notes on single sheets, as opposed to in a notebook?

_____

_____

_____

3 NOTE–TAKING TOOLS
There are some purely mechanical things that you can do simply in the physical handling of material that you gather, which will greatly facilitate your keeping track of it and getting it organized in outline form. A good system for data gathering and note taking will have as a minimum:

1. *The right kind of first recording medium. The best is a supply of individual cards or sheets as opposed to a notebook in which notes are run on with each other.*
2. *One note to a sheet! Never put two subjects or unrelated items on a single sheet. Sometime in the process you'll have to separate them for proper sorting under your outline headings. It's far better to maintain the separation from the beginning.*
3. *A method of physically sorting material by outline point. Standard tabbed file folders are the best.*

On the following page are some note cards which indicate the best way to take notes as details come to you. Notice that you can put just about anything you want to in a note, e.g., data, facts, statistics, visual ideas, reminders to yourself, and so forth. Always use quotation marks where applicable to avoid infringement without credit.

Look at the cards. The card with the single word "leaf" is simply a personal reminder the presenter made to himself as he passed a tree and thought of a possible analogy for his presentation, e.g., "Gentlemen, on the maple tree in my front yard this morning, I found a solution to your network distribution problem." (He had thought of the network of veins in the leaves.) So, he made himself this note and will not lose his idea. The "machine methods" card obviously is a first note on a possible major subject division, which in turn indicated sufficient possibility for further subdivision to warrant an additional individual card for each method. Thus, the outlining process emerges from the data–gathering process. Note also the bibliographical source which eliminates duplicative searching. This is not an elaborate system, yet it answers the need for flexibility and sortability. With a notebook, the process can become a hopeless tangle, with constant recopying, shuffling, and searching. Here are some sample note cards:

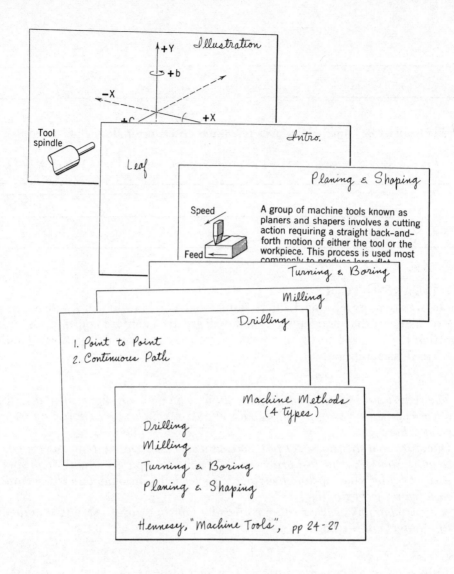

Convert the major subject divisions of your outline to a series of tabbed file folders. This is one of the best organizational devices you can have, because it actually makes your outline a physical method for sorting and dividing your material. Start your folders as soon as you get your first item of information. From the start, you'll have it sorted. Even if you have to change folder titles as you go, you'll be better off. Not only this, but you'll be able to work on any section of your presentation at any time without disturbing or searching through other material. You can also include a folder for notes on your audience, or any other subject such as your objective, the location of your presentation, people involved, and so forth.

The following are sample tabbed outline folders for sorting and storing notes taken during the data-gathering process:

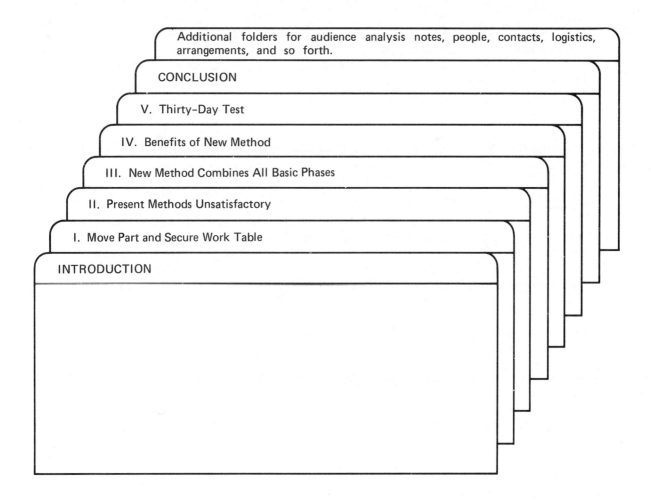

Additional folders for audience analysis notes, people, contacts, logistics, arrangements, and so forth.

CONCLUSION

V. Thirty-Day Test

IV. Benefits of New Method

III. New Method Combines All Basic Phases

II. Present Methods Unsatisfactory

I. Move Part and Secure Work Table

INTRODUCTION

Answers to Question D: We've asked you for only six. Here are the many possible pitfalls that you ought to look out for as you gather details and information for your presentation.

1. *Subjectivity* is probably the number one pitfall, the old egocentricity business, interpreting what you see without sufficient perspective.
2. *Fragmented thinking.* One of the main thinking fallacies—stopping before you have enough information; thinking that part of the truth is the whole truth; thinking that one side of the story is the only valid way of viewing something.
3. *Audience viewpoint.* No matter how many viewpoints there are, failure to take into account the most important one, that of the audience. How will they see the facts?
4. *Failure to isolate*—sufficiently, that is. Hence, neither you nor anyone else will know the exact borders and limitations of what you're talking about.
5. *Failure to integrate.* As you can fail to isolate sufficiently, you also can do the opposite—fail to allow for relationships of this idea with others, with what you already know, or what the audience already knows.
6. *Fact vs. opinion.* Make sure you know the difference, whether you tell your audience or not.
7. *Misuse of evidence.* Using a fact, opinion, or other element to support something that it really doesn't support. This is basically a "relationship failure."
8. *Testimony reliability.* Thinking that just because a "reliable source" says it, it's so.
9. *"Locked-in thinking."* Closing your mind to possible new data.

19

10. *"Black and white thinking."* The tendency to look for conclusions when there are none, or when the reality is that things are not clearly defined.
11. *"Synchronicity."* The imputing of false relationships (causal or otherwise) to ideas because they occur near each other in time or space.
12. *Overresponse.* Emotional or otherwise, placing more weight on something you see or hear than it deserves.

Answer to Question E: Simple, but it's such an important mechanic of the process that we wanted to stress it. A single note to a single sheet gives you sorting flexibility.

4 **CLEAR "UNITS OF EXPRESSION"**
An individual idea within your presentation, of course, can be expressed in many ways. It could be an anecdote, an analogy, a description, an explanation, a picture, a sentence, or merely a word. But, as we said when we talked about sensory communication, if, for some reason, that unit of expression cannot be perceived; that is, if the audience cannot even understand what it is that you're expressing to them, you're lost before you begin. So, "clarity" really becomes a primary watchword.

A recent presenter we heard, for example, was making a presentation on language analysis. He continually referred to "sentence parsing" and "semantic differential," terms common enough to a grammarian, perhaps. They also happened to be keys to his audience's understanding of practically everything else he was telling them. But, the fact was that fully half of his audience did not know what these terms meant. Thus, those people could not possibly have perceived or comprehended his ideas, let alone evaluate or act upon them simply because he was not clear. He had not selected "units of expression" that accurately conveyed what it was that he was saying. How can an idea be made clear? There is no doubt that following all of the "rules" for effective idea support and avoiding the pitfalls will help. But there are some more guidelines that you can follow that will even further increase the clarity of what you say. Following are some examples:

- Think clearly.
- Select and analyze words carefully.
- Avoid jargon and technical terms.
- Define the terms.
- Develop good diction.
- Be concrete.
- Think multidimensionally

Question F: How would you define "clarity in verbal communication"? _____

---

5 **THINK CLEARLY**
Obvious? But we must restate it. There is no way that you can verbalize an idea clearly to someone else if you cannot verbalize it clearly to yourself. If you cannot state an idea to yourself in words that you understand, all you can possibly do is repeat whatever you have heard to your audience. Anyone can pass on words he has heard. It is another matter entirely to digest an idea and then state it as you have comprehended it.

Answer to Question F: Regardless of what it means anywhere else, in this context "clarity" means the conveying of an idea or part of an idea in such a way that it will be perceived exactly as you intend it to be perceived.

Question G: Throughout this course we have repeatedly stressed what is essentially an extrapolation of the basic tenet of pragmatism as a philosophy; that is, that "the validity of an idea lies in its empirical consequences." We assure you that we know exactly what we have said here. Do you? If so, translate this statement into language that anyone could understand.

_____

_____

_____

Question H: Each of the following terms has a special meaning in the context of this course. Translate each so an uninformed audience would have a clearer understanding of what they mean.

1. Functional communication: _____

2. Objective _____

3. Inherent structure: _____

Question I: What is the primary determinant in choosing words to be used in your presentation?

_____

_____

_____

6 **SELECT AND ANALYZE WORDS CAREFULLY**
Many idea presenters wrongly assume that their audiences comprehend more in terms of language and vocabulary than they really do. Not only must you be able to verbalize an idea to yourself, you must also question whether your audience can understand your vocabulary.

7 **AVOID JARGON AND TECHNICAL TERMS**
"AIMS is the equivalent of SCRAP, our program which originally replaced FORTRAP." Jargon, acronyms, and the like usually are to be avoided in presentations. Even informed audiences have to be "right up" on the latest jargon to understand such things. It is better to avoid all such usage. "Differences in word meanings," even before an informed audience, is far preferable to "semantic differential" which probably was coined solely for the purpose of "technological esotericism."

Analysis of your audience helps to determine word choice, but even if they understand the "OK" words, there is far more dignity and clarity in phrasing ideas in plain English.

8 DEFINE THE TERMS

When specialized terms must be used, even with a presumably knowledgeable audience, it is wise to build in definitions. They need not be obviously patronizing. For example, the whole matter of semantic differential could have been cleared up by a simple statement such as, ". . . semantic differential. Thus by finding the differences in word meanings, we are able to . . . ." No one is offended by a definition thus worded. It is merely a restatement. Similarly, for those members of the audience who had never been exposed to sentence parsing ". . . with the parts of speech identified . . . ." The real point here is that "knowledgeable" audiences are rarely as knowledgeable" as the presenter assumes them to be. Wording must be selected and analyzed in advance of the presentation. This does not mean memorizing every phrase. It does mean that the presenter should phrase his thoughts in his mind and then ask himself if his idea will be clear to the least knowledgeable member of his audience. Obviously, he should himself understand the meanings of the terms he is using, or at least have a meaning for them in the context of his presentation and state this fact to his audience.

9 DICTION

Clarity is not only a result of both presenter and audience mutually understanding the meanings of the wording used, but a product of using the *right* words as well. Impeccable word choice is the mark of an expert presenter. Similar words should never be confused. A list of words which are often confused would fill a whole chapter. The only real answer to avoiding misuse lies in personal development. A presenter should not use words in public which he doesn't fully understand. Others might escape criticism *adopting* when they mean *adapting*, having *illusions* when they mean to *allude*, listing things *respectfully* instead of *respectively*, *lying* something down, *suspecting* when they mean to *expect*, or describing the *better* of three things or the *best* of two.

Answer to Question G: The simplest translation of this statement would be, "The end justifies the means." You might also say, "Whether or not an idea is justified can be measured only by the results it produces." And of course, our functional approach to idea presenting (form follows function, measuring everything you do against your objective, and so forth) is, in fact, the pragmatic approach. Simply saying, "ours is a pragmatic approach" would even assume that the audience understood what pragmatism is. Add "empirical consequences" instead of just saying "results" or "outcome" and you have almost pure "technological esotericism," also known as "gobbledegook" and "kleftinobulism."

Answer to Question H:
1. *Functional communication*: A change in a human being, not merely the dispersing of certain information in his direction. Communication is viewed as an accomplished event and not a process. If no change takes place in a person, there has been no communication.
2. *Objective*: A description of audience condition, action, or attitude after the attempt to communicate has occurred. The equivalent of the change in 1 above.
3. *Inherent structure*: The order in which the elements of an idea are first perceived as opposed to the order in which one intentionally presents them.

Answer to Question I: The primary determinant for your choice of wording must be your audience—their vocabulary level, their education, and what is understandable to them.

Question J: Make the following statement more concrete: The user of this keyboard will be at a serious disadvantage.

_____

_____

_____

10 CONCRETENESS

Words are rarely right or wrong in themselves. They are only wrong when they do not do what you as the presenter want them to do. Aside from incorrect use, such as confusion of synonyms, antonyms, similarly spelled words, and generally poor diction, there is the "wrongness" connected with the lack of vividness and concreteness of wording and phrasing. Overly generalized wording is the main offender here.

Answer to Question J: Working with this phrase you might come up with something like the following: "The girl who operates this keyboard will not be able to move the part and press the input key at the same time."

Several things have been done by altering this statement (and we have made the same error here). What does altering this statement say? By making the words in this statement more specific:

1. The term "girl" immediately related the situation to reality.
2. It also is an image word and will help the audience to picture what is being said.
3. A serious disadvantage could be anything. It doesn't advance the idea. Something specific still must be said to clarify it.
4. Action has been added to remove the comment from the academic realm and make it more real.

Add to the original statement the words, "... thus losing valuable production time." Too general. Now substitute "... thus losing five seconds on every operation, multiplied by ... "

Without endlessly listing examples, what can you do to make your language more concrete and thus more meaningful? For every item of information, word, or phrase about which there is any doubt regarding its concreteness, he can ask the simple question:

"How can this be narrowed to the most specific terms possible?"

If you then find that this is too specific for where you are in your treatment, you can simply work back up toward the general until it does not reveal more than you want it to at that time in your idea development. By following this process, you'll be continually moving closer to making everything that you say absolutely clear, and packing your presentation more solidly with clear and meaningful information.

11 MULTIDIMENSIONAL THINKING

There can be no doubt that the real key to your ability to impart clarity, concreteness, and all the rest to your ideas will be a multidimensional thinking approach and your personal creativity, based upon a good thinking vocabulary. A knowledge of the kinds of idea structure available to you, the kinds of rational support, the methods of physical, sensory, emotional, and psychological reinforcement all are a part of your base for clarifying your ideas. Only you can decide, in the final analysis with respect to each subelement of your presentation, when to state an idea verbally; when to restate or repeat it; when an action is better than words; and when emotional appeal, an analogy, a simile, or a metaphor, are the most appropriate. The key is to stay multidimensional in your thinking.

Summary Exercise: Recall that in Segment 13 we gave you a list of the main forms of rational idea support and asked you to be sure that you knew what they all meant. It is in the selection of specific forms of idea support in the idea-gathering and note-taking processes that this knowledge really pays off. So, we don't want you to forget these things. Following is a list of several of those listed forms. Define each.

1. Analogy: _____

2. Antithesis: _____

3. Assertion: _____

4. Definition: _____

5. Enigma: _____

6. Hyperbole: _____

7. Illustration: _____

8. Interrogation: _____

9. Narrative: _____

10. Metaphor _____

11. Onomatopoeia: _____

12. Oxymoron: _____

13. Personification: _____

14. Response point: _____

15. Understatement: _____

Scorable Quiz: Fill in the missing word or words.

1. Two note-taking tools are suggested. What are they?

   a. _____   b. _____

2. The text gives twelve pitfalls to avoid in data gathering. List here any three (words or phrases only).

    a. _____

    b. _____

    c. _____

3. The text gives seven suggestions on how to have "clear units of expression." List here any three (words or phrases only).

    a. _____

    b. _____

    c. _____

4. In this segment, the word "communication" is defined in a very specific way which can be stated in a seven-word phrase, beginning, "Communication is (a) _____ in a (b) _____ ."

Answers to Summary Exercise:

1. Analogy: A comparison of a known idea with an unknown idea; mainly to save words and clarify, not for proof (e.g., the computer and the brain).

2. Antithesis: An idea, usually opposite, set against another idea to emphasize either or both. Relates to two-sided structure.

3. Assertion: The simple, clear statement of an idea.

4. Definition: The verbal setting of the limits of an idea. The act of clearly stating and delineating that idea.

5. Enigma: A statement or an impression with an obscure meaning or a meaning which has been left to be guessed or assumed by the audience (e.g., to arouse curiosity, get attention or interest.

6. Hyperbole: Intentional overstatement for effect (e.g., "there must have been a million of them").

7. Illustration: Synonymous with "example." The main purpose of an illustration is to make an idea clear, not to prove. It means "to illuminate."

8. Interrogation: The main purpose of a question in a presentation is either to get information or lead the audience where you want them to go in their thinking.

9. Narrative: Basically, a chronological form of telling something. An anecdote is told in narrative form.

10. Metaphor: A comparision differing from an analogy or simile mainly in terms of length. Usually stated in a word or two. The comparison is implied; e.g., "the plane knifed through the air."

11. Onomatopoeia: The formation of a word to imitate a sound; e.g., "buzz, swish, plunk."

12. Oxymoron: Literally, "sharply foolish." An intentionally contradictory, incongruous or paradoxical statement for effect; e.g., "clear as mud, "efficiently inefficient."

13. Personification: Attributing human qualities to nonhuman objects; e.g., "the machine chattered incessantly."

14. Response point: Anything done or said by a presenter to ensure that the audience is "with" him or to lead the audience farther. ("Understand?")

15. Understatement: The emphasis, reinforcement, or clarification of an idea by stating it in the negative; e.g., "It took a little effort to accomplish that," "There was *some* activity in sector." (Also known as "litote.")

Answers to Scorable Quiz: (Each correct answer = 10%.)

1. (a) individual cards or sheets, (b) folders for sorting

2. Any three of the following:

subjectivity	fragmented thinking
audience viewpoint	failure to isolate
failure to integrate	fact vs. opinion
misuse of evidence	testimony reliability
locked-in thinking	black and white thinking
synchronicity	overresponse

3. Any three of the following:

clear thinking	careful wording selection
avoid jargon	define terms
diction	concreteness
multidimensional thinking	

4. (a) change, (b) human being

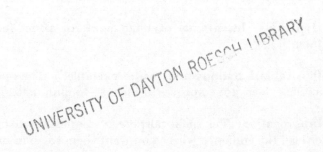

ISBN 0-471-01632-2

EFFECTIVE PRESENTATION
Idea Integrity

UNIT VII

W. A. Mambert

Executive Director

National Communication and Education Association

Wiley Professional Development Programs

Advisory Editor

Steven C. Wheelwright

Harvard Business School

John Wiley & Sons Inc.

New York • London • Sydney • Toronto

Center for
Professional Development
University of Dayton
Dayton, Ohio

Library of Congress Catalogue Card Number: 75-39750

ISBN 0-471-01633-0

Printed in the United States of America.

10 9 8 7 6 5 4 3 2 1

Preparing An Effective Introduction

PREMISE: That an audience's first perception of an idea is extremely significant, because if it is not effective, you may not get a chance to have the rest of your idea heard.

SEGMENT OBJECTIVE: To enable you to see the true purposes of a presentation introduction and to prepare effective introductions for your presentations.

Question A: In this and the two succeeding segments, we are going to be talking about a concept that we call "idea integrity." Before reading on, write here what you think we mean by this term.

_____

_____

_____

_____

_____

1 INTRODUCTION

As we have said, what you really are doing when you decide to make a presentation is to isolate an idea from the larger world of ideas among which it may be found, perhaps in a "random" state. You, in effect, have made the decision that you are going to restructure that idea and re-present it to a special group called an audience with a very specific function (objective) in mind.

Then, also in a very real sense, your task is to reinsert, or reintegrate, that idea back into the larger world of ideas and perceptions which, this time, is your audience's world of ideas and perceptions, and to make sure that it is perceived in exactly the way that you deliberately want it to be perceived and, more pointedly yet, to be acted upon.

In order to do these things most effectively, you must be sure that your idea has, among other things, a very specific identity and that it is perceived as a unified whole, which is precisely what integrity denotes. By definition, it is "the state or quality of being whole and unified." It is singleness and homogeneity. The next question is, not in a general, but in a very specific way:

What can be done to give an idea this essential quality of unity and singleness?

1

The answer to this question is a "big" one. To answer in the fullest possible sense, you could go back to the beginning of this course and merely think of its title as "How to Give an Idea Presentation the Quality of Integrity." For, indeed, everything properly done in the construction of a message does lead to its unity and cohesiveness.

Question B: Look or think back through the segments you've already studied, thinking in terms of what gives an idea presentation singleness and unity. From the material, state below five things that you already have studied that will do this.

_____

_____

_____

_____

_____

Answer to Question A: Most people think of "integrity" has having to do only with personal character and morality. But by definition, the word has a much broader applicability. For it means literally, "wholeness, entireness, completeness, something undivided; that is; an integral whole something unimpaired or uncorrupted (e.g., an unimpaired or uncorrupted moral state.) The term "integrality," although less familiar, is synonymous. Thus, "integrity" is the condition of singleness and cohesive unity. "Idea integrity" is the idea's condition of wholeness, unity, singleness and cohesiveness. It is one of the most significant qualities that your idea can and should have if you want it to accomplish a specific function.

Answer to Question B: If you answered in essence that:
1. singular, clearly stated objective . . .
2. converted to a singular, clearly isolated thesis . . .
3. developed into a single, unified main-thought pattern (structure) . . .
4. directed to a clearly defined audience . . .
5. and adequately supported by the right amount and kinds of rational, physical, and psychological evidence, persuasion and reinforcement related directly to the thesis and objective . . . .

will almost certainly impart the quality of integrity to a presented idea, we congratulate you on having truly grasped the heart of the message of this course so far.

For example, giving your idea a strong, singular main structure mitigates toward its unity. Integrity is further strengthened by adhering to the dictum, form follows function, for its net effect is to link everything done, every supportive element directly to the basic singularity of the message, directly to the end product you are seeking. As you fill in the details, you thus build properly and effectively through the whole presentation a composition process. And, when the time comes for the final verification of the presentation's integrity, you find yourself with an edifice that already exhibits much of the integrity you are seeking. The task, in effect, then becomes one of merely "topping off." And, in this respect, there are three very specific things that you can do. These are:

1. A deliberately planned first perception of your idea
2. A final check of its internal cohesiveness
3. A deliberately planned final perception of your idea

In this segment, we'll look at the first of these: the planned first perception.

Question C: Can you think of some strategic reasons that a deliberately planned first perception of your idea is important? State them briefly here.

_____

_____

_____

_____

_____

2 A STRATEGIC VIEW

This is what we're asking you to do: Take a strategic (and tactical) view of your presentation introduction. Remove it from the realm of "just getting the presentation started" or "warming up" to what you have to say. A proper presentation introduction is in fact a presentation unto itself. It is, if you will, the "presentation" of your presentation. As such, it has some very specific functions. At a minimum, it should:

1. *Get audience attention, for, without it, nothing else will matter. Where there is no attention, there is no reception or perception. Therefore, you might just as well not be giving the presentation.*
2. *Focus that attention on your idea presentation as a single communicative entity.*
3. *Place you and your idea in the most advantageous position and posture that is possible.*
4. *Provide for the audience a transitional link, a "bridge" between their larger world of ideas, people, things, impressions and so forth, into the specific world of the idea you're presenting to them.*
5. *Tell or forecast as much or as little as you deem strategically necessary or advantageous to your objective.*

Question D: List below some particular forms of idea support (see segment 13) that would be good candidates for accomplishing each of the five introduction functions you have just read about.

1. Function: to get attention
   Possible device: _____
   (For answer see heading #6.)

2. Function: to *focus* attention
   Possible device: _____
   (For answer see heading #7.)

3

3. Function: to place idea in most advantageous position
   Possible device: _____
   (For answer see heading #8.)

4. Function: to tell or forecast presentation content
   Possible device:_____
   (For answer see heading # 9.)

> *NOTE . . .*
> *Remember this too: In the actual delivery of your introduction, nobody but you may know that these are the actual functions (your private objectives) that you are trying to accomplish. Hopefully, the elements, actions, emotional appeal, and so forth that you select will simply do the job.*

3 THINK OF HOW YOU FIRST PERCEIVED

If you'll consider for a moment how you first perceived the idea, i.e., sought first to isolate it, then to establish its main parts, its inherent structure, its external relationships, and so forth, you'll have a pretty good idea of what you're now trying to do for your audience (with the added factor that you know the purpose behind what you're trying to do). Nevertheless, the same must take place for your audience in terms of how you want it to see your idea.

As we've said, the well-conceived introduction is considered as a separate communicative entity or increment, with its own set of objectives. Think of it as the handling of the idea of handling your idea. Its final objective is the changing of your audience to a point where it is ready to see or hear your message.

4 THE SAME CHARACTERISTICS AS THE PRESENTATION BOX

As a distinct communicative entity, your introduction should exhibit the same characteristics as the body of your message. It will, for example, have its own structure. In turn, it will draw from the same repertoire of rational, physical, and psychological supportive material, with the possible exception that the "biggest and best" will have been saved for the beginning (and, as you might expect, saved also for the ending).

In other words, structure is structure, whether it is the structure of the whole idea, the subelements of the idea, or the structure of the introduction. The same applies to idea support (rational, physical, or psychological).

Question E: What structure(s) do you think would be the most likely candidate(s) for the outline of an introduction?

_____

_____

_____

_____

_____

Answer to Question C: We gave you the answer in the succeeding text. All of the standard "first impression" reasons apply. No matter how many times humans are reminded of the dangers in thinking and acting on first impressions, most of us continue to think and act on the basis of them. So your audience's first impression of you is likely to be what you're "stuck" with, like it or not. This applies particularly in the rational and emotional dimensions and somewhat at the sensory level too. If, for example, for some reason you touch a "sore spot" at the outset, are too threatening, alienate an audience, and so forth, you're more than likely going to be in deep trouble throughout the rest of your presentation. Similarly, if a rational judgment is made against you in the beginning (some audiences also arrive with preconceived judgments), your evidence and persuasion, no matter how valid, will be considerably weakened. Face the fact that your audience usually will be afflicted with all or some of the "data gathering pitfalls" we cautioned you against in Segment 18.

Answer to Question E: There's obviously no "pat" answer to this question, and, at one time or another, all of the discussed structures would be candidates. Particularly, though, look at the possibilities of:

1. Some form of "in medias res" structure, e.g., picking a most impressive event as a starter and working backward or forward from it.
2. You'll find the orders of familiarity and acceptability of particular use in introductions too for pretty obvious reasons. They start at a point where the audience already is, and then relate directly to their world.
3. The deductive approach, although sometimes a poor candidate because it reveals too much too soon, also sometimes is effective when you want to shock an audience into attention, "get it right out in the open," or in some other way really "hit" them with your idea.
4. Stating a problem (the first half of a two-sided structure) sometimes is also effective, especially if it's something that is directly on your audience's mind, and they are really relating to it when they come to you.
5. Looking at the whole "family" of state, condition, quality, and degree also will give you many more ideas for opening a presentation. Starting with the closest (proximity), the most important, the most relevant, the most immediate, and so forth, all are excellent "openers."

5 THE AUDIENCE ANALYSIS PAYOFF

It is here, when you actually start to think about standing before your audience for the first time, and when you start planning to do this, that your detailed analysis of that audience will really start to pay off. For it is in fact this analysis that is going to give you the base for initially and continually relating to that audience. So this is the place to review also what we have said about analyzing the specific audience/situation, particularly in the area of what an audience's attitude toward you, the idea presenter, is.

Question F: List here ten audience attitudes that would have an influence on how you open the presentation of your idea to them.

_____ _____

_____ _____

_____ _____

_____ _____

_____ _____

Answers to Question F: (See Segment 16.) apathetic, hostile, interested, curious, friendly, unfriendly, apprehensive, enthusiastic, resentful, lively, capricious, receptive, relaxed, happy, unhappy, favorable, unfavorable, sympathetic, condescending, prejudiced, distrustful.

6 HOW TO GET ATTENTION
Following are a few of the many possibilities:

- *Use the basic-motive appeal or tie the subject directly to the interests of the audience. Example: "Gentlemen, today I am going to tell you about a new conveyor device that can cut your product handling time by fifteen percent."*

- *Ask a question which has meaning for the audience and a direct connection with the thesis. Example: "Have you ever stopped to think about how much time is lost in trial-and-error ballistics calculation?"*

- *Arouse the curiosity of the audience. Example: "In the next thirty minutes, I'm going to show you how to add five years to the life of every machine in your plant."*

- *Start with a shocking exclamation. Example: "Gentlemen, you may not realize it, but we are sitting on a powder keg!"*

- *Use an example and give it dimensional meaning. Example: "This dictionary contains 1200 pages; so does this microfiche."*

- *Open with a quotation that bears directly upon the subject. Example: "Benjamin Franklin said, "Knowledge is power. It still is and there is more of it than ever before. In fact, man's combined knowledge is doubling every ten years. Soon it will be eight, then six. That's a lot of power. And today, the real problem is how to get at it."*

7 HOW TO FOCUS ATTENTION
You have your audience's attention in general. Now what do you do to focus that attention on your idea as a unit? Here are some possibilities:

- *The most obvious is the one often most ignored: the direct approach. Yes, you can just come right out and tell them to focus their attention on your idea.*

- *If you can tell them, you can also ask them.*
- *Identify with them. This is good advice in many respects, but here especially. Tell them or let them see that you are "in the same boat" they are with respect to this problem, this need, this requirement, and so forth.*
- *Tell them what your idea is not; that is, verbally eliminate possible other things you could be talking about, thereby clearly delineating the "borders" of what you are dealing with.*
- *Use any supportive device, such as an anecdote, a parable, or an illustration that clearly identifies exactly what it is that you're talking about.*
- *Tell them what your objective is and where they will be, what they will know or have or be able to do after you've finished.*

8 HOW TO PLACE YOUR IDEA IN THE MOST ADVANTAGEOUS POSTURE

This is, do not forget, what a true strategist seeks: the most advantageous posture. Nor is this something that's always easy to get. Following are some things that will help ensure that your idea will be seen initially in the most strategically advantageous way:

- *State it in the audience's language and terminology, not yours.*
- *Make sure that all elements of the introduction are in fact carefully conceived, based on what you know about your audience.*
- *Establish the right relationship with the audience from the outset. Do not apologize for what you are bringing to them. Do not apologize for being unprepared; because if you are unprepared, you shouldn't be there in the first place.*
- *Don't overstate, no matter how sure you are of yourself, that you're right. Humility is "in" this year.*
- *Finally, make sure you have a good title (see Segment 17).*

9 HOW TO TELL OR FORECAST WHAT THE PRESENTATION CONTAINS

Many of the devices already mentioned can be used here:

- *Reveal the pattern to the audience. Simply tell them that here is an effect and that the causes will be shown and so forth.*
- *Summarize the main points.*
- *Tell the audience what they will be able to do after the presentation.*
- *State the thesis outright. As has been mentioned, this is usually the best procedure in most business, professional, or technical presentations—even selling. Most audiences in today's business–technology environment are fairly practical people and will not hold with too much contrived suspense building unless there is real purpose in it.*

Summary Exercise: List here the five main functions of an introduction.

1. _____

2. _____

3. _____

4. _____

5. _____

Scorable Quiz: Fill in the missing word or words.

1. We call a presentation's quality of wholeness and unity, _____.

2. The three specific devices detailed in the text that give a presentation integrity are: the planned _____ , internal _____ , and the planned _____ .

3. The main functions of a strategically planned introduction should be to get (a) _____ , to (b) _____ that attention, to place your idea in the most (c) _____ position, to provide a (d) _____ link between the audience's world and your presentation, and to (e) _____ or tell as much or as little of what your presentation contains as you deem strategically necessary.

4. The most obvious, and yet often ignored, method of focusing audience attention is the _____ approach.

Answers to Summary Exercise:
1. Get attention
2. Focus attention.
3. Place yourself in the most advantageous strategic position.
4. Provide the audience a transitional link into the "world" of your presentation.
5. Tell or forecast the contents of your presentation.

Answers to Scorable Quiz: (Each correct answer = 10%). (1) idea integrity, (2a) first perception, (2b) cohesiveness, (2c) final perception, (3a) attention, (3b) focus, (3c) advantageous, (3d) transitional, (3e) forecast, (4) direct.

LEARNING 20 SEGMENT

Giving The Presentation
Internal Cohesiveness

PREMISE: The introduction and conclusion "box in" the idea, as it were. But the internal parts also must be held together.

SEGMENT OBJECTIVE: To enable you to effectively unify and integrate the body of your presentation through the knowledge of specific devices for doing so.

Question A: We've referred to the presentation introduction as analogous to a bridge, which gets your audience from a given "place" in their world into the momentary world of your presentation. For the moment, let's continue this analogy and think of the whole presentation as a bridge, taking your audience from one place to another in their thinking, feeling, attitude, knowledge, ability, action, and so forth. Let's suppose further that you are explaining this analogy to an actual audience and must put a graphic representation of the idea on the chalkboard as you speak. We shall also make this a review exercise in converting ideas received randomly into a better logical sequence for presentation. You'll notice, too, that we've included some reference to the subject of presentation conclusion, although we don't actually go into this until Segment 21.

Below, you will find:
1. Your "script" of the things you will say to your audience, but not in the sequence in which they ought to be said.
2. A "starter" for your chalkboard illustration

Your Script

○ A. "Your main idea structure is the bridge framework, what ties the presentation together at the most fundamental level.

○ B. Your rational, physical, and psychological supportive elements and devices might be viewed as the actual paving of the roadway, what fills in the "spaces" between the structural members.

○ C. "The introduction to your presentation . . . .

    ○ D. Establishes the outlines of the bridge, determines its outer borders . . . .

        ○ E. And, is the approach to that bridge."

○ F. "Ladies and gentlemen, a presentation of an idea to an audience is very much like a bridge.

9

G. You meet that audience at a given place or time in their thinking, feeling, knowing, doing, or not doing. In a nutshell, your presentation task is to take or lead them, over a gap or river if you will, from that initial place to where you want them to be in their thinking, feeling, and so forth. Let's say that your presentation is the bridge between these two places."

H. "Your presentation conclusion is the exit ramp that leads your audience, with your idea in mind, in hand, or in actions or behavior, back onto the roadway of their own lives, now redirected, over your presentation bridge into the new direction in which your objective said that you wanted them to go.

I. "Your objective-converted-to-thesis is the central structural member of the bridge, stretching its full length, from the time of your meeting to the time of your parting."

Your Chalkboard Illustration

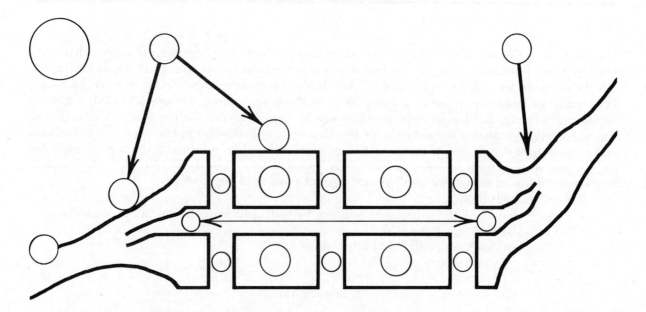

Here's your task:

1. First, resequence the statements into the order and suborder in which you would actually say them to your audience. Use the circles to the left of each to number and letter them.

2. Envision yourself as actually making these statements to an audience, explaining that a presentation is very much like a bridge.

3. As you "say" each statement, enter your number for each in an appropriate circle in the diagram.

4. Notice also that there are more circles in the diagram than there are statements, indicating that you will enter some numbers more than once as you "speak."

10

Answers to Question A:
Your Script: (A) 4, (B) 6, (C) 3, (D) A, (E) B, (F) 1, (G) 2, (H) 7, (I) 5

Your Chalkboard Illustration:

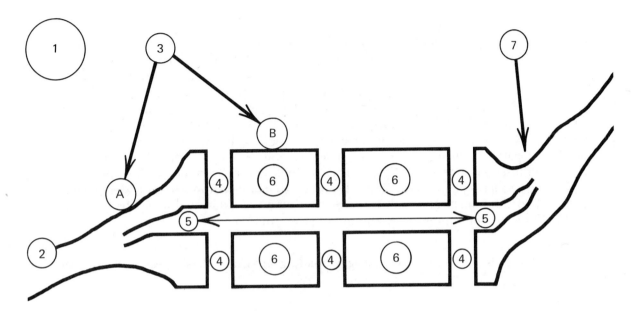

Question B: Now let's review something you read at the beginning of Segment 19. There are three specific things that particularly work to give a presentation the quality of integrity. They are:

---

1   DEVICES FOR BUILDING IDEA INTEGRITY

Internal cohesiveness is something that you should build into your presentation as you construct it. And, after you have absorbed the contents of this segment, you will know what to look for and do as you go. The main reason that we include it here, in between talking about the introduction and conclusion of your presentation, is that it rightfully is a part of the process of giving your presentation integrity and unity, as are the introduction and conclusion.

Like many of the other elements of idea presentation, internal cohesiveness is something that many people talk much about but whose actual anatomy very few people really understand. That is, there are some very specific devices that you can intentionally build into the presentation that will tend very strongly to give it the internal cohesiveness, the effective linking together of its parts, that it should have. There also may be things other than those that we cover here. But if you look for and build into your presentation at least these devices, it's almost a sure guarantee of increased internal unity, of idea integrity.

You also will recognize some of these "devices for building idea integrity" as some of the supportive devices we've already talked about. What else could they be?

11

Answer to Question B:
1. A deliberately planned first perception
2. A final check of internal cohesiveness
3. A deliberately planned final perception

2 STRUCTURAL SINGULARITY

This, of course, is the beginning point. It's why we stressed that your presentation, no matter how it's subelements may be structured, should have a single main structure. If, for example, you begin with a problem-solution approach, this is what you should continue with throughout the whole presentation. If you're going with a general-to-specific idea pattern, stay with it throughout, and so forth. Remember what we've said about your average audience member. He must know what pathway he is on. He not only has a rational need for it; he also has a psychological need for order and pattern. The human mind generally abhors and is "turned off" by that which confuses or is chaotic. People usually think and act at random; but they generally crave order and shy away from disorder. Remember, too, the principle of simplicity, that the human mind takes the path of least resistance and ought to be given that path by anyone who wants that mind to grasp something.

Question C: When is the best time to begin building internal cohesiveness into your presentation?

_____

Question D: Enter the following phrases in their proper places in the flow diagram: (1) a goal-directed manner, (2) a specifically described audience response, (3) a distinct sense of purpose, (4) a thesis, (5) a single main-thought pattern, (6) gives a presentation cohesiveness.

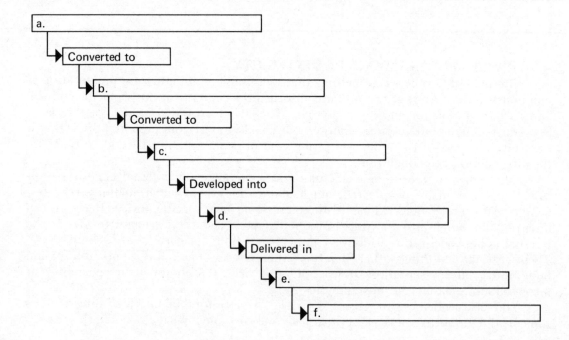

a.

Converted to

b.

Converted to

c.

Developed into

d.

Delivered in

e.

f.

3 ADHERENCE TO OBJECTIVE

There is nothing that will work better to give a presentation internal cohesiveness than keeping your objective ever-present in your mind throughout the entire preparation and delivery processes. We think it is very difficult to overemphasize the need for concentration on objective. It is truly inseparable from anything else you do in the functional idea presentation. Remember, this is what this course is talking about: functional presentation.

You can do many things "wrong" in the course of your presentation. But the one thing you can't do and retain any cohesiveness is lose awareness of your objective. The moment you do, your presentation deteriorates into a meaningless hodgepodge of information and impressions. Often, when all else fails you, when you forget some details, make "unforgivable mistakes," your concentration on what is the intended end product of your presentation will redeem you. It will be like tapping a hidden source of power, for very few obstacles can withstand the force of a person truly bent on accomplishing what he has set out to do.

Take it a step farther in terms of your actual confrontation with your audience. For them, you concentrate on your thesis; never lose sight of it. It is memorized, burned into your mind, and, in the final outcome, must also be similarly etched into their minds and beings, attitudes or behavior, knowing or feeling.

Answer to Question C: From the moment you begin gathering data for your presentation, you ought to be thinking about and building internal cohesiveness.

Answer to Question D: (a) 3, (b) 2, (c) 4, (d) 5, (e) 1, (f) 6.

Question E: State the following outline points in parallel form:
Thesis: "For an efficient system

- As close to its source as possible, capture the data.
- Provide for feedback and control.
- There must be a good storage medium.
- Always disseminate results properly.
- Determine the basic system function.
- Know the user requirements.

I. _____

II. _____

III. _____

IV. _____

V. _____

VI. _____

4 PARALLELISM AND SIMILARITY

Recall our prior discussion of this subject. When ideas are perceived, stated, or constructed in a parallel or similar way, they tend more strongly to be bound together and to have a unified relationship with each other, often even if they actually are unrelated. That is, you can make them look related. The similarity in appearance itself becomes a relationship.

Nor need the parallelism or similarity always be executed at the rational level, simply stating things in a similar way. Visual unity, for example, can be achieved through the intentional omission of variety or change. You might impart parallelism by stating similar ideas in the same type style, all in the same-shaped boxes, color, and so forth.

Answer to Question E: There's nothing complicated about parallel structure. In fact, its simplicity is the key to its effectiveness in giving cohesiveness to a group of ideas. Many presenters shy away from it because it looks boring at the outline level, when the sentences are so close to each other. But envision these as the first statements in sections of a presentation separated by considerable amounts of verbiage, and you'll find that they have a desirable effect on tying the sections together.

Thesis: For an efficient system:
   I. You must capture the data as close to the source as possible.
  II. You must provide for feedback and control.
 III. You must always have a good storage medium.
 IV. You must always disseminate results properly.
  V. You must determine the basic system function.
 VI. You must know the user requirements.

5   CONSISTENCY

Carry through here on the idea of parallelism. Consistency of attitude, behavior, gesture, environment, even mode of attire, the decor of a room, the level of language, humor, and mood, to mention a few, all have a unifying effect on the idea being presented. Absence of such consistency actually can have the opposite disintegrative effect.

Similarly, "mixed emotions," unless it's your specific functional purpose to "mix" them, rarely contribute to the singularity of an attempt to communicate. As we saw when we talked about sensory communication, the same goes for mixing too many sensory effects or impressions at the same time.

Some of these elements have very overt effects on an audiences sense of presentation unity; others are more subliminal (beneath the level of normal perception). Their absence may simply give the audience a feeling that something isn't tied together properly.

For example, if a presentation begins on a relatively informal, conversational level and the presenter suddenly switches his language and tone to that of an elaborate state dedicatory or funereal address, his audience will either consciously or unconsciously be disconcerted, perhaps even experience the feeling that they missed something he said. Actually the inconsistency could be something as simple as a loud necktie or an unpleasant mannerism, anything that breaks the mood, image, or pattern the presenter is attempting to establish and maintain. A change in the style of visual aids, for example, from serious art to slyly humorous cartooning, neither wrong of itself, could work to destroy the unity of the presentation. The basic question which the presenter should ask himself is: "Are what I am doing and saying consistent with the image I wish to convey, with the audience and occasion, and with the objective."

6 REFERENCE

Two subideas within a presentation can be linked together and given relationship by referring to one while talking about the other. You can, of course, do this in the most direct way; that is, you can tell your audience, "This and that are related, and here's why and how." But you can also use reference terminology or transitional phrasing. This type of reference usually is typified by beginning statements with such terms as:

Although	*Moreover*	*Recall that*
Because	*Considering that*	*Therefore*
Thus	*However*	*Since*
In addition to	*In view of*	*But*

These are connectives whose function is to link ideas through subordination, co-ordination, causal, or other relationship. They help to prevent the presentation or parts of it from becoming just a listing of topics instead of a flowing idea.

Such terms tell the audience that something related to the present segment of the idea has already been said or surmised. They tell him that this is not an isolated thought, but a part of a whole, even that if he hasn't perceived the referenced idea, he had better ask a question or find out what it was, or he won't grasp the whole logic flow. Here are some sample phrases that might be found, say, at the beginning of a new subidea where the presenter would be using the device of reference to provide internal transition:

"Recall that we said how important objective was. Now you will see why."

"Although it is important to know about data gathering, what we must do now . . ."

"Based upon the fact that a good strategy is necessary, we must know . . . "

"Moreover, converting your objective to a thesis is just as important as . . . "

Question F: Now you try it. See also how such devices serve an additional function of progressing and developing a logical thought flow. Following is a series of statements with which a novice might begin the sections of his presentation, without transition. Convert each to a clearly transitional statement. Don't worry about logical flow between statements.

1. The instructor had not discussed two key principles in class.
2. Sixty-five percent of the students in this class received failing grades.
3. The examination was not clearly written.
4. Many students did receive high grades.
5. They all misinterpreted two key questions.

1. _____

2. _____

3. _____

4. _____

5. _____

Answer to Question F: This, of course, is only one of many possible ways of stating the ideas. If you did anything like this, you're on the right track in understanding idea transition by reference.

1. Although many students did receive high grades . . .
2. Because of this, sixty-five percent of the students in this class received failing grades.
3. Considering that the examination was not clearly written . . .
4. Since the instructor had not discussed two key principles in class . . .
5. Therefore, they all misinterpreted two key questions.

7 RESTATEMENT AND REPETITION

Many people confuse "planned repetition or restatement" with "inadvertent or unnecessary redundancy." One grows out of intentional planning, the other out of ineptness. Planned repetition, or restatement, obviously will increase the chances of an idea's having the desired effect. As an integrating device, it can be used to extract or or state any salient part of the idea already covered, ranging from a repeating of what the basic structure of your presentation is, its thesis, its dominant emotional mood, or its sensory impressions. There obviously is a close relationship with consistency here, for repeated themes, motifs, words, phrasing, and so forth are a form of consistency. But here, too, you cycle right back into the idea of multidimensional thinking and the almost infinite variety of ways of repeating and restating ideas.

8 RESPONSE POINTS

A very effective way to impart cohesiveness to a presentation is to build into the device that we call "responsive points." Among other things, the response point is to the presenter of ideas to live audiences what the rhetorical question is to the writer, ("What, then, is a response point?") But the response point is much more than a mere rhetorical question to the oral presenter. For he is in an active interchange with his audience. He can actually get and see their responses and thus gains a much greater flexibility than the writer has.

The response point is a form of overt or tacit audience participation intended
primarily to keep that audience on the track on which the presenter wants

them. How often do you, the student, visualize a typical audience member as you prepare a presentation?

Assume that someone is leading you through an unfamiliar forest, perhaps dimly lighted, which is what it often amounts to when someone is hearing or experiencing your presented idea for the first time. Periodically, he calls out, "Are you with me?" Did you see that important landmark we just passed?" What did you see that time? Whatever he says, he's probably trying to do one of two things: to either make sure you're still "following" him, or to keep you with him. And this is precisely what the idea presenter who uses response points is doing. (Isn't that right?)

Most function-oriented presenters also want to know whether they are accomplishing their objective during the presentation. Audience feedback provides some measurement, but you can use this feedback more deliberately by building intermediate responses into your presentation. For example, an instructor asks a test question at the conclusion of a major point. A salesman is more subtle because he usually uses questions to lead his audience. An example is the double-question technique, recognized in many sales presentations. He asks, "Which do you like, sir, the red or yellow model?" "Do you like the office on the seventh floor or the fifth better ma'am?" "Which one of these systems best suits your needs, sir?" Later on he might ask, "Does your company usually purchase or lease?" Such questions can be subtly interwoven into a presentation to the extent that a hearer is not even aware that he is gradually weaving an affirmative net around himself, from which it will become increasingly difficult for him to extricate himself without "losing face" which is a form of ego involvement.

A similar type of response point is that of developing a kind of "cumulative affirmation," which goes something like this. "I'm certain you'll agree that solid state technology is superior, isn't that right?" "Every efficient office needs good records, doesn't it?" The point here is to ask objective-oriented, generalized questions to which any normal person must answer with a yes and to reinforce the questions by actually giving the expected answers. The natural result is the creation of an affirmative atmosphere. After all, the hearer has agreed with the presenter throughout the conversation. True, many of the things to which he has agreed may have no direct bearing on the issue, but human nature is such that it will be difficult for him to do a complete public about face after he has aligned himself with the speaker all along. His pride usually will not let him. An audience must be conducted over such a course carefully and with a great deal of finesse, or they will see through the device.

Sometimes nothing is better than simply coming out and asking a direct question. This should be done only when you are reasonably sure of what the answer will be. And you can be, on the basis of what has gone before.

Regardless of what response technique may be convenient in a given situation, one thing is certain for the presenter operating on an aware basis: every success or failure in the use of these techniques will drive you deeper and deeper into the realm of subtlety, which is precisely where the art of using response points belongs. You will frequently find the most sophisticated of people surprisingly naive when they are confronted with even an amateur use of questioning techniques. For the average presenter, direct test-type questions will undoubtedly be the best method for determining how well the idea presentation is progressing. Unskilled use of leading questions is insulting to the intelligent audience, as is inept employment of any communicative device. Yet if even the novice presenter thinks in terms of response points and objective measurement as he proceeds, he is far closer to making his presentation integrated, purposeful, and functional than he would be if he simply dispensed his message in one-sided fashion.

9 SUMMARIZING

This is a time-honored and proven method of giving a presentation unity and cohesiveness. Do not confuse the process of summarizing with that of concluding. Summarizing may be a device used in concluding a presentation, but it is rarely a conclusion per se. Summarizing not only at the end but throughout the presentation is an excellent way of keeping both yourself and the audience on the track. Obviously, summary embodies the idea of reference as well. It can be directly stated as a summation, or it can simply be implied in the discussion without mentioning that it is a summary.

Summary Exercise: What a coincidence! In this summary exercise, let's use a simple summary as a closing device. The gist of this segment has been eight basic methods of giving an idea presentation internal cohesiveness. What are they?

1. _____   5. _____

2. _____   6. _____

3. _____   7. _____

4. _____   8. _____

Scorable Quiz: Fill in the missing word or words.

1. When is the best time to build internal cohesiveness into your presentation?

   _____

2. According to the text, what is the "beginning point" of internal cohesiveness?

   _____

3. There obviously always is a rational need for idea structure from the simple standpoint of comprehensibility. But audiences have another need for structure. What is it? _____

4. What is the analogy used in the text to describe the presentation structure or framework? _____

5. What is it which, if kept ever-present in your mind, will help to give your presentation internal cohesiveness, perhaps above all other·devices?

   _____

6. As far as your audience is concerned, they probably will hear your objective stated as what? _____

7. What do we call the stating of ideas in similar ways? _____

8. What do we call the maintaining of a singular motif or style?

   _____

9. Two ideas within a presentation can be linked together and given relationship by what device? _____

10. What do we call the use of such devices as rhetorical questions or doing or saying things designed to get the audience to react in some way during the presentation?

   _____

Answers to Summary Exercise: (1) structural singularity, (2) adherence to objective, (3) parallelism and similarity, (4) consistency, (5) reference, (6) restatement and repetition, (7) response points, (8) summarizing.

Answers to Scorable Quiz: (Each correct answer = 10%.) (1) as you construct it, (2) a single main structure, (3) their psychological need for order, (4) a bridge, (5) your objective, (6) your thesis, (7) parallelism, (8) consistency, (9) reference, (10) response points.

21 Preparing An Effective Conclusion

LEARNING 21 SEGMENT

PREMISE: That a presentation should not merely end; it should conclude functionally.

SEGMENT OBJECTIVE: To enable you to construct a functional conclusion.

Question A: List here some things that you think a functional presentation conclusion ought to do.

1. _____

2. _____

3. _____

4. _____

5. _____

Question B: When should you prepare your conclusion?

_____

_____

_____

_____

_____

Question C: Besides time and position in the presentation, what are the main differences between an introduction and conclusion?

_____

_____

_____

1 THE PLANNED FINAL PERCEPTION

A functional presentation should not just end; it should conclude. It should be a strategic move. A good conclusion will answer at least the following two questions:

- *How do you want your idea seen and heard for the last time?*
- *What do you want your audience to do as a result of having heard your message?*

Question D: What will the answers to the above two questions match? _____

If you do the job correctly, your answer to both of these questions will almost perfectly match something that you have already stated earlier in your preparation.

Like a functional introduction, a functional conclusion stands alone as a communicative increment unto itself. It is a separate part of the presentation. Its functions, in fact, are quite similar to those of the introduction. For example, attention is extremely important. If you have had it at no other time during your presentation, you ought to have it here; for this is your last chance to get it. The conclusion also should serve to focus attention on the presentation as a unified whole, to integrate it. And the conclusion should serve as a "bridge" for the audience, leading from the world of your idea into their own world, and, of utmost importance, back into their world changed in some way. For (stop and think about it a moment) if there indeed has been no change, you have just done little more than consume a certain amount of time and energy. You might just as well not have bothered in the first place.

Answers to Question A: As a minimum, a good functional conclusion will:
1. Focus the audience's attention for the final time on the presentation as a unified, integrated idea, and
2. Serve as a final attempt to accomplish the objective, or
3. Seek some measurement that the objective has been or will be accomplished, or
4. Tell the audience what to do next if your objective was to have them do something after they leave your presentation, or
5. Provide the initial step in objective accomplishment if you are seeking some kind of continuing or protracted action, change, response, and so forth.

Answer to Question B: Believe it or not, the best times to prepare the introduction and the conclusion actually are the reverse of the sequence in which they appear in the presentation. The reasons are simple. First, you can't really adequately introduce something in its entirety until you know completely what it is. But the first thing that you do know in functional presenting is where you want to finally end up. So, your objective statement will give you some of your best ideas for your conclusion.

Answer to Question C: Good, functional introductions and conclusions are very similar in both function and content, in fact, they often may be interchangeable with only slight changes in wording or content. They both also use such techniques as summary, reference, repetition, and so forth.

Answers to Question D: The answers to these two questions will almost perfectly match your original statement of objective. What else could it be?

Question E: Name some methods of telling what a presentation has contained.

_____   _____

_____   _____

_____   _____

2 A SINGULAR FOCUS

We have already seen that the average human mind craves order and desires that ideas be presented to it in neat little packages. This is precisely one of the things that a good presentation conclusion will do. It will give the audience a singular focus on what you have told or shown them.

You usually can provide this singular focus by:

1. *Restating your thesis, or*
2. *Telling what the presentation contained.*

There is an old saying in the professional communicating business that you should:

"Tell them what you're going to tell them . . .
tell them what you want to tell them . . .
then tell what you told them."

In doing this, the simplest method is to summarize probably the main points of your outline. But here again, a multidimensional approach is open to you. For, a whole series of ideas can be summed up in an anecdote, an analogy, a picture, or almost any of the forms of idea support.

Answer to Question E: The list of idea support forms will give you many answers to this question. For example, you can:

1. summarize
2. restate
3. use an example
4. use an illustration

5. ask some summary questions
6. tell an anecdote
7. repeat
8. use a quotation

(See Segment 13.)

Question F: State the following four items as two equations in the space provided.

1. Objective Accomplishment
3. Actual Audience Response

2. Stated Objective
3. Planned Audience Response

22

A. ——————————————— = ———————————————

B. ——————————————— = ———————————————

3 THE VITAL COMPARISON
Final preparation of your conclusion should bring you just about full cycle right back to where you started, back to the formulation of your objective. In the final analysis the whole matter will boil down to a simple comparison:

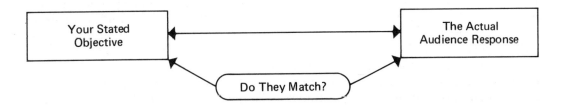

If the answer to this question is yes, you have what we call a "hit" on objective accomplishment. If they do not match, you have a "miss." It's that simple in functional communicating. Remember, too, one of the "constants" we discussed early in the course: There always are only two people, you and the other person, no matter how many other persons there are in your audience group. You are always dealing at the individual level, and people are convinced, decide, believe, know, do, and so forth, at the individual level. Therefore, if you have an audience of twenty people, and three respond as your objective described, you have three hits. The more the merrier!

Answers to Question F:
A. Stated Objective = Planned Audience Response
B. Actual Audience Response = Objective Accomplishment

Question G: If someone told you that you, as a presenter, had to take an "action step," what would you assume he meant?

——————————————————————————————————

——————————————————————————————————

——————————————————————————————————

——————————————————————————————————

4 THE ACTION STEP
There are very few functional-idea presentations which should not and cannot have an action step. For you, the potential idea presenter, an understanding of what an action step is and how it works is as important as anything else we've told you in this course. For, a presentation without an action step cannot be truly functional in the sense of our meaning here.

23

In a nutshell, an action step is:

1. An attempt to precipitate or evoke the actual audience response that you described as your presentation objective; or

2. An attempt to get some measurement, evidence, or verification that the objective has been accomplished.

Do not gloss over these two definitions. They are not mere comments, but very important ideas. What we are saying is that in functional–idea presentation, you must never depart the "field of battle" without a final bid either to accomplish your objective or to know as closely as you possibly can if the audience change you have been seeking has, can, or will take place. The action step "closes the loop" in functional communicating. It is the final "knot," as it were, that ties the whole presentation "fabric" together. It forces the issue.

Other forms of communication may or may not force the issue, but functional presenting always does. The ways that you force the issue may vary greatly, depending on mood and how persuasive, educational, informative, and so forth your presentation is. But force the issue, you must. In some persuasive situations, such as selling, an action step is fairly easy to devise. You might, for example, simply ask for the order, or for a signature on a contract, and immediately you have a measurement of whether or not you've accomplished your objective. In education, too, the action step is fairly easy to devise. You simply give a test or have the learner perform. If the answers to the test or the performance match exactly with what your objective stated you were going to get into your audience's "knowing," or the description of the ability you said you were going to teach him, you have a hit. If there is no match, there is no hit or objective accomplishment.

If a teacher, for example, is doing his job correctly, one of the first things that he will do, usually as a part of his objective–formulation process, is to devise the questions for the examinations that he will give his students. Naturally, he composes his questions, or performance tests, on the basis of what he knows to be the "right" answers or actions that will tell him whether or not the learners have indeed come to know or be able to do what he set out to impart to them. As a result, his whole teaching process will in effect be one of leading (changing) his students to the point where they can answer the questions or do the things which quickly will verify for him whether or not he has accomplished his objective.

Answer to Question G:

1. **An attempt to precipitate or evoke the actual audience response that you described as your presentation objective.**

2. **An attempt to get some measurement, evidence, or verification that the objective has been accomplished.**

5 PEOPLE MAKE SMALL CHANGES

In devising action steps, it is very important to remember, as we've said, that people normally cannot and will not take big steps all at once. This is why you devised a very narrow objective in the first place. Remember, also, that you should have been building response points throughout your presentation. That is, you can and should have a whole series of action steps that tie the parts of the presentation together, that have built affirmativeness, knowledge, and so forth, as you've proceeded. So, ideally, when you arrive at the point of your final bid for action, belief, knowing, and so forth, your "final response point" isn't such a big step for the audience.

The wise presenter thus will give his audience smaller action steps which are more palatable and easier to perform but which subtly commit them to the larger course of action. For example, instead of advocating a complete change to a new system all at once, you might ask them to perform one phase, to try a "thirty-day experiment," to meet with the engineers or designers, and so forth. The point is that you get some action and that you make it realistically performable. To drop a presentation, persuasive or otherwise, without getting some kind of measurement, commitment, or action is in effect defeating the whole purpose of functional presenting.

Remember too that subtlety often will be important. People will make any change quicker and more easily if they think they "thought of it themselves." When the audience member says in his mind, "Aha, it's just as I thought it was all along," or "I think I will do this or that," you have communicated in the highest sense of the word.

Question H: List three ways of forcing issues.

1. _____

2. _____

3. _____

6 HOW TO FORCE ISSUES

Many people are accustomed to avoiding decision. They tend to think that if they never force the issues, they are safe from failure. They also are "safe" from success in so doing. So you must train yourself in the ability to force issues. Here are a few tried and proven methods.

1. *Bluntly and boldly ask for the action; for example:*

    "Will you please sign there?"
    "May I see you next Tuesday at two?"
    "May we submit a written proposal?"
    "Please fill out the card."

2. *Use the choice-question method.*

    "Which model do you prefer?"
    "Can we meet on Monday or Friday?"
    "Would you prefer to lease or purchase?"

3. *Assume acceptance, thus forcing the hearer to stop the process.*

    "Where would you like the system installed, sir?"
    "How many . . . ?"

Answers to Question H: (1) Ask for the action. (2) Use the choice question method. (3) Assume acceptance.

7 DEALING WITH THE INTANGIBLES

Some presentations deal with intangibles not so easily measured. In getting people to believe, to change their attitudes, to feel a certain way, and so forth, devising an action step becomes a little more difficult, but not impossible if you have carefully stated your objective. How do you know when a person has acquired a certain attitude, is feeling a certain emotion, or is reacting within himself the way you intended him to react? In this case, you are in precisely the same position as the teacher. You must decide upon exactly what will indicate to you that this person does indeed feel or have love, compassion, desire, motivation, and so forth. This is where your sensitivity and experience come into play. Do you not already have ways of telling these things? Most of them have to do with the manner in which a particular person behaves, or acts toward you. Only experience and personal development can widen and deepen your capabilities in this area.

No matter how intangible your objective, you'll still want to know, if possible, if the "internal" change in your audience has taken place, if the opinion, attitude, belief, or feeling has indeed changed. How can you do this?

1. *You can ask the other person straightforwardly if he does now believe, feel, know, acknowledge, or think that your case has been proven, and so forth.*
2. *You can, as noted above, test him, either openly or covertly, and observe whether he now acts or responds as if he can do, knows, and so forth.*
3. *You can order or force him. For example, here too you can start to do something that he must stop you from doing or otherwise tacitly accept your message.*
4. *If nothing else, you can tell him that he has indeed now accepted your idea. He at least will have to confirm or negate you, and by this you will still be able to measure.*

There are, of course, situations where you may never know whether or not you have succeeded. In preparing this course, for example, we may never know whether we have accomplished our objective in a given student. Yet, even in such situations, it is often possible to find out. For instance, we could ask you to communicate with us after you have completed the course. And, on the basis of your response, we could get a pretty fair idea of how close we came to accomplishing our objective.

The fundamental point remains that a practical communicator never should leave a situation without some bid for action.

8 DEALING WITH FUTURE ACTION OR CHANGE

The objectives of some presentations may be to merely start some action or change that you want to continue into the future. Here, you'll still want to precipitate a first step in what probably will be a series of actions. You'll want to tell the audience what to do now and next. It might be, for example, that you'll want to come back and give another presentation. How can you precipitate such action? Basically, the same way that you can precipitate any of the other actions we've described here. You can, for example, ask for it, order it, or assume it.

If you want later personal contact, you also can force the issue on this. One of the best methods is to use registration forms or an audience-response card such as that shown. Any presenter can design his own to include multiple-choice questions or other information he wants in order to follow up his presentation with individual members of the audience. An example follows:

```
┌─────────────────────────────────────────────────────┐
│                                                       │
│                    RESPONSE CARD                      │
│                                                       │
│   My reaction to the presentation is: _____   │
│                                                       │
│   _____   │
│                                                       │
│   _____   │
│                                                       │
│   _____   │
│                                                       │
│   _____   │
│                                                       │
│   _____   │
│                                                       │
│                                                       │
│                        NAME_____     │
│                                                       │
│                        COMPANY_____     │
│                                                       │
└─────────────────────────────────────────────────────┘
```

Note that this response card is kept as simple and convenient to fill out as possible and asks for a minimum of personal information to avoid appearing like a device to get a contact. Consider the conditions under which such a card will usually be filled out. A call can be made to ask, "I was wondering what you meant by this, Mr. Jones." If a later contact is intended, getting the rest of the needed information is a simple clerical task. The concentration here is on his opinion and getting a response.

9 "FIRMING UP"

You may wish to "firm up" a commitment already given. This primarily occurs in persuasive and selling situations and is more a repeat action step than a new category. It consists mainly of restating what has been agreed upon so that there can be no possible misunderstanding that an arrangement has in fact been consummated.

- *"Well, sir, then we can consider it a 'deal,' all right?"*
- *"Fine; then you'll have the space ready by the thirty-first?"*
- *"We'll see you on Tuesday at nine."*

10 SUMMARY

The key, again, is to think of and construct both the introduction and conclusion of a message as practically separate communicative increments, each with its special function to perform. Then build them as specialized messages with proper transition into and out of the main message. Whereas effective introductions usually are better prepared after the main body of a message, it sometimes is advantageous to expand your objective into a full-fledged conclusion before preparing the full message. For then you truly will know exactly where you are going and what you are trying to do!

The final and most important step in concluding any functional attempt to communicate is the action step. Every functional communication always attempts to "force the issue" whenever possible.

Regardless of what device or method is used, in many ways the conclusion and action step, for a brief moment or two, are the presentation. For better or for worse, they are the culmination of the deliberate act, stretching right back to the title of the presentation. As such, they should be carefully, excruciatingly, and fully planned.

Summary Exercise: Insert the listed items in their proper sequence in the furnished flow diagram.

Support rationally	Initial conclusion ideas	Establish limitations
Prepare introduction	Finalize conclusion	Select thought pattern
Analyze audience/situation	Convert to thesis	Hit
No hit	No	Yes
Reinforce psychologically	Actual audience response	Support rationally
Check internal cohesiveness	Reinforce physically	Action step
Compare	Match	

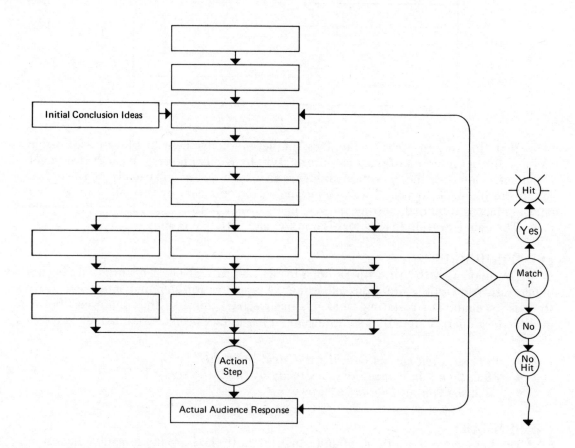

Scorable Quiz: Indicate true (T) or false (F).

1. A conclusion and summary are quite synonymous. _____

2. The conclusion of a presentation is strategically more important than the introduction. _____

3. A functional conclusion should stand alone as a communicative entity or increment unto itself. _____

4. The functions of the conclusion are quite different from the functions of the introduction. _____

5. There are very few presentations that should not have an action step. _____

6. An action step and a response point are essentially the same. _____

7. The way to test the success of a presentation is to compare the stated objective with the audience response. If they match, you've succeeded; if they don't match, you've failed. _____

8. One good way to focus attention on your presentation idea for the last time is to restate your thesis, no matter how many times you've already stated it. _____

9. It is wrong to give an audience a direct order to do what you want them to do. _____

10. You can't have an action step when your objective deals with intangibles such as changes in attitudes, feelings, or beliefs. _____

Answer to Summary Exercise:

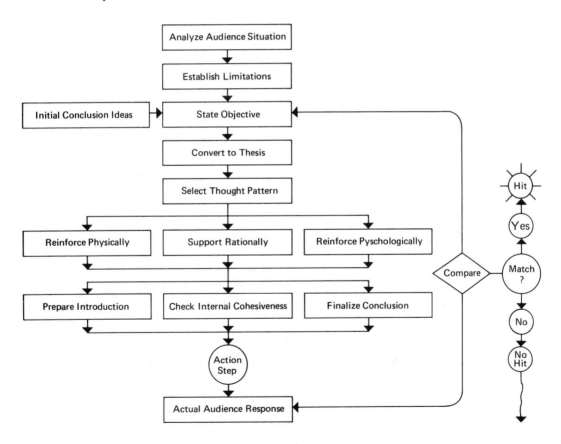

Answers to Scorable Quiz: (Each correct answer = 10%.) (1) F, (2) F, (3) T, (4) F, (5) T, (6) T, (7) T, (8) T, (9) F, (10) F.

ISBN 0-471-01633-0

EFFECTIVE PRESENTATION
Visual And Other Aids

UNIT VIII

W. A. Mambert

Executive Director

National Communication and Education Association

Wiley Professional Development Programs

Advisory Editor

Steven C. Wheelwright

Harvard Business School

John Wiley & Sons Inc.
New York • London • Sydney • Toronto

Center for
Professional Development
University of Dayton
Dayton, Ohio

Library of Congress Catalogue Card Number: 75-39750

ISBN 0-471-01634-9

Printed in the United States of America.

10 9 8 7 6 5 4 3 2 1

Understanding Aids

LEARNING 22 SEGMENT

PREMISE: That aids are means to ends and not ends unto themselves.

SEGMENT OBJECTIVE: That you have a grasp of the reasons for preparing visual and other aids and be able to make your aids an integral part of your presentation structure and supportive material.

Question A: List below what you think are the functions of aids.

1. _____   5. _____

2. _____   6. _____

3. _____   7. _____

4. _____   8. _____

1 WHAT ARE AIDS?

Notice that we do not just say "visual aids" here. This nomenclature is far too restricting for the multidimensional-thinking presenter. The visual, as we have seen, is only one of many sense avenues, not to mention the emotional avenues. So, at the outset, think multidimensionally. Think of an aid as any reinforcement technique, visual or otherwise.

The second important thing to remember is the true role of aids. They are supportive and not primary. The "tail should not wag the dog." That is, as usual, form must follow function. You don't build a presentation around some pictures, for example, just because you happen to have them. In short:

The idea must always precede the aid that supports it.

Answer to Question A: **The right way to view aids, as we call them, is as a refinement of idea-support technique. Therefore, their functions are identical to those of idea support in general, as well as a little more.**

As Idea Support:

1. Define or identify
2. Clarify
3. Prove
4. Strengthen or reinforce
5. Generate mood

In Addition:

6. Save time
7. Increase attention
8. Increase retention

1

2 SENSORY AND PSYCHOLOGICAL COMMUNICATION

This is where all of the principles of sensory communication that we've talked about in Segment 14 are applied. So, we ought to review these first.

Question B: What are the principles and factors which must be considered in sensory communication?

1. _____   5. _____

2. _____   6. _____

3. _____   7. _____

4. _____

Psychological communication is another area where you'll want to be sure that you really understand the principles involved. (They were in Segment 15.) So, let's review these also.

Question C: In Segment 15, we gave seven basic categories of emotional response or reaction. How many can you remember? List them here.

1. _____   5. _____

2. _____   6. _____

3. _____   7. _____

4. _____

Always, as you devise your aids, you should be asking yourself what their psychological as well as sensory effects will be. For example, does a device offend, constitute a threat, and so forth, or, what kind of psychological need (especially the need for order and the abhorence of "chaos," pleasant sensation, shock, and so forth) does or can it fulfill?

Answer to Question B:

1. Same-sense reinforcement   5. Simplicity
2. Other-sense reinforcement   6. Duration
3. Same-sense distraction   7. Path of least resistance
4. Other-sense distraction

Answer to Question C:

1. Ego-extension   5. Pugnacity
2. Ego Survival   6. Gratification
3. Order   7. Conditioning
4. Gregariousness

Question D: Why include visual and other aids in the presentation outline?

_____

_____

_____

3 OUTLINING AIDS

Let's move quickly into the mechanics of preparing your presentation aids. The first point is that pictures, graphics, handouts, and similar material, as another form of idea support, are an integral part of the presentation and should be included in the outlining process like any other individual form of idea support. Many presenters do not do this. Somehow the aid part of the presentation gets separated from the text and becomes a matter unto itself. As a result, although a set of slides, for example, might be excellently designed, they do not really serve their proper purpose of clarifying, supporting, or reinforcing a spoken idea. Too often someone gets an idea for a "great set of aids" and prepares a presentation around them, and the "tail wags the dog." This is probably the main pitfall for inexperienced presenters; they get into the business of designing aids instead of supporting ideas.

One way to avoid this is to include the aid ideas in the main presentation outline where they will remain in proper perspective. Insofar as idea support is concerned, there is little difference between using the word "downward," for example, and using a picture of an arrow pointing downward. Often it is better to convey the idea by impression than by speaking it, especially when subtletly is desired; for example, one might "protest too much" that he is reliable, but the design of the building in which he houses his plant or the brochures that advertise his product can express the same concept in an unspoken way. The preliminary ideas can be sketched or described.

For convenience, it also is wise to keep a separate list of the aid ideas. This will serve the following two purposes:

1. *It will make it easier to work on the execution part of the job, especially when designers, artists, or people other than you are involved in preparing finished art, lettering, photography, etc. These people are essentially interested in the graphics part of the job and must be instructed by you on what to do. The separate list of ideas and sketches is more efficient for this purpose.*
2. *It will give an over-all view of the whole idea flow from the visual standpoint. It will show the whole visual part of the presentation at a glance, just as the basic structure of the text is shown in outline form. The net result will be more unified, cohesive visuals, and a better integration of the individual panels.*

Here is an example of how aids may be sketched as subpoints in an outline.

> *I. A Branch Office Near Every Customer (outline point)*
>   *A. Map—showing representative customer sites spread out in one color and matching branch office sites in another color. (visual idea as outline point)*

II. *No Loss of Centralized Control (outline point)*
   A. *Map—Washington and lines emanating outwards to branch office sites. (visual idea as outline point)*
   B. *Same map as 'A' with a colored overlay square over Washington, labeled "centralized coverage." (visual idea)*

III. *The Principle of Decentralized Coverage (outline point)*
   A. *Same slide as II B with smaller squares over outlying sites. Each screen contains the words "decentralized coverage." (visual idea as outline point)*

IV. *Combined for Marketing Action (outline point)*
   A. *Same map but now with two-headed arrow.*
   (visual idea and visual as outline point)

V. *Marketing and the Customer (outline point)*

   *(visual outline point)*

VI. *Elements of the Program (outline point)*

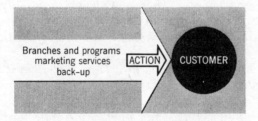   *(visual outline point)*

VII. *Immediate Action is Required (outline point)*

   *(visual outline point)*

4

These graphic representations can also be used later in preparing delivery notes. The mechanics are of little significance; the important thing is that the aids appear where they belong—within the presentation outline itself as support for individual ideas, all aimed at objective accomplishment, all performing an actual function.

Answer to Question D: Because they are another form of idea support and ought to appear as subpoints of the ideas they support.

4 THE STORYBOARD

Professional designers usually prepare what is known as a "storyboard" of the presentation, a series of preliminary idea sketches to show quickly the whole presentation graphically. These usually are done with chalk or charcoal pencil and presented to the client for approval before work begins on the finished art.

Question E: Why prepare a storyboard?

It saves trouble and misunderstanding. You can do this yourself without being a professional designer or being able to draw. Actually no one is better equipped to prepare a preliminary storyboard of the presentation than you. By preparing your own preliminary visual ideas, you are also better prepared to discuss them with a professional designer if you use one. You know better than anyone else the ideas which must be supported. Your purpose need not necessarily be to produce finished art, although you can do this too under certain circumstances, and save a lot of money in the bargain. Do-it-yourself visual aids are discussed later. For the moment, the purpose of the storyboard is to help plan the presentation and to develop a firm idea for each visual panel.

"Below" is part of a storyboard for a presentation about an inventory control system. The subject matter is of little importance here. The main point is that, just as a series of written outline points shows idea flow at a glance, a series of visual "outline points" prepared in this manner does the same for visual idea flow. It is a visual outline.

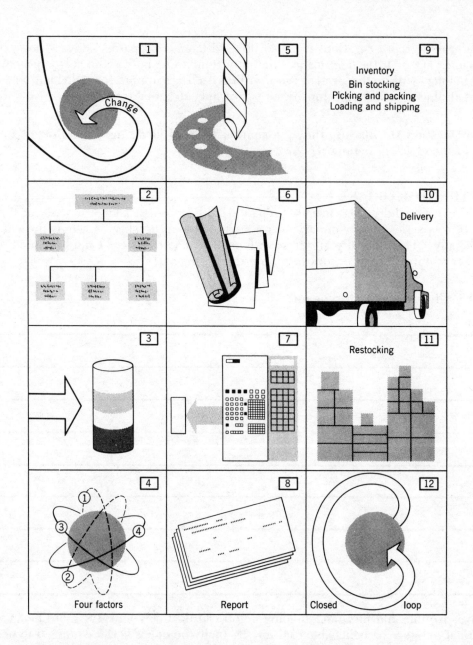

1 Change	**5**	**9** Inventory Bin stocking Picking and packing Loading and shipping
2	**6**	**10** Delivery
3	**7**	**11** Restocking
4 Four factors	**8** Report	**12** Closed loop

Answer to Question E: A storyboard gives you an overall view of your presentation from the graphic viewpoint, similar to the overall view your outline gives from the verbal viewpoint. A storyboard also makes it more convenient for you to work on all of your aids at the same time, just as folders for your outline points help you to manage your "scripting" task.

5 FORM FOLLOWS FUNCTION

You'll never get away from this dictum in functional communication. It should be your guiding light, especially in preparing aids.

Graphic design is not impressionistic art, although some designers try to make it so. It is functional art, and as such has its own set of standards, some of which are similar to those of the "art for art's sake" artist and some are not. The similarities are of little concern here. The only significant questions are: Does the picture, the shape, the color, the type style, the movement, the gesture serve a specific, identifiable function? The function must be identifiable. Nor can one simply use a certain device and attribute a function to it. For example, if a type style with dignity is desired, it should be sought. But to choose the type and then to decide that it has dignity, whether it does or not, is not functional design. Type style, incidentally, might seem like an unimportant matter. Yet it can influence the effect of the whole visual panel. More important, to choose the visual panel itself and then decide what it should do is equally dangerous, because it has not been selected with a specific objective in mind. These things would seem to go without saying, but the truth is that countless presentations are designed backward. The result is that the aids really add nothing to them, except by accident, once again negating the philosophy of functional presenting. How can you avoid such a pitfall? You can begin with the idea and ask these questions:

Does this idea need support or reinforcement?
Of the many methods available, which is the best?
How can I make every element of this support contribute?

In this way you are beginning without any preconceived ideas. You are letting the idea demand and direct its own support. You may well find that what it needs is additional verbal support; an example or illustration, further definition, an analogy or another point, something to hand out to the audience, or that it is sufficiently clear without any further support.

Question F: Here are three series of visual ideas. Notice that each panel contains a single visual idea, and the series develops a larger idea. Notice, too, there are no words or captions. Can you furnish a few lines of script for each of the three series?

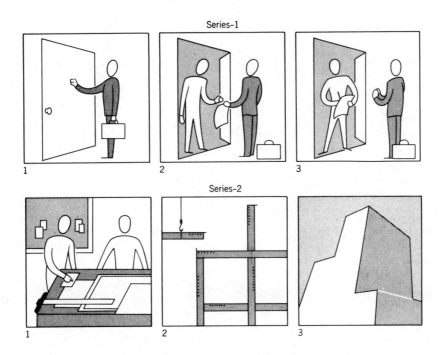

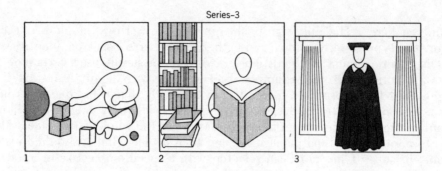

Series—1 Script: _____

_____

_____

_____

Series—2 Script: _____

_____

_____

_____

Series—3 Script: _____

_____

_____

_____

6 SIMPLICITY

Most aids prepared by novices tend to be too complex or "busy." They try to do or say too much for the time and space. It is not unusual to see slides with a minute's worth of reading flashed on a screen for only a few seconds. Many presenters try to make their slides or easel charts do what properly belongs in the realm of verbal discussion, handouts, or other printed material. The point is that visuals should be primarily *visual* in nature. They use the eye to reinforce what is heard by the ear. It is rare that a visual aid can have too little copy, if the presenter and the rest of the presentation do their proper jobs. This is not to say that copy should be eliminated altogether, but if you follow as a rule of thumb the maxim,

The less copy, the better the visual aid,

you will be leaning in the right direction.

An easel chart page or slide is not a full text; it is condensed information. Telegraphic style should be used, with all unnecessary words, symbols, and figures eliminated. Abbreviations sometimes can be used when they do not obscure meaning. Better yet, a completely visual impression. Whatever is viewed should reinforce, restate or support what is said orally, not overwhelm it. Often a purely visual impression is sufficient, without any words.

Elaborate symbology or attempts at subliminal visual communicating by a person who does not understand the psychology of color and shape motivation normally are a waste of time in the average presentation. It is preferable to concentrate upon making the meaning of the visual idea itself absolutely clear on a purely sensory level. Each visual panel should contain only one idea. Abstract art is useless unless it makes an idea clear. Remember, one of the main aims of the visual aid in the first place is to *clarify* ideas which cannot be adequately expressed, emphasized, or proven in words alone within the time allowed.

Answers to Question F: Remember that ours is only one set of possibilities. The main aim here is to sharpen your ability to interchange the verbal and the sensory.

Series—1 Possible Script: "Making personal calls is important. It is the best way to make sales and get contracts signed."

Series—2 Possible Script: "It all starts at the drawing board, and ultimately you see the final structure."

Series—3 Possible Script: "We start building and learning early, do our 'homework' throughout the process, and finally wind up with the desired results."

7 HINTS ON HANDLING DETAILED MATERIAL

The value of putting detailed information in a visual aid is questionable from the standpoint of:

- *Visibility: The more detail, the smaller it must be, and the harder it is to see it.*
- *Retention: What is there to retain a large amount of detail in the audience's mind after it leaves the screen or is erased?*
- *Duration: How much can be read, or will be read, while the panel is in view?*

There are too many factors that work against having large amounts of detail in a visual aid. Although it sometimes will be necessary to do so, it should be avoided as much as possible, especially in presentations with a strong educational slant. The following are some suggestions for alleviating the negative visual effects of large amounts of detail:

- *Try to break information up into clearly defined categories with as few headings as possible.*
- *Use sharply contrasting colors.*
- *Place information in clearly defined visual segments.*
- *Draw borders to separate the informational elements.*
- *Allow plenty of blank space and wide margins.*
- *Consider dividing the visual into more than one panel.*

- *Try covering parts of the information and progressively exposing it.*
- *Use overlays to gradually build a complete panel.*
- *Be sure exposure is long enough for full comprehension.*
- *Use additional simplified panels to summarize the detail and to show over-all concepts.*
- *Consider handout material to be used in conjunction with displayed or projected information.*

Summary Exercise: Following is a presentation outline. Many of the ideas in it can be expressed visually, but we'll only ask you to do a few. For each of the points marked with a check, describe or sketch in the space to the right how that point might be expressed in a visual way.

OUTLINE	YOUR VISUAL IDEA
I. The Variator is highly efficient and durable. √ A. It uses microcircuitry. B. Its housing is constructed of tufflex. C. Its moving elements are made of templon.	I.A:

II. The Variator will have many uses.
 A. As a guidance and control device
   1. In space flight
   2. In conventional flight
   3. In automotive travel
√ B. As primary power
   1. In tools
   2. In appliances
   3. In hobbies and crafts
	II.B:

III. The Variator took fifteen years to develop
 A. Gromnich's work in microcircuitry (1953–1957)
   1. Based on transistor development
   2. Based on cryogenic discoveries
√ B. Development of Tufflex (Rocket Nose Cone)
   1. XYZ Corporation (1954–1956)
   2. ABC Corporation (1955–1957)
 C. Discovery of Templon (1965)
 D. Use of materials in space flight (1966–1967)
	III.B:

Scorable Quiz: Fill in the missing word or words.

1. Aids are another form of _____ .

2. The true role of aids is _____ and not

   _____ .

3. _____ thinking will make for more creative aids.

4. Aid ideas should be included in the presentation _____ .

5. A means of quickly showing an overall view of the visual content of a presentation is to make a _____ .

6. The dictum "_____" is especially applicable in the preparation of aids.

7. The value of putting detailed verbal information in visual aids is questionable from the standpoint of visibility (a) _____ and

   (b) _____

8. Often, a completely visual impression is sufficient, without any

   _____ .

Answers to Summary Exercise: There is, of course, no way that you could exactly duplicate our ideas, nor should you have to. The whole aim is for you to be as creative and flexible as you can. Following are some ideas.

I.A.: It uses microcircuitry. Try microscope, or perhaps a slide photo of an actual micro–circuit, or better yet, you could pass an actual sample around to members of the audience.

II.B: How about a montage of photos of power tools or of people using power tools.

III.B: Tufflex was first used as a rocket nose cone. Why not show a rocket?

Answers to Scorable Quiz: Each correct answer = 10%. (1) idea support; (2) (a) supportive, (b) primary; (3) multidimensional; (4) outline; (5) storyboard; (6) form follows function; (7) (a) retention; (b) duration; (8) words.

LEARNING SEGMENT 23   Do It Yourself Visual Aids

PREMISE: That you should be able to make visual or other sensory statements of your own ideas.

SEGMENT OBJECTIVE: For you to have a basic ability to make your own visual aids.

Question A: Let's test your ability to express verbalized ideas visually. Following is a series of simple ideas. Below each, describe or sketch a visual idea that would express each without the use of words.

<table>
<tr><td>1. "Time is money."</td><td>2. "It's a long haul to a solution."</td></tr>
</table>

3. "Coffee break"

Answers to Question A: Remember again, in this area of aids, there are no single "right" answers. (But some are more wrong than others!) Compare your ideas with ours: For "time is money" you might have drawn an hour glass and a dollar sign, side by side. For "It's a long haul," you might have drawn a person climbing up a mountain. For "coffee break," you might have drawn a steaming cup of coffee.

1 DO IT YOURSELF

Learn to prepare your own visual aids. Most professional designers and artists greet such amateur attempts with anything from indulgence to disdain. But creativity is not anyone's exclusive province. With a little native ingenuity, you can produce highly effective visual aids, if you follow the basic principles discussed here and stay within the limits of your mechanical capabilities, which you can extend as far as your motivation leads you. In many cases, time and expense will leave you no other choice than to create your own aids anyway. A major part of the philosophy behind this cause is that a specialist need not nor should not remain restricted to his own specialty, but should have a broad base. If nothing else, he should know the possibilities open to him.

Sometimes it is appropriate to create visuals "spontaneously" during the presentation. The chalkboard is undoubedly the most popular and simplest device for doing this. The visuals actually should be created in advance and merely copied from memory or notes at the time of presentation. An easel and paper can substitute for the chalkboard, using a variety of writing materials such as felt pens, grease pencils, chalk or charcoal. These give the added advantage of varying color. The basic rule for such on-stage visual aid creation is to know exactly what is to be written or drawn. Follow these basic guidelines:

1. *Have samples in delivery notes.*
2. *Writing or drawing surface should be clean.*
3. *Write and print legibly.*
4. *Do not crowd the board.*
5. *Do not block anyone's view.*
6. *Work large enough for all to see.*
7. *Do not apologize for lack of artistic talent.*
8. *Generalized drawings and key words are better than detailed work.*
9. *Draw or write quickly.*
10. *Do not stand silent or with back to the audience too long.*
11. *Face the audience frequently. Maintain audience contact.*
12. *Erase or cover the work after discussing it.*
13. *Never leave exposed any illustration not in active use.*

2 SOME BASIC GUIDELINES

Three guidlines to consider are: visibility, unity and consistency, and appropriateness. Audience size is the main factor to consider with respect to visibility. Will the person in the back row be able to see as well as those in the front? Color and typography also are important. The best way to test visibility is to test the material at the same distance and with the viewing conditions under which it will actually be used. Particular attention should be paid to selection of sharp and vivid type styles for the copy and to the use of contrasting colors, which do not vibrate or run together. Shapes should have clean lines and sharp separations from each other. Renderings and shaded sketches are usually poor choices as visuals because they tend to look busy and to confuse the eye.

Unity and consistency in visual aids are usually referred to as "motif." It is rare that a presentation's purpose can be served well by switching design motifs in the middle of it. Abrupt changes in color combinations, type styles, basic formats, etc., have the same effect of discontinuity as choppy, abrupt changes in language, pace, or mood in the spoken part of the presentation. This is not to say that such changes cannot be made, but when they are they should be accomplished in smooth and appropriate transitions. As you prepare your visual-aid ideas and look at the final panels, you should consciously look for such abrupt change. This is often done mainly by "feel," yet even the amateur can sense when something seems not to fit.

The last of our three guidelines is appropriateness. Both the presenter and the organization to which he belongs will have an existing image when his presentation comes along. Admittedly, it takes a lot more than graphic design to build a corporate or organizational image. Yet no presenter should attempt to work in the design environment of his organization without studying its current policies on design and image. In the process he will probably learn more about design, too. Another question you must ask yourself is:

"Is my design proper and consistent with both the existing image and the occasion?"

Question B: What is the effect of abrupt changes in motif?

_____

_____

_____

_____

Question C: List at least five guidelines for using a chalkboard.

_____

_____

_____

_____

_____

Question D: What is the main factor in determining the visibility of a visual aid?

_____

Answer to Question B: Abrupt changes in motif are disconcerting to the senses and can have a disintegrative effect on your thought flow.

Answer to Question C: Review the list under heading #1 of this segment.

Answer to Question D: Size of audience.

3 BASIC CONSIDERATIONS IN SELECTION

Before getting too deeply into any visual aid project, it is wise to check on the following factors:

- *Are the necessary equipment and facilities available?*
- *Is the aid right for the audience and room size?*
- *How does this aid method compare with those used in the rest of the program?*
- *Is there sufficient artistic talent available?*
- *Is there enough time to produce the job?*
- *Is there money in the budget? Who will pay for the work?*

Obvious questions; yet frequently when the bill comes it is realized that no one ever authorized the work. Thousands of dollars may be paid for a one-time presentation or excessive overtime work done to meet the deadline.

4 USE OF EXISTING MATERIAL

Many organizations have collections of film strips, slides, movies, recordings, and similar material, or someone who knows where to get them. Most of them are standardized packages describing a specific item of equipment or a concept, or telling a self-contained story or message. They can serve two purposes:

1. *Use in the presentation as background, introduction, or direct supporting material.*
2. *As a source of ideas for you in preparing your own aids.*

Such material can save considerable time and effort in explaining basic technology or concepts for which your preparation would merely be duplication of work already done, often on a more professional level, but it should not be used merely as a filler. It should actually contribute to your objective.

The best way to decide whether to include such a package as a part of your presentation is to review the material to be sure that it really fits and contributes to your own message. Most material, when included as a part of another presentation, requires careful introduction and explanation to the audience so that they may understand why it is being shown and what it is intended to do.

Another method of using existing material is to "cut and paste." For example:

1. *Collect magazines, manuals, brochures, pictures, and so forth, and use them to cut and paste. Be careful of using copyrighted or trademarked materials.*
2. *Use colored paper to cut basic shapes and silhouettes.*

3. *Stick to simple shapes and vivid colors. Avoid shading, shadowing, and attempts to produce dimension or depth.*
4. *Use preprepared press–down lettering, available in art stores.*
5. *Use plenty of blank space.*

5 SOME OTHER SUGGESTIONS

Other suggestions include team presentation, an audience "plant," the audience as an aid, an assistant, displays and exhibits, and demonstration material.

Question E: Following are some presentation "reinforcement needs." List opposite them what you think would be the best aid or device for handling them.

REINFORCEMENT NEED	YOUR IDEA FOR A DEVICE
1. A response to reinforce a point	
2. Several demonstration items at a certain time in your presentation.	
3. A series of questions and answers in your presentation.	

Team presenting is an excellent way to add variety and interest to a presentation; for example, two presenters can engage in a conversation, a mock telephone call, or question-answer session before the audience after the fashion of some television news-reporting teams.

Another type of human aid is the *audience "plant,"* or "shill," who is given specifically planned questions to ask the presenter. This adds variety, sparks audience interest, and can be used to start a general question–answer period.

Audience members themselves can be used as aids by the presenter who has strong enough control. The visiting expert or someone known to have special knowledge of a given point might be referred to for on-the-spot testimony or to answer a question asked by another audience member. The presenter must know his man and be able to gauge the situation well enough to do so. He should never place an audience member (or himself) in an embarrassing position from which there is no graceful retreat. Obviously, arranging the matter beforehand is the safest way.

Depending on the nature of the presentation, *an assistant* might be required for a variety of duties such as operating projection equipment, passing out material, helping in demonstrations, etc. Depending on how extensive his role is, he should be thoroughly versed in what is expected of him.

On occasion it is effective to provide literature racks, to display working or static examples of the technology, or to produce automatically operated audiovisual displays. *Displays and exhibits* range from simple automatic projector tape recorder mechanisms to elaborately designed sets staffed with personnel. Many displays and exhibits, are major productions and need not necessarily concern the average presenter. Yet they should be mentioned as a matter of familiarization. You should consider display or exhibit as one of the aids open to you.

Demonstration is undoubtedly one of the best presentation aids. Sometimes the presentation itself will be a demonstration. Some keys to good demonstrating are: (1) a clear reason for doing so; (2) adequate introduction to the audience; (3) flawless performance by the presenter; (4) flawless operation of the device or equipment; (5) visibility for all audience members; (6) impeccable appearance of the device or equipment; (7) audience participation in a demonstration usually adds to it in terms of attention and interest.

Demonstrations at business shows and similar events are slightly different, although all of the principles of functional presenting apply to them. Rarely will you be completely on your own in such cases. These are usually well-coordinated team efforts that involve professional display and exhibit people, producers, directors, and rehearsals.

Answer to Question E:

1. A good place for an audience "plant" or "shill."
2. Obviously, an assistant is needed.
3. A good place for dialogue, either a second person on the podium or an "audience member."

Question F: Following is another list of presentation situations. In the space provided, list what you think would be the best supportive aid in each case.

THE SITUATION	YOUR SUGGESTED AID
1. The operation of a new machine.	
2. Detailed printed description of a mechanical device you mention in your presentation.	
3. The arrival of Professor Gromnich as you are beginning to describe his invention.	

Question G: List here at least five "aids," other than visual.

_____

_____

_____

_____

_____

Answers to Question F:
1. A demonstration of the actual machine in operation would be best. Second best, at least have it on display. Third choice would be some photos or slides.
2. Definitely, handouts, or a literature display is called for here.
3. He's classed as the "unforeseen occurrence." You'd better acknowledge his presence, and even might invite him to say a few words. And you'd better be accurate in what you say about his invention.

Answer to Question G: (1) team presenting; (2) the audience plant; (3) the audience itself; (4) an assistant; (5) a demonstration.

6 THE UNFORESEEN OCCURRENCE AS AN AID

Recently, a presenter we know arrived at the podium for a presentation a minute or two before he was scheduled to go on. The audience had already assembled, leaving him no opportunity to check the facilities. With his easel charts under his arm, he sat down in the front row to be introduced momentarily. A minute later he arose and walked to the easel which had been provided for the flip chart presentations. It was only when he attempted to hang his charts that he discovered that the holes in the charts did not match the pegs on the easel. A hundred pairs of eyes immediately became aware of the dilemma. He glanced around with barely a moment's hesitation, bent down, removed his shoe laces and, to the accompaniment of a hearty round of applause, used them to tie his charts to the easel. Turning to the audience, he began his presentation with the unrehearsed quip,

> *"Ladies and gentlemen, although this presentation is operating on a shoe-string . . . ,"*

and he had the kind of opening that did what few planned openings could have done better.

7 MAKE YOUR OWN SLIDES

This is not as difficult as it may sound. Anyone with a rudimentary knowledge of photography and lighting can produce his own 35mm slides for little more than the cost of film and its development at a corner drugstore. The key again is to stay within your own limitations. Stick to basic shapes, clear outlines, sharp colors, and minimum copy on a panel—and work to improve your design sense.

For the presenter who has no drawing or sketching ability whatsoever, simple "stick man" art, combined with verbal explanation as necessary, often will suffice.

Artwork can be "pasted up" on a flat surface, using prepared lettering or press type, mounted on a wall or other vertical surface, and photographed with the proper focus like any other scene. Actual objects such as parts and equipment can be arranged against an appropriate background and similarly photographed. With a little experimentation, considerable quality and professionalism can be attained.

Visual ideas abound everywhere—in a colorfully wired electronic part, a few bricks from a construction site, a closeup of part of a piece of equipment, part of a picture in a magazine, a simple cut-out or silhouette and a thousand other things. The creativity—or the restriction—is solely in the "eye of the beholder." Most people are restricted from doing things like this by an unwarranted sense of inadequacy and a reluctance to step over into another discipline. To the professional communicator, the boundaries of no disciplines are sacred. He ranges freely wherever the requirements of his message take him.

8 PREPREPARED EASEL CHARTS

These are more familiarly known as flip charts and can be prepared in almost any size desired. The methods for drawing or lettering them also vary greatly. There are various lettering sets, tracing and template outfits, and chartmaking supplies available in stationery and art supply stores. Felt pen is the most popular and cheapest method for making this type of visual, which can serve a very wide range of technical presenting needs. Care should be exercised in lettering and drawing. All of the basic rules for graphics—simplicity, visibility, clearness, unity—should be followed. Smaller desktop charts of this nature can be carried in a looseleaf binder-type easel, also available in most stationery and art supply stores. There are a great many variations of such equipment and supplies on the market. It is recommended that the reader visit a fairly large art supply house and familiarize himself with what is available to him if he wishes to prepare his own visual aids. There is no reason why he can not do so, if he recognizes his own limitations as well as using his own native creativity.

The Desk Easel is a specially designed looseleaf binder

The Standard Easel
and the Desk Easel

Question H: List five methods of projecting or displaying information.

1._____   4. _____

2. _____   5. _____

3. _____

9 BASIC METHODS OF PROJECTION AND DISPLAY

Size of audience, basic purpose, and environment are the main influences on the kind of projection or display medium required. The principles of design remain constant. Projection techniques, such as slides, opaque, or overhead projection should be used for larger groups. Easel charts and chalkboard are usually effective with a hundred or fewer people. For very small groups desk size easels may be used. Another thing to consider is how many times the presentation is to be given. If it is for a single event, it will be uneconomical to go to a great deal of expense to produce color slides, for example, when easel charts, foils, or overhead transparencies are cheaper. Some of these will project in color and can be dressed up considerably with a little imagination. Many presenters tend to be overelaborate anyway, often thinking in terms of the most elaborate medium when other methods of projection or display will do just as well.

There are many manufacturers and models, but only a few basic kinds of projection equipment with which the average presenter need be concerned. If you do not own the needed equipment, the classified telephone directory listings under audiovisuals or audiovisual equipment show where it can be rented. For more detailed information, the National Audio Visual Association, Inc., 3150 Spring Street, Fairfax, Virginia 22030, produces an annual audiovisual equipment directory containing three hundred pages of available equipment. Avoid old or manually operated equipment.

Now let's take a look at different projection and display techniques:

Almost all *slide projectors* accommodate standard 2 X 2 in. slides. The main characteristics to watch for are the following:
1. *Number of slides held without changing tray or carrier.*
2. *Pushbutton, remote slide changing, forward and reverse, remote focusing, and random access.*

There are basically two types of projected images: opaque and transparent. *Opaque projectors* cast an image on a screen directly from an original. They do not produce the clearest of images, but are often quite suitable for projecting flow charts, engineering drawings, and similar visual support, especially in classroom environments or where extreme vividness, sharp color, and high resolution are not critical. Their main advantage is that they do not require special mounting, copying, or photographic work. A clear original image may be used. Most makes perform comparably.

Overhead projectors look and function very much like opaque projectors. The primary difference is that the overhead projects through a transparency and reproduces in color. Of the two types of pictures, most presenters prefer to project transparencies because of their resolution and versatility. Most models perform comparably. Material for do-it-yourself transparencies is available in most art stores. Information can be typed, drawn, traced, or written on acetate sheets, which then can be placed directly in the projector for viewing on a screen. Blank acetate sheets also can be used for "live" writing and drawing during the presentation. The same rules apply as in using the chalkboard or easel paper.

Flannel and magnetic boards are made in various sizes and materials and can be used to substitute for extensive writing or drawing at a chalkboard or easel during the presentation. The board is covered with felt, flannel or similar material. Each picture or element of the aid is prepared in advance on material backed with this same type of soft, cohesive substance. The presenter then merely attaches the element, which sticks to the board, instead of drawing or writing. A variation of this principle is the magnetic board which uses a thin sheet of painted or porcelain-covered steel and small magnets glued to the back of the visual elements. Most of the time these methods will be too much trouble. The same effect can be obtained with easel charts or chalkboard. Chalkboards with metallic content are also available to permit a combination of methods.

When a movie is to be shown, you will often have to take the *movie projector* that is available. If possible, get a projectionist with it. It is very difficult to run a projector and conduct a presentation simultaneously. This, incidentally, is why it is important to have a remotely controlled slide projector when the presenter must flash his own images on cues for which he, as the presenter, can provide the best timing. A movie is best run by a skilled projectionist if for no other reason than to keep the presenter out of trouble, but no matter who runs the projector, it should be positioned, threaded, and focused before the presentation begins.

There are so many *tape recorders and record players* on the market that the only sound advice is to try the equipment for fidelity and trouble-free operation. Most of the better known electronics trade names are quite reliable.

Larger organizations sometimes use *closed-circuit television* for presenting information. This entails some additional technical considerations in terms of contrast ratios and other clarity factors. Knowledge technicians however, are almost always available in such cases.

To lay down a specific set of rules as to which form should be used in a given situation defeats the flavor of creativity which is necessary to the producing of effective visual idea support. The late Thomas J. Watson, founder of International Business Machines Corporation, while attending one of his company's early sales meetings, is said to have coined what is perhaps one of the most familiar visual aids in American industry. It also is the prime rule for creating any other aid—and in fact for creating presentations themselves.

The meeting apparently had bogged down. Walking to the chalkboard, Mr. Watson picked up a piece of blue chalk and wrote five letters. When asked to explain what he meant by them, he refused to do so—merely referring the questioner again to the five letters: THINK.

Answer to Question H:

1. Slide projection
2. Opaque projection
3. Overhead projection

4. Flannel and magnetic boards
5. Movie projection
6. Tape recorders and record players
7. Television projection

10 PLANNING AND USING HANDOUT MATERIAL

Printed handout material can help or hinder a presentation, depending upon when it is distributed and how it is used. Like all other elements in the functional presentation, it should serve a function. If it is distributed before the presentation, there should be a specific reason for doing so. The one thing that a presenter does not want to do is compete with his own handout material in the crucial moments of beginning. Nor does he want to interrupt the idea flow or risk losing attention during the presentation without a very good reason for doing so. If he distributes material at the close of his presentation, what function will it perform? In short, the simple act of providing printed material in connection with a technical presentation, so often taken for granted, also can and should be reduced to a deliberate act—aimed at a specific function. The following are guidelines for the use of such material:

1. *Hand out material only at the time when it is necessary to advancement of the presentation per se. Never permit it to compete with the presenter and what he is saying.*
2. *Do not be afraid to ask or direct the audience to put handout material aside and pay attention to the speaker.*
3. *Make sure that the appearance of the material is up to the standards and image of the rest of the presentation. Too much so-called handout material is really verbal padding or stock room surplus.*
4. *Material handed out before the presentation usually should be confined to such matters as agendas, schedules, outlines, accommodations and similar information necessary to the business of the presentation.*
5. *It is sometimes expedient to bring the audience to a common level of awareness with respect to the subject, definitions, or assumptions before the presentation begins. In such cases, ample time should be allowed for reading the material. The audience then should be asked if there are any questions and specifically requested to set the material aside if they do not do so on their own. They cannot read and listen at the same time. The presenter is in control and should remain so.*
6. *A handout can often be the best form of visual aid, especially in a relatively complex presentation. It can serve to increase attention. For instance, an outline, with space in between the points for note taking, can be used to motivate the audience to follow the idea flow more easily. They will also tend to pay closer attention as they follow along.*
7. *Material handed out or made available for pickup after the presentation should be designed to serve one or all of the following three functions:*
   a. *Add supporting detail which could not be covered during the presentation.*
   b. *Contribute to the desired audience response or action step.*
   c. *Get information from the audience.*
8. *Handout material also includes samples, novelties, favors, and souvenirs. These can often be expensive. Their value is sometimes questionable, unless they serve as direct reminders of the subject of the presentation.*

Scorable Quiz: Indicate true (T) or false (F).

1. **It is advisable never to make abrupt changes in visual mood or motif.** _____

2. **Visual statement of an idea takes the place of verbal statement of an idea.** _____

3. **Abrupt changes in color combinations, type styles, and other aspects of visual motif have the same general effect as choppy, abrupt changes in language, verbal pace, or mood in the verbal portion of a presentation.** _____

22

4. An audience "plant" or shill might be classified as an aid. _____

5. Audience size shouldn't have any real effect on the kinds of aids planned. _____

6. Audience size is the main factor in determining the visibility of an aid. _____

7. The best place for displays and exhibits is near where the presenter is to stand to be sure that they have proper attention. _____

8. Handout material should be passed out at the time it is mentioned in the presentation. _____

9. Team presenting can also be classed as an aid. _____

10. It is perfectly acceptable to use an assistant before or after, but not during, a presentation. _____

Answer to Scorable Quiz: (Each correct answer = 10%.) (1) F, (2) F, (3) T, (4) T, (5) F, (6) T, (7) F, (8) F, (9) T, (10) F.

ISBN 0-471-01634-9

EFFECTIVE PRESENTATION
Preparing To Face The Audience

UNIT IX

W. A. Mambert

Executive Director

National Communication and Education Association

Wiley Professional Development Programs

Advisory Editor

Steven C. Wheelwright

Harvard Business School

John Wiley & Sons Inc.
New York • London • Sydney • Toronto

Library of Congress Catalogue Card Number: 75–39750

ISBN 0–471–01635–7

Printed in the United States of America.

10 9 8 7 6 5 4 3 2 1

Preparing Notes For Delivery

LEARNING **24** SEGMENT

PREMISE: That podium notes, like all else in the strategic presentation, ought to be planned carefully.

SEGMENT OBJECTIVE: That you learn to prepare meaningful delivery notes that will effectively support your actual delivery of your presentation to an audience.

Question A: Briefly define each of the following types of presentation delivery.

1. Impromptu: _____

_____

2. Memorized: _____

_____

3. Manuscript: _____

_____

4. Extemporaneous: _____

_____

Question B: Which of the methods above do you think is normally the most effective? Why?

_____

_____

_____

1 **THE FEWER, THE BETTER**
Generally speaking, the fewer notes, the better your delivery. The function of notes should not be so much to help remember information as to remember to include activities and ideas already stored in the memory, or to direct yourself to do something

that you might forget to do in the general press of many things to do and say. In reality, what you need more than notes is a script or scenario as your "stage director," to cue you and prompt your preplanned actions. Preparing podium notes is a highly personal matter. Good technique is whatever works for you in delivering your message and maintaining contact with your audience. There are, however, some basic guidelines which should give you a flexible foundation upon which to build your own system.

There are times when nervousness or other such factors will almost force you to use extensive notes; but you will never be a good presenter until you overcome this weakness. Surmounting it is a direct function of your preparation and the confidence it will give you and how often you practice and force yourself into presentation situations in which you must rely upon your ability to think, instead of to read.

Answers to Question A:
1. **Impromptu: No particular preparation has been made for the occasion. Usually called on unexpectedly, the presenter relies solely upon skills and knowledge available to him on the spur of the moment.**
2. **Memorized: Material is repeated or recited word for word.**
3. **Manuscript: Material is read to the audience word for word as printed.**
4. **Extemporaneous: Everything is prethought and planned in detail except that the exact wording and phrasing of the main body are not committed to memory, but the thoughts are. The presentation is delivered from a written or memorized outline.**

2 WHAT DELIVERY NOTES SHOULD CONTAIN

Delivery notes should contain the entire sequence of what you will do and say at the podium. This includes:

- *The subject matter of the presentation in abbreviated form.*
- *Directions for movements, gestures, readings, passing out handouts, use of the blackboard, and similar stage activities.*
- *Cues for the use of visual aids such as charts or slides.*
- *Any information to be written on a blackboard, easel chart, or similar medium during the presentation.*
- *Podium samples of each individual aid.*

3 WHAT THE PODIUM NOTES SHOULD NOT CONTAIN

Podium notes should not contain:

- *Handout material*
- *Material to be read to the audience*
- *Material to be held up, shown, or demonstrated*

Such supplemental material should be numbered and kept in a separate pile in the exact sequence in which it is to be used. When your presentation includes this kind of support, you will be working with two sets of material. The main reason for this is that carrying notes and often bulky demonstration or reading material in a single sheaf is both confusing and awkward. It is far better to keep the presentation outline itself as a single sequence of events and merely key the supporting material.

4 ADVANTAGES OF EXTEMPORANEOUS DELIVERY
Some of the advantages of extemporaneous delivery are:

- *It is more natural and intimate and affords better audience contact.*
- *It is more believable and convincing.*
- *It enables you to remain flexible and adapt your actual words to the occasion and temper of the audience.*
- *It forces you to become involved and to think, instead of merely reading to your audience.*
- *An audience has more confidence in a speaker who displays enough confidence to speak spontaneously.*

Rarely, if ever, should the entire presentation be written out in manuscript form and carried to the podium. The only time that a manuscript is permissible is when the presentation is a highly significant formal statement or matter of record, or where exact wording and programming require no deviation from a set plan.

Answer to Question B: The best presentations are delivered extemporaneously. Sometimes a complete draft of the text might be written out to fix the thoughts firmly in mind, but it is never carried to the podium. Some parts of the extemporaneous presentation may be read or memorized.

5 DISADVANTAGES OF A MANUSCRIPT OR EXCESSIVE NOTES
Some of the disadvantages of a manuscript or excessive notes are:

- *They hinder spontaneity and naturalness.*
- *They restrict movement and platform performance.*
- *Audiences don't like to be read to—they know how to read.*
- *Manuscripts are boring and easily confuse a listener.*
- *They cast suspicion on your ability and knowledge.*
- *They restrict rapport and audience contact.*
- *You'll tend to use them as a crutch. This would destroy much of your motivation.*

Question C: Convert the following to delivery notes.
1. Sentence: **There are three basic elements in any presentation—the presenter, his audience, and the contents of the situation.**

Your Delivery Note:

2. Sentence: Are the necessary equipment and facilities available?

Your Delivery Note:

---

3. Sentence: A good objective is narrow, measurable, and stated in terms of audience behavior.

Your Delivery Note:

---

4. Sentence: Extemporaneous delivery is more natural, affords the presenter greater flexibility, and allows better audience contact.

Your Delivery Note:

---

5. Sentence: Your need to draw an illustration of the two-way flow of information between you and your audience.

Your Delivery Note:

---

6 MAKE THE NOTES INCONSPICUOUS

Never mention your notes to an audience. "It says here in my notes . . . ," "I lost my place in the notes," and similar comments are made only by amateurs. The presenter should actually make an attempt to play down and screen from his audience the fact that he is using notes. This does not mean that he should go to disconcerting extremes to hide them. The audience may know and probably expects that he has some notes on what he plans to say to them. Yet, the less he relies on or calls attention to them, the better his contact with the audience.

A card slightly larger than a standard business calling card is the ideal size. These may be cut from larger cards. Experiments have shown this to be the best all-around size. Used properly, they can hold everything that larger, bulkier sheets can hold. A fair-sized stack can be held inconspicuously in the hand or pocket, and they are easy to slip out of the way during the presentation.

Sample Note Card
(Actual Size)

I. Continuous Path

   A. Three-axis

   B. Two-axis

II. Point to Point

   A. Machining center

   B. Tapping cycles

   C. Milling capability

III. Tool Selection

IV. Rotary Table

7 YOUR SENTENCE OUTLINE: A GUIDE

If you followed our advice and you prepared a sentence outline, this is where the effort will bear fruit. For you already will have an excellent base from which to prepare the notes you'll use in delivery. Now, what you do is reduce your sentences to key words to help you remember each thought at the podium.

You do not memorize your presentation word for word, but you do memorize its main points and thought pattern. Your podium notes then become memory keys, in case you forgot something. You should keep samples, material to be held up, and similar aids separate from your actual delivery notes, and merely key your cues into the notes.

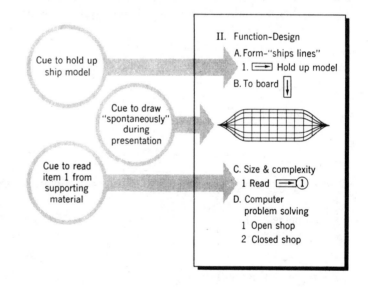

To illustrate, here is an example from a sentence outline:

Ship design today often entails processes too involved and time--consuming for available manpower.

Converted to delivery notes, it might read:

Ship design today . . . Involved . . . time—manpower.
or
Involved Ship Design

8 INCLUDE MINIATURE AID REMINDERS

Remember that each aid is a sub-element of your presentation thought flow. Therefore, it also is part of your delivery sequence. You can increase the overall smoothness of your delivery by including miniature aid reminders in your podium notes. It makes for better synchronization of what you are saying with what you are projecting or displaying, especially if equipment breaks down. In any case, it frees you from looking anywhere but in your notes to find out where you and your aids ought to be in the delivery sequence. In other words, the miniature aid serves the same function as a key word reminder.

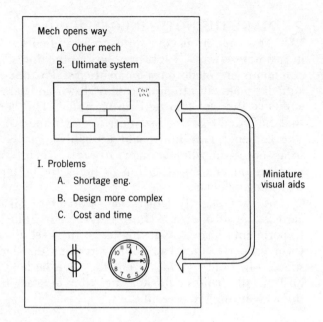

Answers to Question C: There are samples. Compare yours with ours.

1. Probably a combination of words and graphics would be best, e.g.

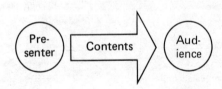

2. Probably a couple of key words plus symbolic emphasis on the question.

Equipment ? ? ? ?
    Facilities ? ? ? ?

3. Simple outline will do, e.g.

I. Good Objective
  A. Narrow
    B. Measurable
      C. Behavioral

4. Same, basic outline form would be best, e.g.

I. Extemporaneous Delivery
  A. More Natural
    B. Greater Flexibility
      C. Better Aud. Contact

5. Probably a basic statement of the point, plus your own cue to go to the blackboard, plus a sample of what you want to draw. The note card at right shows an example.

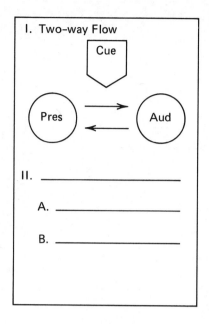

9 STANDARDIZE YOUR METHOD

The symbols and other "memory joggers" you use in your notes are personal. But, standardizing your system will help you. You can use color codes, for example. If you know that a red arrow always is your reminder to write on the chalkboard, you'll be able to look ahead in your notes and always stay on the track. Similarly, if you always start a major point on a new card, you'll have better transition. A blue circle might be a slide projector button and so forth.

10 A FLOW CHART OUTLINE

Obviously, this may be an excellent way of handling your delivery notes because of its graphic visibility. You can even devise your own system of symbols for cues, aid reminders, main points, and the like. Sometimes, if you're using "flip charts," you can write your delivery notes very lightly right on the chart and appear as if you're not using any notes at all. Also, easel charts themselves can serve as your delivery notes. A sample flow chart appears on the next page.

11 DISADVANTAGES OF MEMORIZED PRESENTING

Among the disadvantages of memorized presenting are:

- *Causes continual worry over forgetting, making good audience contact almost impossible.*
- *One thing forgotten usually destroys the whole presentation.*
- *Involves a great deal of non–creative time for the sheer mechanics of memorizing.*
- *Does not allow for spontaneity or adaption to audience reactions.*
- *Restricts animated delivery.*

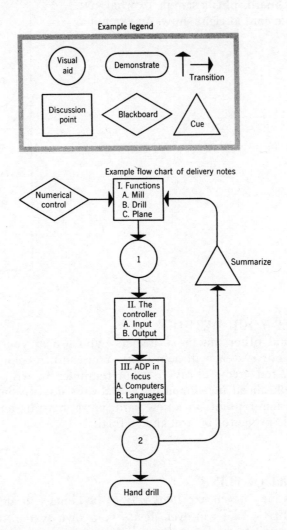

Example legend

Visual aid

Demonstrate

Transition

Discussion point

Blackboard

Cue

Example flow chart of delivery notes

Numerical control

I. Functions
A. Mill
B. Drill
C. Plane

1

II. The controller
A. Input
B. Output

III. ADP in focus
A. Computers
B. Languages

2

Summarize

Hand drill

Question D: When would you use a full manuscript of your presentation for delivery?

_____

_____

_____

12 MANUSCRIPTS

As we've said, manuscript delivery is undesirable because it reduces direct audience contact. But there are times when this type of detailed delivery is desirable; e.g., when you want the record of your presentation to be exact. We'll talk about manuscript delivery later. For the moment, we're concerned only with the manuscript as a form of delivery notes. In any case, the physical appearance of your manuscript will be important. Proper spacing, typing, indenting, underscoring, capitalizing, numbering, lettering, color coding, and so forth, all can be used as effective devices for smooth delivery.

In preparing a manuscript, follow these rules:

- *Use cards or stiff paper for durability and ease of handling.*
- *All manuscripts should be typewritten, double- or triple-spaced.*
- *Allow at least 1 1/4 in. margins all around to make reading easier.*
- *Number all pages.*
- *Include visual or other aid cues right in the manuscript in the order in which they are to appear.*
- *Do not staple or put the sheets in a binder.*
- *Use only one side of the card or sheet.*
- *Try to end points or thoughts at the ends of pages, instead of placing only a few lines of an idea at the bottom of one page. If a new thought begins near the bottom, start a new page—especially at transitions between main points.*
- *Do not end a page in the middle of a sentence.*

Observe how these rules are applied in the sample manuscript below. Notice the use of spacing and the "buttons" that indicate visual aid projection. Every time the presenter using this manuscript sees a numbered circle, he knows to press his projector button.

Answer to Question D: Only when you wanted the record to show exactly what you've said, e.g., a statement for the press, when there are legal implications, when you might be called to task at some later time, and so forth.

13 SUMMARY

There is no point in needlessly complicating speaking-note procedures, but there is great value in proceeding systematically. The fact that most presenters do not do so has prompted the inclusion of the foregoing suggestions. The worst thing that could happen is for the procedure to dominate the presentation. This is not the intent here. These ideas should be viewed as suggestions only. The individual should select or combine from them what suits his individual needs. If these merely awaken in him a recognition of the value of preparing his delivery notes as any other technician would prepare to do a job, this chapter has accomplished its purpose.

Summary Exercise: Convert the sample manuscript under heading #12 to note cards, as discussed.

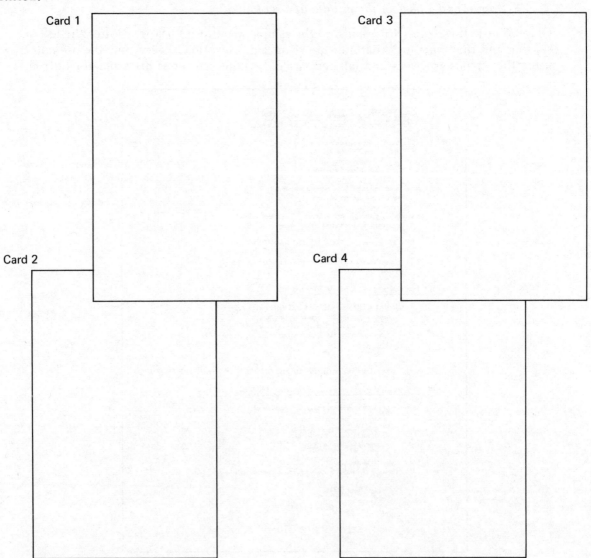

Card 1

Card 3

Card 2

Card 4

Scorable Quiz: Circle the correct answer.

1. Impromptu delivery is
   a. being fully prepared, but having no notes
   b. presenting without notes or prior preparation
   c. knowing your outline, but having no notes

2. Extemporaneous delivery is
   a. presenting with a scenario of preprepared notes
   b. presenting from a detailed text
   c. memorizing the entire presentation

3. A complete set of notes should not contain
   a. cues for use of aids
   b. podium samples of aids
   c. handout material

4. Extemporaneous delivery
   a. restricts your movement at the podium
   b. forces you to become involved in your presentation
   c. is too loose and disorganized

5. Delivery notes should
   a. be as concise as possible
   b. not have stage directions in them
   c. be memorized

6. Aids should be
   a. fully described to the audience
   b. restricted to a single medium
   c. keyed into the delivery notes

7. Flow chart outlines
   a. may suffice in lieu of regular delivery notes
   b. are good for planning, but not actual delivery
   c. often confuse the audience

8. Standardized notes
   a. are too restrictive
   b. facilitate delivery
   c. don't permit the use of cues

9. Miniature reproductions of aids in delivery notes
   a. prevent spontaneity
   b. serve the same function as key words
   c. make notes needlessly bulky

10. The best physical size for notes is
    a. 8 1/2" x 11" sheets
    b. a small spiral notebook
    c. cards that can be hand-held

Answers to Summary Exercise: Compare your note cards with these. Notice the aid keys, abbreviations, and indentations. If you've really thought out each point of your presentation, note cards like this can literally be held in the palm of your hand, giving you both spontaneity and complete freedom of movement.

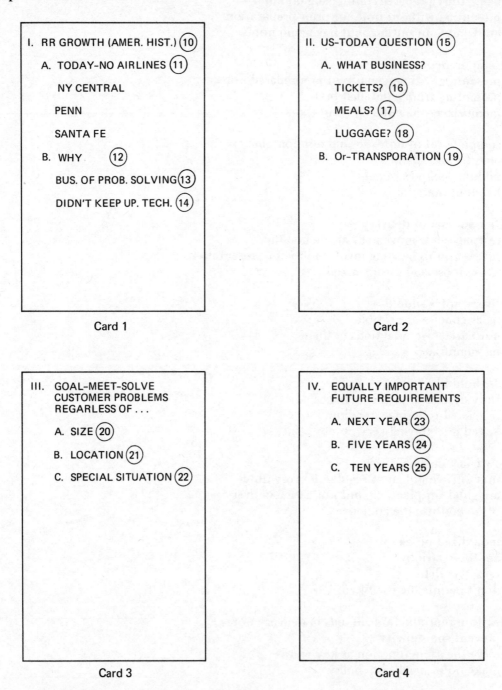

I. RR GROWTH (AMER. HIST.) (10)

  A. TODAY-NO AIRLINES (11)

    NY CENTRAL

    PENN

    SANTA FE

  B. WHY (12)

    BUS. OF PROB. SOLVING (13)

    DIDN'T KEEP UP. TECH. (14)

Card 1

II. US-TODAY QUESTION (15)

  A. WHAT BUSINESS?

    TICKETS? (16)

    MEALS? (17)

    LUGGAGE? (18)

  B. Or-TRANSPORATION (19)

Card 2

III. GOAL-MEET-SOLVE CUSTOMER PROBLEMS REGARLESS OF . . .

  A. SIZE (20)

  B. LOCATION (21)

  C. SPECIAL SITUATION (22)

Card 3

IV. EQUALLY IMPORTANT FUTURE REQUIREMENTS

  A. NEXT YEAR (23)

  B. FIVE YEARS (24)

  C. TEN YEARS (25)

Card 4

Answers to Scorable Quiz: (Each correct answer = 10%.)   (1) b, (2) a, (3) c, (4) b, (5) a, (6) c, (7) a, (8) b, (9) b, (10) c.

Rehearsing The Presentation

PREMISE: That rehearsing, or prethinking, your presentation is a major key to smoothness of delivery!

SEGMENT OBJECTIVE: That you develop a workable system for privately practicing and rehearsing the delivery of your presentation with the aim of eliminating as many bugs and *faux pas* in the actual delivery as possible.

Question A: What would you say is the first principle of good rehearsal?

_____

_____

_____

_____

1 WHAT IS REHEARSAL?
What is a presentation? It is a thought process or, more correctly, a thought transference process with certain supporting behavior. It is thinking in public. Rehearsal, therefore, more than anything else, is thinking. Recall your whole presentation process. It has been first a process of producing the thought, the idea, and then developing the support, the proof, the reinforcement. So it is with rehearsal. It is first and foremost a thinking process. Then it is a processing of doing and practicing in private what must be done in public. The one thing that you do not want your rehearsal to become is a mere rote process of mechanical memorizing and repetition. Thinking, therefore, is the first principle of good rehearsal. Memorize the actual thought pattern of the presentation.

We call this approach to rehearsal "prethinking the presentation." It is a thinking and exercising process, a getting involved in your presentation at a mental level where all you do really need are a few reminders or key words to trigger you to relive and re-experience with your audience what you have already lived and experienced. This is the key to good extemporaneous delivery, the best method for maximum contact and interaction with a live audience.

Answer to Question A: The first principle of good rehearsal is thinking.

13

Question B: What should you memorize as a part of your rehearsal process?

_____

_____

_____

_____

_____

Question C: List at least five things that you can or should do in prethinking your presentation.

_____

_____

_____

_____

_____

_____

_____

_____

2 HINTS ON PRETHINKING YOUR PRESENTATION

In prethinking your presentations, you may find the following suggestions helpful:

1. *Know the outline of your presentation inside out. Make it a mental picture or pathway in your mind (which is what you want it to become for your audience, also).*
2. *Repeatedly travel this mental pathway. Become totally familiar with each "signpost," that is, your subpoints, supportive devices, aids and so forth.*
3. *As you come to each element along the pathway, envision yourself actually reliving and retelling what you are mentally experiencing to your audience.*
4. *Test yourself to see if a key word will trigger your recall of a specific element; for example, an anecdote, an example, or a list of details. From this point you can retell in your own words without further reference to written notes.*
5. *Some other things may be committed to memory:*
   Your very first statement to your audience;
   Your very last statement to your audience;
   Any special quotations or similar material that you want to quote verbatim.

Answers to Question B:
- Your thought sequence pattern
- Your very first statement to your audience
- Your very last statement to your audience
- Any special materials that you want to quote verbatim

Answers to Question C:
- Know your outline completely.
- Rethink and relive each part of your presentation in your mind.
- Envision yourself actually talking about each element to an audience.
- Commit your first and last statements and special material to memory.
- Carry rehearsal reminder cards.
- Repeatedly review your objective and thesis.
- Sketch and doodle your illustrations.
- Mentally picture anecdotes, stories, examples, and the like.
- Relive your original thinking processes.

3 SOME OTHER HELPS

The "divide and conquer" method of rehearsing is good whether the presentation is complete or not. Many of its elements can be practiced almost anywhere, at any leisure moment. The net result, when the time to deliver arrives, will be a prethought presentation. With such a technique, it is easy to see why key words are sufficient in the delivery notes.

1. *Make preliminary note cards for various portions or subdivisions. Carry them in pocket or purse and mentally rehearse them whenever possible.*
2. *Go over and over your objective thesis.*
3. *Repeat to yourself quotations, statistics, and similar parts to be recalled by key words.*
4. *Sketch and doodle with illustrations to be drawn or written during the presentation.*
5. *Repeat and mentally picture stories and anecdotes over and over in the mind until they can be recounted without referring to a single note.*
6. *Relive the thought processes which originally brought about a particular conclusion, premise, or idea in your own thinking.*

Question D: List at least five things you can do to rehearse the use of your aids.

_____

_____

_____

_____

_____

Question E: When should you rehearse?

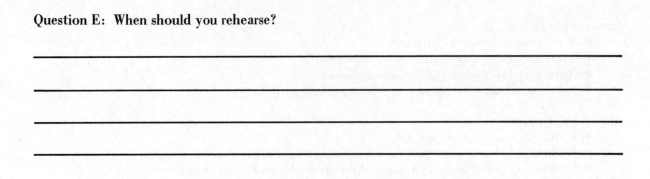

4 AUDITORY REHEARSAL
The more experienced you become, probably the more introspective your rehearsals will be. You'll know your style and method of delivery. You'll already have made and corrected many of the mistakes normally made in delivery. If you are well informed on your subject, you'll have pre-established methods of getting points across. Many of your facts and supporting material will already be committed to memory. In effect, you'll engage in a kind of auditory rehearsal because you'll be able to visualize and mentally "hear" your own performance. Yet, even there, an actual auditory rehearsal can have value. You may wish to practice and polish specific effects, smooth out the use of your visuals, or just try your ideas out on someone.
The areas of auditory rehearsal we will consider here are:

- *Choosing an auditor*
- *Using the microphone*
- *Speaking before an auditor*
- *Timing the presentation*

5 CHOOSING AN AUDITOR
You can serve as you own auditor by recording your presentation, listening to it (or observing it, if you use video tape), making notes, rerecording it, and so on. But this method lacks the objectivity which other people can provide. The best way is to choose one or more reasonably qualified persons to act as "rehearsal critics." Sometimes it may even be advisable to assemble a group approximating the size of the real audience, and have them ask questions that the public group might ask. If possible, auditors should have at least the following qualifications:

- *Technical knowledge sufficient to criticize or check the accuracy and validity of the presentation's substance.*
- *The ability to evaluate you objectivity. (This normally rules out people who are emotionally involved with you.)*
- *Interest and willingness to serve as critics.*
- *If possible, they should have taken this course.*

6 USING THE MICROPHONE
Many people are unduly influenced by the presence of a microphone. With the modern equipment and techniques available today, there is little difference between speaking with or without one. Sound engineers, when present, give all of the necessary

16

instructions and signals, and monitor and adjust the equipment to fit the individual. With public address systems, you'll hear your own voice and be able to adjust to the proper distance from which to speak.

7 SPEAKING BEFORE AN AUDITOR

Simply pretend that your auditors are your real audience and make the presentation exactly as you would under the actual conditions. It is important that you convince yourself as much as you possibly can that they are a real audience. Do not act the presentation, but get right into the spirit of it as a real-life situation. Both you and your critics should decide whether a given rehearsal is to be all or part of the presentation, and then there should be no interruptions. All comments should be reserved until that portion has been delivered in its entirety. Partial rehearsing is less desirable than going through the entire presentation each time, but these days time restrictions often preclude this. Yet there should be at least two full rehearsals: one to find the mistakes in the total version, the second to correct them. Additional rehearsals are determined by available time and the need for further polishing.

The rehearsal, like the presentation itself, should be extemporaneous. As already explained, this does not mean that you speak "off the cuff." It means that you know precisely what you want to say or do but do not memorize word for word. Thus, each time that you rehearse, the presentation will come out a little differently. Many things will be said almost identically each time, but will still be expressed in language spontaneous and fresh to the moment. This is the most personal and real form of communicating.

8 TIMING THE PRESENTATION

Do not forget this important matter. If your presentation runs over in rehearsal, so it will under actual conditions. The presentation should always be planned to run just a little under its time limitations. Rehearsals tend to compress information. This margin of safety will allow for this and ensure that the actual presentation will not run over. It is also good psychology to end a little early.

9 REHEARSE YOUR AIDS

Actually using the aids during the presentation often proves to be a stumbling block to the person without practice in coordinating what he does at the podium with what he says. The only solution to this is practice—rehearsal. To arrive at a podium without ever having pressed the projector button at the spot in the presentation where it will be pressed under actual conditions is taking a foolish chance. As far as visual aids are concerned, rehearsal should include as a minimum the following:

- *Thorough familiarization with the content of each individual aid.*
- *Actual practice in the use of any equipment to be used.*
- *Actual performance of any act to be performed during the presentation. For example, if a blackboard illustration is to be drawn, it should be practiced at least once in advance on the blackboard.*
- *Any demonstration should be rehearsed from beginning to end at least once.*
- *Preview of all movies, film strips, and similar material obtained from libraries or other sources.*

- *Time each aid to be sure that it is exposed long enough for comprehension, but not too long. Also time other activities to be sure that they fit proportionately into the time allowed for the presentation itself.*

- *Proofread all handout material in its final form. Also check quantities against anticipated attendance.*

10 WHEN TO REHEARSE

You should begin to rehearse the moment you first phrase your thesis. Your notetaking also undoubtedly produced a particularly pithy phrase or two which you would want to state to your audience in almost precisely the original wording. These should have been mulled over in the mind, brooded upon, perhaps even tried out on people and refined in conversation. This should certainly have been done with the thesis, if nothing else. If at all possible, it is good to live with a presentation and its parts as much as possible before it is given. Become a little militant about the thesis or some particular part of it. Make it a personal matter.

When should the delivery notes be ready in their final form? There are too many variables involved to state a specific length of time. As early as possible, is the only answer. The longer they can be carried before the presentation, the more familiar they become—and the less they will be needed. The whole presentation package—notes, aids, and handouts—should be ready in time for at least two complete dress rehearsals, but parts of the presentation can be thought about and rehearsed before this.

Last minute rehearsals are undesirable. They create undue tension and nervousness and do not allow sufficient time for correcting mistakes and polishing delivery. Ideally, the first full auditory rehearsal should take place at least a week before the presentation date and be conducted in surroundings in which it will not be disturbed or interrupted. If a microphone is to be used in the actual presentation, one should be used in rehearsal, preferably a live one, but a dummy can be used for familiarization. If possible, use the room in which the presentation will be given. If not, use one as similar to it as possible.

11 REHEARSING A MANUSCRIPT PRESENTATION

One of the occasions where manuscript speaking might be warranted already has been mentioned. Assuming that one has been decided upon and prepared as suggested, the following rehearsal procedure should be followed:

- *Silently read, absorb, and ponder each thought several times just as for any other form of presenting. Just because it is to be read does not mean that it is only to be read. The aim still is to make it appear as little like reading as possible.*

- *Read the manuscript aloud several times.*

- *Learn to lift the eyes from the paper as often as possible to maintain contact with the audience.*

- *Do not over-dramatize the reading. Every word should not be spoken at the same level of emphasis.*

- *Learn to pause between important ideas and at transition points.*

- *The natural tendency is to read too rapidly. Make a conscious effort to read slowly and deliberately.*

- *Use a colored pencil to make additional cue marks during the rehearsal, underscoring words that need additional emphasis, inserting additional pauses where they are required (. . .), and so on.*

- *Have the final manuscript retyped and completely clean.*

- *See that the manuscript is placed on a surface high enough so that there is no need to bend over or strain to see the print. Make sure the surface is large enough to allow for moving used pages aside.*

- *Try not to turn the pages. Instead, simply slide them aside. Use the manuscript like an open book, keeping two unread pages up at all times. This prevents stumbling, breaking of thoughts, and so forth.*

The following diagram shows how manuscript should be handled:

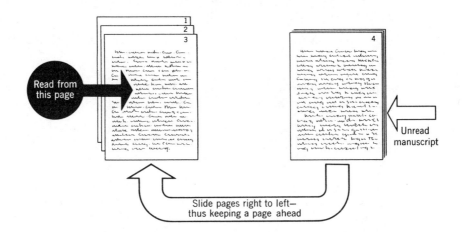

12 "REHEARSING" THE IMPROMPTU PRESENTATION

By definition, an impromptu presentation allows no time for rehearsal. Yet, if one stops and thinks about it a moment, an impromptu presentation can be rehearsed—and has been. A person is rarely asked on the spur of the moment to present a subject about which he knows nothing. Usually the contrary is true, and this is exactly why he is asked to "say a few words." This person also usually is aware of the possibilities of his being asked to do so. Following are a few guidelines for the prospective impromptu presenter:

- *When attending a meeting where the possibility of being called upon exists, find out as much as possible about the subjects to be discussed.*

- *Carry a notebook or blank note cards.*

- *Perhaps even carry a few cards with generalized outlines.*

- *Keep a repertoire of "canned" introductory comments.*

- *Listen actively to everything being said. Form opinions, think of thoughts or facts which are missed by the speakers.*

- *Keep a running commentary of notations on these things.*

- *Be alert for comments made by the speakers, which could be used to introduce and tie in impromptu remarks.*

- *Watch for patterns and outline points emphasized by the regular speakers.*

- *When called upon, there almost always will be a few minutes of advance warning. Utilize this time fully. Immediately do the following things:*

  - *Quickly scan the notes just taken and attempt to extract a central idea and jot down a key word for it.*

  - *Quickly establish a pattern and jot down a key word for each point in it.*

  - *Use a single card or sheet for such notes.*

  - *Arise slowly. Glance around the audience. Begin with something from the personal repetoire, perhaps a story or a joke which can be told with ease, allowing additional time to marshal forces and glance at the notes just made.*

  - *Form mental pictures. Try to get on an organized mental pathway already thought out.*

- *Do not be afraid to decline the invitation. It is far better and wiser to do so than to fumble in a completely unprepared manner.*

The key to impromptu speaking is to be always prepared and expecting to be called upon. A wise prospective impromptu presenter sitting in an audience will always be preparing "a few remarks." In short, for the real professional, there is no such thing as impromptu presenting.

13 A REHEARSAL CHECKLIST

A checklist will make the rehearsal far more meaningful and useful than simply asking someone to judge the presentation in a generalized way. It is both good planning and considerate of the persons who are asked to assist in auditing the rehearsal to provide them with a guide to their criticism. It also would be quite difficult for them to note everything which needs to be noted without some reminder of what to look for. A critique is worthless unless it is clinical and objective. At this stage, you are looking for what is wrong with your presentation more than for what is right. The critic must be merciless. (Better he, than the audience.)

Criticism should center upon both the subject matter and the main points of good presenting as discussed in the foregoing chapters. Although, ideally, the critic should read this book as a foundation for his criticism, the assumption is that he has not done so. The following checklist is designed to be selfexplanatory. Use it if you are now in the process of preparing a presentation.

REHEARSAL CHECKLIST	Time Start Finish	Excel- lent	Good	Fair	Poor	Remarks or Exceptions
Presenter's Attitude						
1. Is there appropriate enthusiasm and sincerity?						
2. Does the presenter seem convinced?						
3. Does the presenter seem "real"?						
4. Is he nonegocentric?						
5. Does he suffer from stage fright?						
Content						
1. Is the information valid and accurate?						
2. Does the presenter display full grasp of the subject?						
3. Does he appear to have a reserve, to know more than he is telling?						
Objective-Thesis						
1. Is there a clear, central idea?						
2. Is it sufficiently stressed?						
3. Does it run through the whole presentation?						
4. Is everything said and done relevant to it?						
Structure						
1. Is there evidence of a single, main structure?						
2. Is it integrated, unified, and easy to follow?						
3. Is it sufficiently supported with appropriate detail?						
4. Is the detail concrete, valid, and specific?						
Introduction						
1. Does it get attention?						
2. Say what the presentation contains?						
3. Relate the presentation to the audience's world?						
Conclusion						
1. Does it tie the presentation together?						
2. Focus attention on the presentation as a unit?						
3. Relate back to the objective-thesis?						
4. Tell the audience what to do next?						
Audience Awareness						
1. Does the presenter understand and empathize with them?						
2. Does he speak from their point of view?						
3. Does he use their language?						
4. Is there audience contract?						
Aids						
1. Are they clear and easy to see and comprehend?						
2. Does each clearly support or reinforce its related idea?						
3. Is there a single visual motif-unified and harmonious?						
4. Is there too much detail?						
5. Are they "busy"?						
6. Are they exposed sufficiently for comprehension and retention?						
Delivery						
1. Are language, diction, and pronunciation cultured and appropriate?						
2. Is the presenter poised and relaxed?						
3. Is the voice clear, well-modulated, relaxed, and in proper volume?						
4. Are there irrelevant gestures, actions, mannerisms, etc.?						
5. Has the presenter a good physical appearance?						
6. Does he look at the audience-everyone-and maintain contact?						
7. Is microphone used properly?						

Answers to Question D:
1. Thorough familiarization with the content of each individual aid.
2. Actual practice in the use of equipment to be used.
3. Actual performance of any act to be performed during the presentation.
4. Any demonstration should be rehearsed thoroughly at least once.
5. Preview of all movies, film strips, and similar material.
6. Time each aid to be sure that it is exposed long enough for comprehension, but not too long. Also time other activities to be sure that they fit into the time allowed for the presentation itself.
7. Proofread all handout material in its final form. Check quantities against anticipated audience.

Answer to Question E: You should start rehearsing as soon as you formulate your thesis. As you continue to gather data, you can rehearse the various elements as you build them into your presentation. In short, you can and should rehearse throughout your preparation process.

Scorable Quiz: Fill in the missing word or words.

1. Good presentation rehearsal is best described as a _____ process.

2. The main thing that should be memorized is the _____ of the presentation.

3. Having someone else listen to your presentation is called _____ rehearsal.

4. The presentation should always be planned to run just a little _____ its allotted time.

5. _____ delivery is the best method to ensure freshness and spontaneity at the podium.

6. There should be at least _____ rehearsals.

7. The "_____" method of rehearsal permits practice of parts of the presentation almost anywhere or anytime.

8. You can serve as your own auditor by _____ your presentation.

9. All movies, film strips, and similar materials obtained from libraries or other sources should be _____ .

10. A wise prospective impromptu presenter will always have "_____" ready.

Answers to Scorable Quiz: (Each correct answer = 10%.) (1) thought, (2) thought pattern, (3) auditory, (4) under, (5) extemporaneous, (6) two, (7) divide and conquer, (8) recording, (9) previewed, (10) a few remarks.

Understanding Stage Fright

PREMISE: That, like everything else in the functional presentation, you should and can control your own emotions, trepidation, and motivation.

SEGMENT OBJECTIVE: That you understand the anatomy of self-motivation and stage fright in order to better control them as a basis for effective delivery.

Question A: What do you think are the causes of stage fright?

1. _____

2. _____

3. _____

1 **THE ANATOMY OF STAGE FRIGHT**
We've seen enough cases of stage fright, or "buck fever" as it's also sometimes called, to know that no course in effective presentation would be complete without some mention of how to deal with this self-defeating phenomenon.

If you don't experience some form of stage fright as you finally face your live audience for the first time, you're lucky indeed, and you might skip this segment. But you're also in a very small minority among professionals and amateurs alike. For, few idea presenters, even people who deal with audiences daily, ever completely overcome it. Most professional performers freely admit to "pre-opening jitters." Professional salesmen frequently admit to the same feeling before taking a call. In some ways it would not be completely beneficial to overcome such feelings, for two basic reasons. First, it is beneficial to maintain a certain amount of tension in the human mechanism. Humans function better when they are "keyed up" a bit, so long as the tension isn't such that it interferes with normal functioning and operation. Second, a complete absence of such tension can result in laxness, or even an attitude of condescension toward an audience —which is worse than fear of audience.

So, the trick is to find and strike the happy medium between too much and too little tension, stage fright, the jitters, or whatever else you might call it.

Controlled tension is power.

Question B: List here some things that you think one might do to overcome or control stage fright.

1. _____

2. _____

3. _____

4. _____

5. _____

Question C: What is the primary source of stage fright?

_____

_____

_____

Franklin Roosevelt's famous dictum, "We have nothing to fear but fear itself," applies here. When any fear is brought out into the light of day, squarely faced and its anatomy dissected, as it were, to be seen for what it really is, this is half of the battle of dealing with it. At first glance, to say that shyness or reluctance to display oneself is a form of egotism might seem contradictory. But this is precisely what stage fright is: it is defense and protection of the ego, the self.

In the early days of his Evolution, man faced dangers constantly. His body instinctively geared itself for defense by glandular activity which, on the signal of danger, stimulated his physical mechanisms to a point of maximum preparedness and performance. As he became more civilized, the need for physical defense diminished. With his socialization, danger took on a different connotation, that of danger to his ego, his inner self. Basically his glandular responses, triggered by his senses and mental perception, never learned to recognize the difference between psychological and physical danger. Thus, when the danger signal is received, they still stimulate and tense the whole human mechanism for defense. Some psychologists undoubtedly would shudder at such a short and quick description. But, essentially, this is the anatomy of stage fright. Allowing for the complexity of man's psychological behavior, it is basically an ego defense reaction, and you should understand this as the first step in building a base for dealing with it.

The first key there is to be aware of is that all of the emotional drives we described in Segment 15 are at work in you the same as they are in your audience. Once you know, for example, that you too can be ego defensive, need recognition, acceptance, approval, and so forth, you have a better chance of controlling such needs in yourself as they might affect or interfere with your dealing with or controlling someone else.

The key question is to constantly ask yourself exactly what motivating forces the other person is evoking in you in the course of a communicative interchange. The next step, then, is to make a decision as to whether or not you want to let that force continue to work unchecked. Then you must decide upon the degree of control that you want to exercise over your own emotions and through a conscious effort of will to exercise that control.

Answers to Question A: For individual cases there may be other reasons for what we commonly call stage fright, but in most cases, you'll be able to fit the causes under one of these headings:
1. **Lack of preparation**
2. **Fear of failure or some form of ego defense**
3. **Lack of self-motivation**

Answers to Question B: Here are some of the more important things you can do to deal with stage fright. You can:
1. Understand the anatomy of stage fright.
2. Learn how to convert it to "delivery energy."
3. Be fully prepared.
4. Once again, use your adherence to functionalism.
5. Understand the anatomy of self-motivation.

Answer to Question C: At its very roots, it is a defensive mechanism stemming from man's primitive reaction and preparation to face "danger."

Question D: Without looking back at Segment 15, list here at least five forces that might be at work within you which could cause stage fright.

1. _____   3. _____

2. _____   4. _____

5. _____

2 CONVERTING THE ENERGY

The motive forces we've described are, in a very real sense, a form of psychological energy. One thing that professional communicators and performers often have learned to do is to take this energy that exists within themselves (and which can have an interfering or disruptive effect on their delivery) and actually channel or convert it into a positive force that gives their delivery dynamism, enthusiasm, or extra intensity. If, for example, you are propelled primarily by the desire to make money, or by the need for acceptance or praise, you will find that when you link your effort to your desire to make money or to get praise, your efforts will gain considerable strength and momentum. A key, of course, is honesty in deciding what does motivate you.

One presenter we know actually verbalizes to us how he personally converts his tenseness into delivery energy on occasion. He scans his audience, and perhaps picks up some vibration of, say, hostility, disbelief, a "show me" attitude, or the like. In a very real way, he has learned to respond to such real or imagined reactions by exerting an added conviction and intensity in his argument.

Another male presenter we know says, "I intentionally play my tension to the women in my audience. I take advantage of the natural polarity and attraction of the sexes. As some female reaction bounces back to me, as I pick up return vibrations from one or more female audience members, I've learned to rechannel this energy back into my delivery and spread it to the whole audience."

Question E: What do we mean by "converting the energy"?

_____

_____

_____

_____

Answers to Question D:

- Ego extension
- Ego survival or security
- Gregariousness
- Pugnacity
- Ego gratification
- Conditioning
- Some experience, impression, or fear stored in your unconscious mind. (Reread Segment 15 for more detail.)

Answer to Question E: Stated as simply as possible, this is the process of using your tension or nervousness as extra "emotional fuel" to give your delivery increased dynamism, enthusiasm, intensity, urgency, and so on.

3 A WELL-PREPARED MESSAGE

What else can we say? This whole course is designed to help you to have this essential ingredient. It is difficult to shake the confidence of a person who knows that he has "the goods." Unanimously, preparation is recognized as the cornerstone of confidence. There is no substitute for knowing that one has a full grasp of his subject, for knowing precisely what you are going to say and why and how you will say it, and having answers for any conceivable question that might arise. If there is to be any real confidence, it must rest on full preparation. If you have done what the preceding segments have suggested, you will have this foundation and can be confident.

4 CONSTANCY TO PURPOSE

Benjamin Disraeli once said, "Constancy to purpose is the key to success." In the final analysis, your commitment to your presentation's stated objective, no matter what else you forget to say or do, can be the presentation's salvation and redemption. For there are few things that can stand in the way of a person who wants something so badly that he can "taste it."

The best way to describe it is that you should have "an urgent message" to deliver. The truth is that information by itself is composed of cold, hard, dry facts. But if you do your job right, they must become something more. When they are put together, they must have life, and you are the one who gives it to them. William Jones wrote, "In almost any subject, your passion for the subject will save you. If you only care enough for a result, you will most certainly attain it." The deeper this passion, this feeling of having an urgent message to deliver, this conviction in the validity and useful-ness of what is being presented, and a belief that it should be presented, the greater will be your chances of success. Many studies of human success—and of successful idea presenters, have revealed this central self-motivation to be the primary eradicator of fears. Although there are many ways of saying it, the matter goes directly back to what was said at the beginning of this course. Perspective still lies at the base of effective presentation, and runs through it like a life-giving artery. When a person really believes that he has an urgent message to deliver, few fears or obstacles can stop him from delivering it.

It is true that we may not necessarily be speaking here of great battles and noble causes, but self-commitment is made of the same "stuff" in any situation, and full commitment to the cause of the moment is a no-turning-back affair. In the words of Professor William James: "When once a decision is reached and execution is the order of the day, dismiss absolutely all responsibility and care about the outcome."

This is not foolhardiness—unless the will to win is foolish. It is far more foolish to undertake something without a belief that it will succeed. If you have done all that you

26

can in preparing and delivering the message, what else could be done anyway? The chances are excellent that you and your presentation will both succeed. Even if the presentation is a failure, you will have succeeded.

A prepared presenter with a firm belief in his message, fully committed to his goal, needs only one other thing—the strength to pursue it through *to the end*. Napoleon said, "Victory is will." For the idea presenter, persistence is the simple mechanism of wholeheartedly doing each next thing, until there are no more "next things" to do. This also ties directly back to the stress placed upon objective development. If the presentation has a specific goal which has been articulated and reduced to something which can be seen—and if each step in the presentation leads closer to it—nothing need be done but to take the steps. This is also one of the reasons that it is so important to narrow the objective to something realistic and small enough to handle. This is the real secret of functional presenting. It is the accepting of only two possibilities—success or failure. Once the goal is seen clearly, nothing remains but to strive toward it with all of the strength and facilities available and to either succeed or fail in its accomplishment. Stopping anywhere short is automatic failure—hence the importance of persistence, which is colloquially, but eloquently, summarized in this poem by Robert Service:

> It's easy to cry that you're beaten—and die
> It's easy to crawfish and crawl;
> But to fight and to fight when hope's out of sight,
> Why that's the best game of them all!
> And though you come out of each gruelling bout
> All broken and beaten and scarred,
> Just have one more try—it's dead easy to die,
> It's the keeping on living that's hard.

Finally, there is no surer way to overcome stage fright than what we call the "as for me" attitude. There are many stories and examples of this in literature and history. The idea is embodied in Patrick Henry's famous statement, "I know not what course *others* may take . . . *as for me* . . . " Embodied here are several important ideas:

1. *In the final analysis, you can't answer for anyone else's actions, reactions, or attitudes—only your own.*
2. *Succeed or fail, sink or swim, you're stuck with the consequences of your own actions and decisions.*
3. *Thus, if you know you've done all you can and your motives are right, you succeed or fail with a clear conscience. And, if your audience doesn't believe, buy, learn, nor do—that's their problem.*

Question F: Read the following poem, and explain it on the lines below.

Like the little Hindu
You do everything you "kin" do
And if you lose your skirt or pants,
You'll just have to let your skin do!

_____

_____

_____

Answer to Question F: A bit elementary, perhaps; a childish ditty; yet, if you think about it, the thought is profound. For the little Hindu knows the same thing that St. Paul knew: "Having done all that I can . . . I stand or fall." Or Martin Luther: "Here I stand; I can do no otherwise. God help me. Amen."

Scorable Quiz: Indicate true (T) or false (F).

1. Stage fright is a very primitive human reaction. _____

2. Stage fright is basically a form of ego defense. _____

3. You should work to relieve all such tension. _____

4. A complete lack of tension can result in laxness. _____

5. Most professional performers don't have stage fright. _____

6. One good way to overcome stage fright is to act as if you don't have it. _____

7. The key question is to ask yourself what motivating forces another person might be evoking in you. _____

8. There is such a thing as an effort of sheer will that can overcome your own emotional reactions. _____

9. You can't rechannel the "energy" of stage fright because it is a basic human fear. _____

10. In the final analysis, you can only answer for your own actions. _____

Answers to Scorable Quiz: (Each correct answer = 10%.) (1) T, (2) T, (3) F, (4) T, (5) F, (6) T, (7) T, (8) T, (9) F, (10) T.

LEARNING
27
SEGMENT

Understanding Self-Motivation

PREMISE: That is it possible and often necessary for an idea presenter to give himself a "pep talk" prior to delivering a presentation.

SEGMENT OBJECTIVE: That you have available some tools for improving your own motivation, as necessary.

NOTE...
This segment is for reading only. No exercises or dialogue are included.

We feel it appropriate to give you a few hints on how to "tune yourself up" prior to facing an audience. There is always a danger of belaboring the obvious in speaking of such fundamental matters as self-confidence and self-motivation. Yet many people today are cynical and disillusioned; they find it difficult to muster within themselves a feeling of energetic conviction. In one respect, the reasons for lack of self-motivation are a complex part of our accelerated changing times. On the other hand, it remains a simple matter of how the individual, himself, looks at things.

1 THE "MOTIVATION LOOP"

There is no intent here to philosophize upon the ills of our age, other than to get the matter of self-motivation, an essential of good presenting, into proper perspective, and to point out that regardless of environment, self-motivation stems from within the individual himself—not from external influences. There are also specific devices which you can apply to yourself when you find that you are lacking in your own motivation. At first glance, these devices seem artificial, one of the reasons that many people reject them without even testing them. In a sense, they are artificial because they are based on the premise that externally contrived personal actions can actually alter genuinely internal personal feelings. The person with the genuine feeling doesn't need them. Take, for example, this premise: "In order to be successful, one must look and act successful." Stated in terms of the presenter: "In order to be a good presenter, one must look and act like a good presenter." The average opinion is that by so doing, one is deceiving himself. Just because you act a certain way does not mean that you are that way—which is true. Yet let the skeptic ask himself: "When should a person

29

start to act like a good presenter? *After* he has become one?" You cannot become one *until* you begin to act like one. And, if you don't feel like one, what is better than to act like one? There is no intent here to make the discussion sound like double-talk. The fundamental premise of self-motivation is that personal actions trigger personal feelings, just as surely as personal feelings trigger personal actions. When the personal feelings are lacking, there is no better way to get them than to begin acting as if they were present. The best way not to be nervous is to act as if you are not nervous. The best way to succeed is to behave like a successful person. And the best way to be a self-confident, self-motivated presenter is to behave like one. This is the whole essence of positive thinking. There is no mystery, other than the fact that man is a mysterious creature to himself and that, unlike the lower animals, he can control himself with his own mind in a kind of "closed-loop" fashion. Every person is already in either a positive or negative version of this loop. In either case, to change, the entry point is at the "action" stage. A graphic representation of this motivation loop follows:

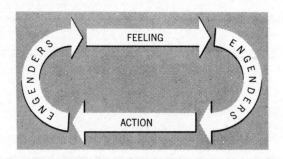

2 SOME SPECIFIC ACTIONS FOR SELF-MOTIVATION

There is no intent here to advance a new theory or to give any great new formula for success, or for any of the suggestions that follow to be construed as a panacea or as the ultimate solution to self-motivation. They are merely suggestions which have been found to work effectively in a great majority of the instances in which they have been tried.

The Self-Motivation Monologue: This amounts to nothing more than giving yourself a "talking to." This may seem foolish at first, but it is amazing how well it works. You can increase your own confidence and motivation simply by consciously speaking to yourself as you would to another person, much as you might counsel a child that he can "do it if he tries." Technically, this is known as rationalization. People use it every day to convince themselves that they can afford this or that item, that "one more for the road" is all right, that "tomorrow, I'll start dieting," and so forth. It is known to work in these cases. Why not put it to good use here, also?

Imitation: Theodore Roosevelt is said to have kept a picture of Abraham Lincoln ever handy. When he was faced with a decision or dilemma, he asked himself what Lincoln would have done in a similar instance and simply imitated him. One can also paint a mental picture of the ideal speaker or presenter and imitate him.

The Value of Dress and Grooming: The military has long recognized the motivational power of dress and grooming. Many sales organizations stress the value of personal appearance not only from the standpoint of the outward *impression* it creates, but because of what "feeling sharp" does for the inner person as well.

Music Hath Charms: Everyone has his favorite musical passage—the one that lifts his spirits just a little higher, puts a bounce in his step, or makes him want to "swing."

It may be a march, a sonata, or the overture of a Broadway show. Try listening to your favorite just before going on to make a presentation.

An Inspiring Motto: Every person should have one or more literary passages or mottoes which inspire him. As does music, these have the power to lift the spirits, to give that little extra flair, to cause the head to be held a little higher. Each person is different, and should be. If you do not have one of your own, a quick perusal of *Bartlett's Familiar Quotations* will provide many from which to choose to suit your needs. One should be printed on a small card and carried to the podium. Let it work its magic. For example, at the top of every note card we use in making presentations is the single word, "SMILE," printed in red ink to make it stand out. Countless times, a glance at it and a brief thought of all that it embodies have brought a presentation back to the human level, re-established audience contact, overcome a momentary loss of confidence, and many other things.

Inspirational Reading: The shelves of libraries (in which institutions good idea presenters spend a great deal of their time) are replete with material for this purpose. Every idea presenter should possess at least one anthology of inspiring monographs on the lives of great men, "truths to live by," or similar material. The choice is entirely personal, but the inspirational value of great thoughts and the examples of great men cannot be denied. A passage read just before the presentation can lift both it and the presenter to a higher level.

> *"Whenever is spoken a noble thought,*
> *Whenever a noble deed is wrought;*
> *Our hearts in glad surprise*
> *To higher levels rise."*
> — *Santa Filomena*

Contrived devices? Yes. But their validity has been proven too many times to be denied. It is also true that they will only work for the person who enters into the spirit of them and permits them to work. Even a mundane idea presentation, lost in significance among the great issues and causes of our day, is most effective when you put something of yourself into it. These suggestions—in fact, those contained throughout this course—will never work for countless thousands of people.

3 A MOTIVATIONAL COUNTDOWN

Some of the devices and techniques discussed here may seem like considerable work to put into such an everyday matter as making a presentation. It is true that experienced presenters may have already found and developed techniques which work very well for them. Yet the quality of most presentations given today would seem to indicate otherwise. They are "everyday matters," which is part of the reason that so many have so little effect on their audiences or are remembered no longer than it takes for their audiences to return to their daily routines. We remind you that part of the intent of this course is to help the average presenter to lift the average presentation above this mundaneness and to make it something special for both himself and his audience. If you have prepared and rehearsed thoroughly, much of what is necessary to accomplish this has already been done. It remains but to face the audience and to deliver the goods.

Before doing this, it is wise to engage in what might be called a final "motivational countdown" in order to arrive at the moment of delivery ready to perform at peak effectiveness. Many professional presenters do this in one way or another. Here are some suggestions for preparation in the final moments before delivery. They should be modified to suit individual needs.

1. *Be fully prepared and rehearsed at least twelve hours before the presentation, with notes complete and in their final form, all aids, equipment, and other matters finally arranged.*
2. *If the presentation is to be given in the morning, do nothing more to it or with it after the close of activity on the preceding day. Use the evening for recreation or some activity entirely unrelated to the presentation.*
3. *If it is to be later in the day, do essentially the same thing during the earlier part of the day.*
4. *Two hours before going on, take one last look through the notes. Make sure your note cards are in order and briefly run through the thought sequence pattern. Then put them away and do not look at them again before going on.*
5. *From here on, think only in a generalized way of how valid the message is, how much it needs to be told, and how important it is to the audience. Attempt to build a militant, motivated feeling about the whole matter.*
6. *Visit a valet shop, shoeshine parlor, or barber shop. If possible, change into fresh clothes, take a shower, or even drop into a store and buy something new. In short, perform some kind of "freshening up" exercise.*
7. *Then take a walk, read an inspirational passage, listen to some music, or engage in a light conversation unconnected with the subject.*
8 *Plan on arriving for the presentation about fifteen minutes early, no earlier, since waiting can build tension. Take a look around to be sure that everything is in order.*
9. *If the meeting is already in session, slip quietly into a back row and listen. Observe the audience as much as possible. See if they seem bored, alert, friendly, or active toward the present speaker.*

When called on or announced, walk slowly and confidently to the podium. Glance downward momentarily to be sure of the footing. Hold notes in the hand or set them on the rostrum, pause for five or ten seconds, look directly and pleasantly at the audience and begin.

Scorable Quiz: The text gives six specific actions for self-motivation. List any five.

1. _____

2. _____

3. _____

4. _____

5. _____

Answers to Scorable Quiz: (Each correct answer = 20%.) Any five of the following: the self-motivation monologue, imitation, dress and grooming, music, an inspiring motto, inspirational reading.

Improving Voice And Speech

LEARNING SEGMENT 28

PREMISE: That the voice and speech are the primary tools used in oral presentation and as such ought to receive consideration and practice in improvement.

SEGMENT OBJECTIVE: That you have a basic self-help method to use for improving your voice and speech.

Question A: Indicate true (T) or false (F).

1. There should be as few pauses as possible to maintain audience attention. _____

2. The level of breathing is quite important to good speech. _____

3. You should eat a good meal about an hour before your presentation so that you will be relaxed and content. _____

4. You should generally speak as rapidly as you can without slurring or running words together. _____

5. You should pay full attention to the pronunciation of all word prefixes and suffixes. _____

6. A cultured, educated voice is always to be desired. _____

1 VOICE IMPROVEMENT

The voice is your primary tool as a presenter. A good one is important in making the presentation effective. What constitutes a good voice? Usually it is the natural voice of the presenter, functioning in well-modulated tones, with sufficient variation in volume, properly pronouncing the words which are spoken. Without taking special voice training, what can the average presenter do to evaluate his own voice and to improve it where necessary? There are basically two things:

- *Listen to it as others hear it.*
- *Practice speaking properly until it becomes a habit.*

Serious physical or psychologically based speech defects are a matter for a doctor or a trained speech therapist. Most poor speaking is a result of carelessness and bad habits. There are many technical terms used in the study of speech to describe the various mechanics, organs, and functions involved. It is not necessary to go into these here. The emphasis, rather, is on specific steps that the presenter can take to evaluate and improve his own speaking.

Question B: What constitutes a good speaking voice?

_____

_____

_____

Answers to Question A:
1. **False. Pause is an effective tool for emphasis and often should be built intentionally into your speaking.**
2. **True.**
3. **False. Eating before a presentation diminishes body resonance and also will tend to dull your thinking and action.**
4. **False. Use of the voice, like anything else in making a planned, strategic presentation, should be carefully planned. Generally, you will want to vary speaking speed as your intended effects vary.**
5. **True. It is important to both your credibility and your being understood.**
6. **True. Although you might at time intentionally want to lapse into colloquialism or informal delivery.**

Answer to Question B: Usually a good voice is your own natural voice, used with well-modulated tones and controlled variations in volume, properly pronouncing the words you are speaking.

2 **LISTENING TO YOUR OWN VOICE**
If possible, a good recording of the voice should be made and listened to. It is wise also to compare it with the voices of other speakers, preferably good ones. To record effectively, follow this procedure:

1. _Use high-fidelity equipment if possible. However, good office dictating equipment can suffice._
2. _Choose about five minutes' worth of text on a familiar subject._
3. _Practice reading this aloud several times, making sure of pronunciation, punctuation, pauses, and so forth._
4. _Test the recording equipment for proper microphone distance and recording volume._
5. _Start the equipment, pause for ten seconds, breathe deeply, and begin to read._
6. _Remain as relaxed as possible. Reading in solitude will help._
7. _Keep the voice natural and conversational. Do not strain or hurry. Speak from as deeply within the body as possible with comfort. Look ahead for ends of sentences and paragraphs to use as pauses for breathing._
8. _Strive to read with feeling and to pronounce each word with properly accented syllables. Do not attempt to affect or dramatize. Pay particular attention to full pronunciation of all prefixes and suffixes. Do not slur or glide over syllables in the middle of words._

Aside from recording and evaluation in a formal speech class, this should give you a recording sufficient for self-evaluation and practice. Where video tape systems are available, you will have opportunity to see and hear yourself. It will not take an expert to pick out the main faults, just careful listening and objectivity. Listen to the recording several times. Pick out a particular part of it and play it several times, listening to the way individual words are pronounced. Gradually your ear will develop a new sensitivity and alertness. The average person rarely hears all that comes to his ears in terms of subject matter. Fewer still are sensitive to the quality of the voices which bring these messages to the ears. Human subjectivity is of a nature that even fewer hear themselves accurately and objectively. The average person is usually quite surprised the first time he hears his own recorded voice. Not an uncommon response is, "That doesn't sound like me." This is because the sound absorption, conduction, and resonance of your own body structures and cavities tend to distort what you hear. You also will discover imperfections which you never knew you had, such as dropped endings, slurred syllables, and accents. Most of these can be corrected with practice, and there are few life activities where more opportunity for practice is afforded than in speaking.

Question C: List here as many checklist type questions as you can think of that you might ask in analyzing your own speech.

_____

_____

_____

_____

_____

_____

_____

_____

_____

3 THE ROLE OF EMOTION

Emotion can be a tool in speaking as well as a hindrance. The person who can get emotionally involved in his subject, put something of himself into it, will carry such feeling over into his physical speech. This kind of emotion will actually have the effect of displacing the emotions of nervousness or fear. Hence, part of the reason for having an urgent message to deliver.

4 RELAXATION AND NATURALNESS

The ability to relax and be natural tie directly to the emotions and self-confidence of the speaker. But tenseness is also physical and can be alleviated to a large degree by conscious efforts to relax various parts of the body—particularly the jaw, throat, and neck muscles. The speaker should consciously tell himself that he is engaged in a perfectly natural, real-life situation. There is no reason why he cannot be mentally and emotionally relaxed at the podium—if he has prepared properly.

Question D: Why will your voice sound "higher" to you when you listen to a recording of it?

_____

_____

_____

5 SPEED IN SPEAKING

Rapid speaking causes words to run together or syllables to slur, endings to drop, and poor enunciation. Speaking too slowly causes the voice to drone or drawl and become monotonous. Proper speed regulation adjusts to the nature of what is being said. Generally, phrases to be emphasized are spoken more slowly. Increased speed builds tension unless it is deliberate and controlled to attain a dynamic effect. Speaking too rapidly also has a tendency to raise the pitch of the voice, giving a strained, harsh, or twangy quality.

Answers to Question C: Here are a few questions to ask in analyzing your own speech. Use this as a checklist and add any other items that you think might be necessary in your particular case; e.g., a regional accent that ought to be curbed or modified.

☐ Are the mood and general temper appropriate to the occasion?

☐ Does the hearer have to strain to hear?

☐ Do variations in the voice, such as inflections, volume, and emphasis convey variations in meaning, or is it monotonous?

☐ Is the voice friendly, harsh, uncultured, accented, pleasant, or unpleasant?

☐ Are the words enunciated clearly?

☐ Are any words mispronounced?

☐ Is the speed slow, fast, or does it vary appropriately with what is being said?

☐ Are ends of sentences and thoughts obvious in the voice alone?

☐ Are there any impediments such as faulty "s" sounds, one of the most common?

☐ Can the geographical extraction of the speaker be determined from his voice?

☐ Does the voice quiver or betray nervousness?

☐ Does the voice strain or occasionally break?

☐ Is the posture of the speaker erect and poised?

☐ Does the voice seem to have feeling and reality, or does it sound contrived and affected as if the speaker were reciting as opposed to conversing?

☐ Does the voice sound as if the person feels inferior, confident, relaxed?

Answer to Question D: Because of the resonance and conduction within your own body.

6 VOCAL QUALITY
There are many technical ways of describing vocal quality. Basically, if you attempt to generate your voice from as deep within your body as you can with comfort and naturalness, the net effect will be improved quality, including both tone and volume. You will find that this also has a tendency to relax you. Since you are relieving your throat, neck, and jaw muscles of some of the work which they should not be doing anyway, you will also find yourself better able to use them in shaping the sounds which come from deeper within your body.

7 AVOID AWKWARD STRUCTURES
It is never possible to avoid awkward structures completely. If there is a speech impediment such as difficulty in pronouncing the "s" sound, try not to include any structures or phrasing that will emphasize the difficulty or cause stumbling. For instance, a person with this particular difficulty should avoid a statement such as, "Several specific sedimentary solutions serve to satisfy . . . ." When one of these crops up in rehearsal, take a moment to rephrase it. Then practice in private to eliminate the trouble.

8 THE VOICE AS A WIND INSTRUMENT
Fundamentally, your voice is a wind instrument. Air is forced from within the body through the vibrating voice mechanism to produce sound which can be varied in tone and pitch by constriction or relaxation of the throat. Volume is controlled by forcing out more or less air. The "wind" thus produced is formed into specific kinds of sound as parts of words by the modifiers—tongue, lips, jaw, teeth, and palate. Most people are unaware of the occurrence of these activities in everyday speech. In consciously practicing speech improvement, it is necessary to become more aware of them and even to overemphasize them while practicing. This will lead to better voice production and control under regular speaking conditions.

Question E: In the diagram, indicate with an arrow the area of the body from which the best breathing for speech should come.

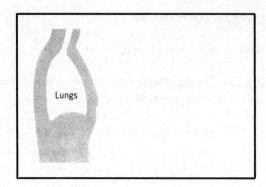

A simple exercise can bring all of these into focus, including the necessity for control of breathing. Practice the following a few times:

1. *Standing erect and relaxed, take a normal deep breath.*
2. *Start slowly reciting the alphabet aloud.*
3. *Overemphasize the pronunciation of each letter.*
4. *Take particular note of the escaping breath.*
5. *Try saying a few letters in higher and lower pitch.*
6. *Note how the throat constricts with the higher sounds and relaxes with the lower.*
7. *Note how long the breath lasts. Start the alphabet over if some air remains.*
8. *Note the differences in placement of the tongue, lips, and teeth with each letter.*
9. *Note how much better the voice feels and sounds as the pitch is lowered and how it is easier to concentrate on using the modifiers.*
10. *Try increasing the volume and note the more rapid escape of air.*
11. *Continue to practice and try variations in pitch and volume. Try to lengthen the use of the same amount of breath. Concentrate on conserving it.*

This is by no means a complete speech improvement exercise. Yet, it will provide you a better awareness of the voice and what it is doing—and can do.

Answer to Question E: In the practice exercise just given, you should have become more conscious of the flow of air and how it affects your volume, pitch pronunciation control, and the length of your speech. Ordinary conversation is normally spoken in short sentences or phrases and requires less concern with breathing. To read and speak in public it is usually necessary to take in larger amounts of air and to coordinate the intake with the natural phrasing of the material being spoken. There are three basic methods of breathing:

- Clavicular: The upper parts of the chest are used. This is probably the least desirable method, because only a small amount of air can be taken in, usually not sufficient for sustained vocalization. Also, this type of breathing tends to make the speaker more tense and high-pitched.

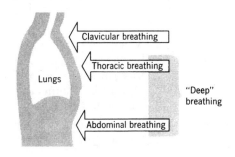

- Thoracic: This is normal chest breathing. Ordinarily, it provides sufficient air for normal conversation and even for some public speaking.

- Abdominal: Most experts recognize this as the most desirable form for public speaking. Some call it abdominal thoracic breathing because it actually involves using the abdominal muscles to help expand the chest cavity to its fullest capacity. It is sufficient to describe it here as deep breathing. It furnishes the greatest amount of air for sustained public speaking.

To breathe deeply, stand erect with shoulders thrown comfortably back and chin inclined slightly above the horizontal. This should be a natural posture and not exaggerated. Then simply draw air deeply into the body. Hold the breath for a few seconds and begin to speak. It is not necessary to wait for the air supply to become exhausted before replenishing it. Air should be inhaled at normal pauses in speech.

9 THE USE OF PAUSE

"Empty time" is rarely considered as a tool by the nonprofessional speaker. The tendency is to speak too rapidly with very little pause, mainly because silent time at the podium seems longer than it really is. Learn to pause after saying things which the audience should weigh carefully. Pause gives a statement more weight. A pause after a complex thought often gives the audience time to comprehend it. It has already been pointed out that pauses serve for breathing. They can also give you time to think, to rally for the next point, check your outline, and find your place.

10 A CULTURED, EDUCATED VOICE

In summary, these are the main things that the person seriously wishing to develop himself as a presenter should seek. In addition to the vocal qualities, which have been touched on briefly here, a cultured voice displays accurate pronunciation and correct grammar and language usage. Oddly, it is not the unfamiliar words and aspects of the language that cause the most trouble. Usually, when a person encounters them, he looks up the correct pronunciation or use. The trouble comes from everyday habits and practices about which no doubt arises—such things as wrong accents on word syllables, omission of syllables, or dropped endings. In usage it is such errors as misuse of words, disagreement of subject and verb, and the use of slang and colloquialisms. The net effect of correcting all such errors is the production of a more cultured voice.

11 VOCAL ANIMATION

One method of conveying feeling and meaning is through the use of vocal animation. Perhaps the most common is the interrogative inflection—upward at the end of a sentence to indicate that it is a question. Moreover, inflection or emphasis can be used in many other ways. Try pronouncing the word "Oh":

1. As a question
2. In anger
3. In surprise
4. With lack of concern
5. Undecidedly
6. With pleasure
7. With enthusiasm

Practice reading aloud and using inflection and emphasis. Learn to vary the voice, to live the words as one does in actual, everyday, uninhibited conversation. Learn to animate. Put real-life feeling into the spoken word instead of speaking in a professional monotone.

Question F: Your general physical condition also plays an important role. List here some aspects of your physical condition that can affect your speaking voice.

1. _____

2. _____

3. _____

4. _____

5. _____

Summary Exercise: Try an experiment with the following sentence, repeated seven times below. Speak it aloud seven times, each time placing vocal emphasis on the italicized word. In the space provided, indicate the mood or emphasis that is caused by your shift in vocal emphasis; e.g., "makes it a question."

SPOKEN SENTENCE	MOOD OR EMPHASIS
1. *This* will change the technical presenter's entire way of speaking.	
2. This *will* change the technical presenter's entire way of speaking.	
3. This will *change* the technical presenter's entire way of speaking.	
4. This will change the *technical* presenter's entire way of speaking.	

5. This will change the technical presenter's *entire* way of speaking.	
6. This will change the technical presenter's entire *way* of speaking.	
7. This will change the technical presenter's entire way of *speaking*.	

Scorable Quiz: Circle the correct answer.
1. The most desirable form of breathing for public speaking is
   a. thoracic
   b. abdominal
   c. clavicular

2. The most desirable posture in breathing for speech is
   a. standing erect
   b. relaxed with shoulders dropped
   c. a natural slump

3. Pauses in speaking
   a. should be kept at a minimum
   b. are fully acceptable
   c. should be no more than ten seconds long

4. Colloquialism and slang
   a. should be avoided
   b. is always acceptable
   c. should fit the occasion

5. Vocal animation
   a. is phoney and should be avoided
   b. is too manipulative
   c. is a valid means of conveying feeling and meaning

Answers to Question F: Good general physical health is much to be desired under any circumstances; but there are some specific things which a presenter can do to sharpen his performance. They include the following:

   1. Moderate use of alcohol and tobacco before a presentation.
   2. Little or no eating immediately before going on. Heavy eating dulls the senses and affects voice resonance.
   3. Sufficient rest before presenting—even a short nap if it is late in the day. This relaxes the whole body and mind and particularly the voice mechanisms.
   4. Dental and oral health.
   5. Good posture, as a mechanical speech aid, for appearance and for its self-motivational value.

Answers to Summary Exercise:

   1. Conveys that there are other things, but this will be the deciding factor.

2. Indicates that someone has said it will not.
3. Implies that something, perhaps undesirable or against the rules has been going on, and one perhaps in authority says all of this is going to change.
4. There are other presenters, but this especially affects the technical presenter.
5. Emphasizes that the whole thing will change, not just part of it.
6. It may change the *way* but not necessarily other aspects. Perhaps not the theory behind it.
7. Could be a question. Or a slight variation of the inflection could indicate speaking but not walking, for example.

Answers to Scorable Quiz: (Each correct answer = 20%.) (1) b, (2) a, (3) b, (4) c, (5) c.

ISBN 0-471-01635-7

EFFECTIVE PRESENTATION

At The Podium

UNIT

X

W. A. Mambert

Executive Director

National Communication and Education Association

Wiley Professional Development Programs

Advisory Editor

Steven C. Wheelwright

Harvard Business School

John Wiley & Sons Inc.
New York • London • Sydney • Toronto

Center for
Professional Development
University of Dayton
Dayton, Ohio

Library of Congress Catalogue Card Number: 75-39750

ISBN 0-471-01636-5

Printed in the United States of America.

10 9 8 7 6 5 4 3 2 1

LEARNING SEGMENT 29 — Correct Podium Behavior

PREMISE: That delivery of the presentation is the "moment of truth." Naturalness is the best guarantee of successful face-to-face delivery.

SEGMENT OBJECTIVE: That you have at your command the essentials of effective face-to-face presentation delivery.

Question A: What do you think are the three most important things to keep continually in mind as you deliver a presentation to a live audience?

1._____

2._____

3._____

1 THE MOMENT OF TRUTH

To this point, in a sense everything you've done has been theoretical. But now the presentation comes alive, actually comes into being. It hopefully becomes something *real*. It is a pity, however, that so many presenters continue throughout the delivery process to treat it as essentially *unreal*, partly as a result of fear, but perhaps more as a product of how they have been conditioned to behave. The art of delivery too often is treated as a mystical rite. Frequently, when a person mounts a podium, a metamorphosis is supposed to take place. The simple act of talking to people suddenly becomes a complicated process of following prescribed genuflections, rituals, and incantations presumably intended to cast some kind of spell.

An otherwise perfectly natural person will often attempt to superimpose all sorts of ritualistic nonsense over his naturalness. This is not to say that certain devices cannot be used to advantage in delivery, but the fact is that speakers often are taught and conditioned in a way that causes the devices to dominate. They fail to realize that the exalted matter of "public speaking" is nothing more than talking to real people, and that what it takes to do it is to be a *real* person. This in no way negates the value of polishing delivery technique or of training the voice and personality. The mistake occurs when these things are put first. The real focal point of good delivery is you as a person—how you feel, what you believe, and how much you and your subject are a part of each other. In short, the whole matter of delivery rests upon your perspective, as does everything else in the presenting situation. Any other foundation is false footing.

Question B: What would you say are two or three basic things that you can do to be more "real" at the podium?

1._____

2._____

3._____

Answers to Question A:
1. Your objective
2. Your audience's feelings, attitudes, and reactions
3. To be your natural self

Answers to Question B: The first step in establishing your "realness" is to dispense with the artificiality that "public speaking" tends to impose and to identify with your own message. Lack of realness usually is caused by one or more of the following:

- Fear
- Lack of a basic sense of involvement in the situation
- Overconcern with the mechanics of "proper" podium behavior

The presenter who really wants to deliver a message effectively to an audience must recognize that his delivery effectiveness stems from deep within himself. If you find it difficult to identify with your own message, you will have extreme difficulty in getting your audience to do so, regardless of your lack of stage fright or polished podium behavior.

Abraham Lincoln has probably been cited as an example in this case more than any other speaker, mainly because he is almost universally recognized as one of the best idea presenters this nation has ever produced. Yet it is well known that his twangy voice was not particularly adapted to public speaking. He rarely made a gesture other than a movement of his head, and his podium appearance left much to be desired. Yet he reached people. Why? Because, above all else, he identified not only with the message but also with his audience. He actually felt what he was saying. Your presentation admittedly may not be a "Gettysburg Address." But what it takes within you to put it across, within the scope of its significance, is of the same order as what it took to convey that classic presentation.

2 ESTABLISH THE RELATIONSHIP

This is the old "first impression" principle again. Unfortunately, how you first appear to your audience probably is going to be what you're stuck with throughout your presentation. Stated as simply as possible, this means that whatever you want your total relationship with you audience to be, you should establish that relationship from the very first moment that you begin to deal with that audience—because, for better or for worse, it will be very difficult for you to change once it is initially established. For example, if you first approach an individual or a group feeling inferior to them, your natural tendencies will make you continue to feel inferior, no matter what ensues in the relationship. At the very least, it will be very difficult to break out of that inferior mode.

The classical example of this is the "I knew him when" syndrome. Consider your immediate family. They know you as you really are, if anyone does. They know all of your weaknesses. They have seen you at your worst moments. A relationship is firmly

2

established. It is very difficult for you to put on your best social behavior for these people. Take the person who gave you your first job, or the one who trained you to become the expert you may perhaps be today. He knows. You cannot hide from him. You will always feel a certain inferiority to him.

Now put this principle to work in the new relationship that you are establishing. How you feel or make yourself feel inside yourself makes the difference. If you feel uncertain or like a petitioner, you will be one, and be treated like one. On the other hand, if you approach the other person feeling equal to him, you will be equal to him, and the tendency will be for him to treat you as equal. In other words, he will act upon his first impression. This is not to say that first impressions cannot be changed. But it is extremely difficult to do so. By far the more strategic and effective approach is to enter the situation with the emotional, rational, and physical flavor in which you want the interchange to continue.

Question C: What is the "petitioner syndrome"?

_____

_____

_____

_____

_____

Question D: Indicate true (T) or false (F):
1. A slightly relaxed slump is the best podium posture. _____
2. An occasional ethnic joke is OK. _____
3. Never apologize for your notes or lack of preparation. _____
4. An occasional personal reference is OK. _____
5. It sometimes is all right to be stern and disciplinary toward your audience. _____

3 GENERAL PODIUM BEHAVIOR
No one in the room should have control but you, regardless of who is in your audience. This does not mean that you become a dictator. But it does mean that you are not afraid to end a question period, wait for a latecomer to be seated (if appropriate), stop until lost attention is regained, and so forth. Such things should not be elaborate, exasperated, foot-tapping affairs. All dealings with your audience should be conducted with the utmost of tact and diplomacy.

- Watch your posture. *Do not lean on anything. Do not place weight unevenly on one foot. Stand with both legs straight, knees relaxed, shoulders back and chin slightly higher than horizontal. The collar should be felt pressing lightly at the back of the neck.*

- Avoid personal reference. *Keep examples from personal life at a minimum. If an example or story must be told, make it about someone else, no matter to whom it really happened. Avoid first person pronouns as much as possible.*

- Use humor wisely. *All humor should be in unimpeachable good taste. Do not do impressions or imitations or attempt to speak in any dialect. Avoid reference to race, religion, personal beliefs, and special interest groups.*

- Avoid apology *unless someone has been misunderstood or inadvertently offended. But do not apologize for lack of preparation, dropped items, or confused notes.*

- If the place is lost, find it. *It is far better to pause and do this than to continue in a hopeless fumble. If the notes are numbered, have been checked just before going on, and are handled as recommended, there is little chance of their becoming too disarranged to straighten out in a moment or two.*

- Pace your delivery to the audience. *Watch for responses. If faces, questions, or other reactions indicate that an idea is not getting across, slow down. Ask a question to see if it has been understood. Do not be so rigidly bound to the predetermined pattern that the presentation is lost because of an unforeseen misunderstanding of an important point.*

- Do not argue. *Never engage in a personal argument or personality conflict with an audience member, no matter who is right.*

Answer to Question C: It is a basic psychologically subservient mode in which many people approach their presentation audiences, as well as many other people and situations in life. For example, in many relationships, most of us are conditioned to be authority conscious, or are inherently subservient to systemized ways of doing things. As a result of this conditioning, you could enter an interchange with half the battle lost because the other person starts out with the psychological upper hand. This is where the ability to throw off your inhibitions can stand you in practical stead. Be aware of the effects that a given relationship can have on your basic mental set, and consciously counteract it. Respect (if it deserves your respect), but do not be intimidated by, authority. Second, keep in mind that any relationship can be changed. Third, whenever possible, establish the kind of relationship you want from the outset. Do not enter situations in the "petitioner" mode.

Answers to Question D: (1) Rarely true, (2) False, never, (3) True, (4) True, (5) True.

4 ANIMATION AND GESTURE
Most of the antics and gymnastics taught and written about animation and gesturing in the name of good delivery are quite useless in the real world of idea presenting. Students "gracefully" wave the arms, effeminately lead with the wrist, learn how to smile, how to frown, how to negate. There are supposed to be special gestures for affirmation, division, negation, rejection, and practically every other feeling or idea. By the time a student learns them all, he is literally a robot. Merely naming a feeling or concept sets the automatic "gesture servomechanism" into motion.

Question E: Names the basic types of gestures.

1. _____   2. _____

3. _____   4. _____

5. _____   6. _____

This would be extremely humorous, except for the fact that these things are actually being taught today. For example, a modern, widely used speech textbook typically divides gestures into "basic types," then proceeds to tell its reader:

To point with the index finger.　　　　*Head gestures.*
Precisely how to indicate giving and　*Torso gestures*
taking.　　　　　　　　　　　　　　*Hand and arm gestures.*
How to reject.　　　　　　　　　　*"Empathetic" (sic) gestures.*
How to show determination.　　　　　*Locative gestures.*
How to caution.　　　　　　　　　　*Hand positions in gesture.*
How to divide.　　　　　　　　　　　*The "Gesture Zone."*
How large or small to make a ges-
ture.
How much vigor to put into one.

Most of this is worthless nonsense. Gesture and animation are so personal, so much a part of the individual engaged in them, that the person "sold" on his subject does not need to be told what part of his body to move when he speaks. Any gesture that emanates from anywhere other than from within the being of the person, which is where a message also should come from, is invalid. No gestures or movements should appear to have been planned. They all must be completely spontaneous. The only rule for any kind of animation is naturalness.

A gesture must grow so spontaneously out of a speaker that he is almost unaware that he is even making it. Perhaps one of the best teachers of effective gesturing and animation is the young child who has not yet learned to pose or affect behavior. There are other examples. By coincidence, on the day that this is being written, we stopped momentarily on the way to the office to "sidewalk superintend" a construction project. Our eyes were caught by a prework meeting, called by the foreman who had mounted a stack of building material, and by his classic display of spontaneous gesture. Although out of earshot, he appeared to be giving a combination of instructions and "dressing down." No doubt he had never studied speech formally. He certainly was not so aware of his gestures as this observer was. He negated, affirmed, cautioned, and divided. He warned, approved, and pointed. His fingers gathered imaginary material from the air. His arms described arcs and his head said who was "boss." It is certain that he knew nothing of the "gesture zone," "torso gestures," or "empathetic gestures," but he did know what he wanted to say and knew that it had to be said.

Answer to Question E: TRICK! Why bother to name them since we've just finished saying that this type of categorization is wasted effort. All gestures should be spontaneous extensions of yourself and what you are thinking and feeling. The audience should be just as unconscious of a gesture or movement as you are. It should be to them so much a part of what is being said that they are aware of nothing but the idea. If they sense that you are acting or affecting your movements, they will become a "show" in themselves and detract from the message. The less attention called to the fact that you have had any formalized or special speech training, the better. People always suspect those who are supposedly "trained" to influence them.

5 A REALISTIC CHECKLIST FOR PODIUM BEHAVIOR

Speaking completely without animation usually makes for a dull and colorless presentation. The person who does so is not making full use of his communicative powers. Such a person would do well to become a little more aware of what the hands and body are doing while he is talking. Although there are no specific rules for animation and gestures, below is a checklist for a few practical considerations:

- *Concentrate on the idea, the message itself, upon believing, and becoming sold on it.*

- *Put the full being and personality into conveying it, out of which will arise the necessary physical movements. Trust to the impulse of the movement.*

- *Do not step out of character. Let the gesture be merely a magnification or accentuation of normal expression. For instance, a normally reserved or conservative person should not attempt to be overly effervescent unless he really feels that way.*

- *Suit the action to the audience. An average gathering of businessmen doesn't normally expect "hellfire and brimstone" at a weekly luncheon. But they will react favorably to sincere drive and enthusiasm almost any time.*

- *Eliminate irrelevant movements, such nervous mannerisms as toying with notes, shifting from one foot to the other, and jingling change in the pocket. Concentration upon the message and completely forgetting self will help tremendously in doing this.*

- *Beware of repeating the same gesture over and over. It will degenerate from emphatic idea support into a mannerism.*

- *Practice making gestures smoothly, unless they are meant to convey abruptness. Learn to follow through and complete each movement in a flowing manner.*

- *Most gestures and movements are best confined to the upper part of the body, to avoid making the audience shift the center of their attention.*

- *Make a gesture of emphasis long enough in duration for it to register with the audience, just as a visual aid must remain long enough for comprehension.*

In summary, spontaneity and naturalness and feeling for the subject are the keys to all movement at the podium. Affectation is the enemy. When you are wrapped up with your subject and intent upon reaching your audience, you will make your own gestures.

6 GOAL-DIRECTED DELIVERY

Here we are again! The objective still is the major key and we can't ignore it. As we've stressed numerous times, your well-conceived objective runs like a central thread throughout the entire presentation process. It merely acquires different "clothing" as the presentation situation progresses. It begins within your own sense of function and both an emotional and intellectual need to present your message to your audience. It then becomes your stated objective, a thesis structured in a single thought pattern, and now takes the form of goal-directed delivery culminating in an "action step."

Even though you presumably know your objective and think you'll not stray from the mainstream leading to it in the live situation, the best of presenters can use all of the reminders he can get. The basic premise is that your presentation must serve that function as articulated by the objective statement. If you lose sight of the function—the objective—your presentation almost immediately deteriorates into a meaningless mass of information, and the best you can hope for are a few by-product effects. Just as thesis is a refinement of objective, goal-directed delivery is a refinement and application of the concept of awareness—in this case, awareness is of objective.

The effective professional salesman practices goal-directed presentation almost instinctively. If the goal of his presentation is to get a signature on a contract, he keeps this thought uppermost in his mind, and every move he makes is an attempt to move closer to the signing. Often, when all else fails him, when he forgets details or his phrasing or makes "unforgivable" mistakes, his sense of goal direction will redeem him almost as if he were tapping a hidden source of power—which in effect he is, for very few obstacles can withstand the power of a man with a purpose.

I.   Continuous Path

A. Three-axis

B. Two-axis

II. Point to Point

A. Machining center

B. Tapping cycles

C. Milling capability

III. Tool Selection

IV. Rotary Table

A good way to make sure that you'll always have your eye upon your objective during delivery is to devise a keyword for that objective, (see illustration), and print it in red at the top of each note page or card so that you'll use it throughout your delivery.

Question F: Generally speaking, how long should you expect to remain at the podium without a break period?

NOTE . . .
Before filling in your answer consider how long you like to listen to someone else speaking.

_____

_____

_____

_____

Answer to Question F: Generally, an audience should not be expected to remain interested and at maximum attentiveness for more than an hour and a half at a time. There is no hard and fast rule, however. If the presentation is longer, a break should be scheduled. If they have been promised a break, they should get it—on time. Yet there is always the exception when interest and attention are such that a break would destroy the mood. When scheduling a break, make it at a natural dividing point in the material. It also is wise to summarize briefly upon reconvening.

Summary Exercise: This exercise is based not only on what we've covered in this segment, but upon much of what we've said throughout the course about such things as sensory reinforcement, attention, control of your presentation situation, and so on.

1. Assume that you are fully prepared to deliver your presentation. Here are the conditions:

    a. You'll have an audience of twenty people.

    b. You'll have some slides.

    c. You'll also have some easel charts (flipcharts).

    d. The room you'll be using is a classroom with tables, each of which normally seats three persons.

    e. You'll want no one sitting behind anyone else.

    f. You'll want to be able to move freely and get close to each person.

    g. You'll need space for your slide projector.

    h. You'll need a chalkboard.

2. You'll need scissors and glue for this exercise to cut out the self-explanatory diagram elements given.

3. Your task is to "set up" your presentation room in a way that will meet the above requirement as fully as possible. Simply cut out the elements and paste them onto the room diagram that follows:

You'll find it easier to cut out each element if you cut out the whole page first.

Chair	Chair	Chair	Chair	Chair	Chair	Chair	Chair	Chair	Chair
Chair	Chair	Chair	Chair	Chair	Chair	Chair	Chair	Chair	Chair

Table	Table	Table	Table
Table	Table	Table	Table

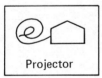

Projector

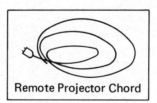

Remote Projector Chord

Easel

Lectern

Your Presentation Room

Chalkboard and Permanent Screen

Scorable Quiz: Indicate true (T) or false (F).

1. Your audience's first impression of you is likely to stick. _____

2. An occasional personal reference is quite acceptable. _____

3. There is no need to try to make every presentation a "masterpiece." _____

4. It is best to avoid all humor in the average business presentation. _____

5. If you lose your place in your notes, you should proceed as if nothing has happened. _____

6. You should not apologize for lack of preparation. _____

7. It is all right to engage in an occasional disagreement with an audience member. _____

8. It is all right to order your audience to do something. _____

9. You should always use the index finger to point. _____

10. All gestures should be kept above the waist. _____

11

Answer to Summary Exercise:

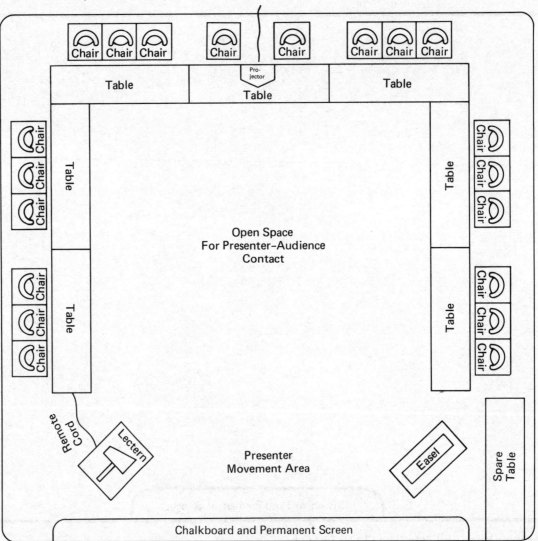

Our surveys have revealed that most presentations in the professional and business world are, in fact, given to twenty people or less, and that many of them are given in conference rooms or classrooms very similar to what we've depicted here. So, you really have a pretty average situation here. If you've set up your room similarly to the way we've shown here, chances are you have a fairly good sense of presentation room layout. This "U" shape is very effective for maximum presenter movement and close audience contact. Notice that the lectern and easel are offset to allow a clear view of the screen. We've used one seating space for the slide projector, thus keeping it from obstructing any audience member's view. A remote control button is a must. Notice that we gave you a spare table (on purpose) and that it's set aside.

We admit that this isn't the only possible way to lay out a presentation room, but it is a tried and proven on which follows all of the principles of sensory reinforcement, effectively uses things at hand, minimizes distraction, and focuses attention.

Answers to Scorable Quiz: (Each correct answer = 10%.) (1) T, (2) T, (3) F, (4) F, (5) F, (6) T, (7) F, (8) T, (9) F, (10) F.

Getting And Maintaining Audience Attention

LEARNING 30 SEGMENT

PREMISE: That attention is a critical factor in delivery because without it nothing else done has any effect.

SEGMENT OBJECTIVE: That you become aware of the critical nature of audience attention and have some means at your disposal for getting and maintaining it.

Question A: Name some things that you think contribute directly to audience attention.

1. _____
2. _____
3. _____
4. _____
5. _____
6. _____

1 **A CRITICAL FACTOR**

The reason that attention is such a critical factor should be quite obvious. If there is no attention, there can be no presentation, for the simple reason that there will be no one to hear or see that presentation. It will be exactly like transmitting a radio message out into space without any receiver to pick up that message. Without attention, you might just as well pack up your notes, your aids, your projector, your easel charts, or whatever else you've brought with you, and go home. You'll be delivering your presentation to an empty room.

Despite this, many presenters begin and continue through their presentations without the slightest awareness of whether or not the audience is even listening to them. The major cause of this, of course, is stage fright. Because of his concern with himself, the presenter has very little time to devote to observing the audience and ensuring that they are paying attention, that he actually has contact with them. The main ways of overcoming stage fright have already been discussed, but perhaps should be reviewed briefly here, since they will place you in a sufficiently confident and secure frame of mind to devote some of your energies to being concerned with your audience's attention and reactions.

13

Question B: List here some things that can get in the way of your maintaining your own awareness of whether or not you have audience attention, and your use of devices to get and maintain it.

1. _____

2. _____

3. _____

4. _____

5. _____

6. _____

2 OBSERVING AUDIENCE ATTENTION

There is only one way to find out whether or not an audience is paying attention. That is to look *at* them, not through them. The best way is to look directly at individual faces and into the eyes of individuals. This does two things:

> *1. It reveals whether they are looking and listening.*
> *2. If they are not, it makes them look and listen.*

This is why all speech teachers worth their salt make an important issue of eye contact. It is the only way to talk directly to people. The speaker should make every effort to get and hold the eyes of his audience. This may be difficult with larger groups. Sometimes it is necessary to concentrate only on the first few rows and use them as a gauge of the rest of the group. Yet it is possible with a little practice to look into the eyes of people fairly far back in even a large audience, or to make them sense the eye contact.

The larger auditorium audience does pose an additional problem to a presenter, especially if you are working from a stage or in a darkened room. Here you must rely more on your voice and other devices to maintain audience contact. Fortunately, except for the larger convention-type meeting, the average presenter deals with more easily handled groups.

Other gauges of how well an audience is listening to you are such things as shuffling feet, movement, scribbling, and general restlessness. You must prevail over all of these, if you are to get and maintain attention. Refer also to the next segment on audience feedback.

Answers to Question A: The answers to this question can be found throughout this whole course. For, in a very real way, everything that you do in proper preparation of your presentation contributes to audience attention. More specifically, however, here are some of the important things:

1. First and foremost, your effective dealing with yourself—your own emotions, ego, hangups, inhibitions, stagefright, and so on, will release you from yourself enough to concentrate on your audience and their attention.

2. Thorough prepartion and having your "ducks in a row."

3. That sense of function and an "urgent message to deliver."

14

4. Persistence and commitment to attaining your objective.
5. Self-motivation.
6. A continual awareness of your audience members as individual persons, and not as merely a faceless mass.

Answers to Question B: To answer this, you can go back primarily to our segments on idea structure, rational support, physical and sensory reinforcement and psychological reinforcement. Probably the major detriments to audience attention are:
1. Lack of order and structure.
2. Inept use of detail, evidence, and facts.
3. Failure to consider the principles of sensory reinforcement.
4. Failure to consider the emotional or psychological content of a situation.
5. Failure to effectively introduce your presentation.
6. Lack of audience or contact.

Question C: What do you think is meant by "developing a feeling of mutuality"?

_____

_____

_____

> NOTE . . .
> Under the following headings we will discuss some ways to get, maintain, or ensure audience attention.

3 DEVELOP A FEELING OF MUTUALITY

Most presenters unconsciously place themselves in opposition to their audiences, and this comes through in their delivery. People are more likely to listen to someone who agrees with them. It is almost always possible to find some area of agreement with which to begin, even if it is nothing more than the mutuality of the audience's and speaker's joint presence. But it can usually go deeper than that. You should work from the assumption that both you and your audience are on the same side, both mutually seeking a solution, seeking to learn, to find the benefits of this or that technology. It would be possible here to cite many examples of how successful presenters have done this.

The word is *tact*—ingenious tact—the kind of finesse of which only a person truly willing to study human nature can become capable. Lincoln had it. If one takes the time to study what he did and said, it will be seen. A contemporary newspaper reporting on one of his speeches on the controversial slavery issue commented,

> *For the first half hour, his opponents would agree with every word he uttered. From that point he began to lead them off, little by little, until it seemed as if he had got them all into his fold.*

Said Lincoln himself, "My way of opening and winning an argument is first to find a common ground of agreement." This is perhaps the best piece of advice which could be given to a novice presenter who wishes to win audiences.

Answer to Question C: We mean here that no matter how unacceptable your idea might be to an audience, how much you may know that you basically disagree with them, you will never win them over, cause them to believe or accept, if you set yourself in opposition to them from the outset (no matter where you hope to lead them, they aren't there yet). No one ever won an argument. So, the trick is at least to start "in the same boat" with them.

4 ACT FRIENDLY

A smile is the universal act of warmth and friendliness. Some races may rub noses; others may touch cheeks or shake hands to show friendship and affinity. On the first confrontation, a smile is understood in any language or culture. In fact, it can usually do more to start a presentation off right than anything else you might do in the first seconds of your presence before an audience. And the remarkable thing is that it will do something for you—inside. Try this experiment with the next audience. Do not be afraid of ten seconds of silence upon arrival at the podium. There is no rule that one must begin to speak immediately upon setting foot on the podium. Say nothing. Look around at the audience. Look into the faces of as many individuals as possible and smile in as friendly a way as possible. This will relax both you and your audience. Continue to smile as occasions present themselves, look at people, interact with them, warmly and disarmingly—and sincerely—and see what happens.

Question D: Recall our discussions of sensory distractions and reinforcement. Here is a list of things that you might find in a presentation room. Some are outright negative factors or distractions, some are potential devices. Without going into any detail, indicate with check marks in the columns to the right which line of defense or offense you would take with respect to each:

Item	Eliminate	Nullify or Compensate	Use as Device
1. A burned out light bulb			
2. A vase of flowers on the podium			
3. An easel chart you're not using			
4. Some extra chairs			
5. Some more comfortable chairs			
6. A spotlight			
7. A chalkboard			
8. A question from an audience member			
9. A heckler			
10. Your body			
11. A rainy day			
12. A noisy conversation next door			
13. Someone who "knew you when"			

16

5 USE YOUR AUDIENCE'S LANGUAGE

Part of the larger philosophy of speaking from the audience's point of view is through the use of their language. It identifies you with "their side." They will automatically feel more closely in agreement with the person who speaks as though he is one of them. A speaker before an audience of naval personnel who repeatedly refers to "ropes" and "boats" instead of "lines" and "ships" is automatically an outsider with extra work to do in building a feeling of mutuality.

In a sales presentation to a group of scientists of the National Aeronautics and Space Administration we recently attended, the presenter repeatedly pronounced the acronym "NASA," with a long "a" as in day, instead of with the accepted "a" as in cash. A small enough matter, yet it told this audience that this person definitely was an outsider, that perhaps his lack of familiarity with their name might be an indication of his knowledge of their problems as well. Thus, the more you are able to couch your ideas in your audience's terms, the better are your chances of establishing a true rapport with them; and you gain one more advantage in your attempt to hold their attention and ultimately reach and win them.

6 TIE YOUR MESSAGE TO A BASIC EMOTIONAL APPEAL

If you've adequately analyzed your audience, you'll know what their fears, desires, and needs are. For example, if they are deeply concerned with their children's welfare, their jobs, the continued existence of their organization, of their financial welfare, and you can link your message to one of these, you're going to maintain attention. Review the segment on psychological and emotional reinforcement.

7 ELIMINATE DISTRACTION

The presentation room you set up in the previous segment was designed to eliminate distraction. Remember the principles of sensory reinforcement and sensory distraction. Work consciously to eliminate all distractions. Here are some examples:

- *Physically arrange the audience so that they are not distracted by late arrivals. Try to group them so that there is a minimum of space between them.*
- *Do not permit guests to remain on the podium during delivery.*
- *Remain aware of audience comfort—ventilation, heat, cooling, and so forth.*
- *Eliminate unnecessary material from the podium—any attention getter other than that connected directly with delivery. For instance, bright flashes of color, such as flowers, signs, or unused equipment. Keep visuals covered unless they are actually in use. Keep the chalkboard clean.*
- *Check lighting to be sure that it focuses on the podium and directly on the speaker. The podium should be the best lighted spot in the room.*
- *Dress conservatively and impeccably. Be pleasant to look at! Do not wear highly reflective colors or jewelry.*
- *Stay on schedule so that the audience will not be distracted by concern with lateness.*

Answers to Question D:
1. *Eliminate* it.
2. *Eliminate* it since normally, you wouldn't want any "competition" visually distracting from yourself.
3. *Eliminate* it for the same reason as the flowers. Simply cover it.

4. *Eliminate* unused chairs since they might indicate missing audience members, hence lack of interest in your presentation or thinking that it's not important enough to attend. Also, a "closely packed" audience is easier to deal with for you, as well as having a positive psychological effect on audience members.

5. *Use* the more comfortable chairs, provided they're not too comfortable and their use might relax your audience more than you want.

6. *Use* or *eliminate*, depending on where it is.

7. *Use* or *eliminate* any "leftover" writing on it. (Same reason as for flowers and unused easel chart.)

8. *Use*, if at all possible, to progress your presentation in the direction you want to go.

9. *Eliminate* the heckler. First wait to see if the group will eliminate him for you. If not, this is one of those times when you may have to take a stand.

10. *Use* it, of course; dress it right, use it as a "visual" aid through gestures.

11. *Nullify or compensate*. The duller the day, the "brighter" you must be to compensate for it.

12. *Eliminate*, *nullify*, or *compensate* with your own volume and increased attention getting.

13. *Nullify* or *compensate*. Decide right now that in *your* presentation room you have no one to look up to. You are in control. There is no manager or leader in that room but you when you are in control and giving your presentation.

8 BE VIGOROUS AND ENERGETIC

Most presentations are not intense enough. The average audience is lulled to sleep by a kind of droning monotony. A really energetic presenter actually can lose a pound or more of weight in the course of delivering an hour-long presentation. This will give some idea of the vigor and energy which can and should go into it. There is an old saying that, "The first thing to do when the audience goes to sleep is to prod the speaker." If you are dull, the audience will be dull also. If you are alive, alert, intense, enthusiastic, they will be unable to keep from paying attention to you. Of course, this ties directly back to your own motivation. If you are not sufficiently motivated, you will not be able to make your words come alive with this kind of intensity.

9 COMMUNICATE WITH PEOPLE

Never once in the course of the presentation lose sight of the fact that you are speaking to people. Keep what is said on a personal level. Speak directly to individuals. Never slip out of focus and begin talking to the room in general. We recently stood among a group of people watching a demonstration of a new product at a business show. The demonstrator obviously had his talk "down pat." He knew precisely what he was talking about; the technology was exciting and significant, the audience was obviously interested. Yet it was also obvious that they were not listening to what he was saying. They toyed with knobs and dials, fingered the equipment, milled about while he droned on, almost in the fashion of a sightseeing tour bus driver. His head appeared to be on a programmed swivel like a prison yard searchlight. He spoke with an unseeing stare. Not once did his eyes make contact with the people standing in front of him. Not once did he talk to a person. Before he had finished, most of the audience had satisfied their curiosity, touched and handled what they wanted to see, and had moved on to other displays and demonstrations in the business show (and to presenters who talked to people). There's something to be said about control here, too. For, if you place your people right, and control them properly, you'll not have them ahead of you doing and thinking things that you don't want them to do yet.

10 FURNISH VARIETY AND RELIEF

People don't like too much of the same thing over a long period of time. Although all of the principles of consistency for idea integrity apply, you'll also sometimes want to furnish variety and relief as an attention-maintaining mechanism. Try to alternate activity and speaking. Intersperse things such as chalkboard use, demonstration, lecturing, and audio-visuals so that no single one occupies too long a period. Do not "bounce" all over the podium, but furnish the audience enough variety of action and speech so that they will have some opportunity to participate and stay alert by shifting their attention.

11 LET THE AUDIENCE PARTICIPATE

Direct participation by audience members is one of the best ways to keep their attention. When appropriately used, audience participation usually will focus the eyes and ears of almost every audience member on what's happening. You should almost always be alert to possibilities for letting people in your audiences *do* and *say*. You may simply ask questions. You may ask for volunteers to demonstrate, use the visiting expert, and so on.

Question E: With what else in the presentation process do these "attention-getting mechanisms" overlap?

_____

_____

_____

Answer to Question E: Obviously, these attention-getting mechanisms overlap with just about everything else that you plan and do. Good idea organization will evoke closer attention than poor thought flow. So will a clear thesis, concrete and vivid detail, and many other things. Good audience attention is a product of the entire presentation planning and delivery process. The principal guideline to using devices for getting and keeping it is the same as that for using any other aid, device, or idea support technique. The device should never dominate or eclipse the idea it is intended to support. Further, these are only a few of the many possibilities. There is hardly any limit to such methods and techniques for getting and maintaining attention. Suspense, humor, controversy, shock, noise, and many others can be used. Most of them, however, grow out of the same foundation—the creativity, imagination, and showmanship of the presenter, combined with his knowledge of the people and the situation.

12 USE NOVELTY AND UNIQUENESS

Your personal creativity and native ingenuity should come into play. Ideas abound everywhere in magazines, television commercial ideas that can be adopted to presentations, things you see in your daily work, humorous situations, and so forth.

A presenter dryly describing, for example, the organization of his department function basically has just another "organization chart" presentation. But suppose that he were to mount the podium and begin to speak. Suddenly, a phone rings. There is an instrument on the lectern. He ignores it at first, trying to continue. Finally he gives up, excuses himself and answers it, right before the audience. It is an engineer (off-stage voice) with a series of questions relating to the organization. It is "highly irregular," but because it also is a pressing situation, the questions must be answered on the spot (while visual support flashes on the screen). Humor meaningful to the audience is injected, such as, "Why aren't you at the meeting?" Suddenly, the presentation time has been used up, and the presenter "never got a chance to talk to the audience." But they've learned what he had come to tell them, and in an attention-getting way.

13 USE THE AUDIENCE'S NATURAL CURIOSITY

There are many ways of using the audience's natural curiosity, ranging from hinting, to a "surprise," to out and out staging. Innovation, inventiveness, and creativity are again the watchwords here. Covered material, a wrapped package, or the unexplained absence or presence of an element of the presentation tend to arouse curiosity and hence attention. Even silence or blank space might sometimes be used. Suppose, for example, that a series of slides were flashed on a screen in absolute silence—pictures of several product applications, then some competitive equipment, then a customer, then an engineer at his drawing board. No sound or speech. A desired momentary or prolonged audience response during this part of the presentation might well be something like, "What's going on here?" "Somebody fouled up . . . forgot the sound." Curiosity and attention are aroused. Then the spoken part of the presentation begins.

> *"You have just seen the pieces of a real–life problem–solving situation. Recognize them? Some of them fit together pretty readily. Others require some nondimensional thinking. Gentlemen, we are in the problem–solving business . . . ."*

Suddenly, the audience finds that they have assembled the problem pieces. They have participated, mainly through their own curiosity. And they paid attention.

14 A TIME TO BE UNEQUIVOCAL

As the saying goes, "There is a time to be everything under the sun," and there is a time to be unequivocal, too. This is good advice in many ways. No presenter should be afraid to take a stand, to come right out and let his audience know that "this is the way it is." Hedging weakens the whole presentation. From the standpoint of attention, an unequivocal statement can make an audience really sit up and take notice. For example, "Gentlemen, you've undoubtedly heard some manufacturers say that the most automated plant is the best plant. This is not true!" Right or wrong, this is clear and unequivocal. If spoken with proper emphasis and self-effacement, it has the ring of a person who knows what he is talking about and is not afraid to say so. An audience will notice and respect it—even if they disagree.

Are these all of the things we could say about getting and maintaining audience attention? Obviously not. But we can just about guarantee you that they and the kind of thinking they represent will put you well on the road to becoming a good getter and maintainer of audience attention.

Summary Exercise:
1. What is the best way to find out if an audience is paying attention?

---

2. Why are empty chairs undesirable?

_____

_____

3. What sensory communication principle is involved in removing flowers from the podium area?

_____

_____

4. What is probably the best way to get and maintain audience attention?

_____

_____

5. What are the limitations you should observe in using attention-getting mechanisms?

_____

_____

Scorable Quiz: Fill in the missing word or words.

1. The best way to determine if audience members are attentive is to _____ them.

2. If there is no attention there can be no _____.

3. Audience members will automatically feel closer to someone who uses their

   _____.

4. The universal act of warmth and friendliness is a _____.

5. Never once in the course of a presentation should you lose sight of the fact that you are

   communicating with _____.

6. _____ by audience members if probably the best way of maintaining their attention.

7. What sensory communication principle is involved in arranging chairs for an optimum view

   of the presenter? _____

8. What is the primary source of your own intensity and creativity? _____

9. People don't like too much of the same thing over a long period of time. What device can you use to alleviate this? _____

10. If you have something like covered material, or the unexplained absence or presence of some element of your presentation, what device are you using? _____

Answers to Summary Exercise:
1. Watch them, obviously. But you can't do this if you're not sufficiently free from your own emotional involvement, inhibitions, or subjective interaction with them.
2. Mainly, empty chairs come under the heading of sensory distraction, and also are a form of psychological distraction. They tend to disunify the audience or at least to indicate that someone is missing. A tightly packed audience is far more desirable than a scattered one. It's better for you in concentrating on them and better for them in the feelings they have.
3. The principle of sensory distraction. Anything on the podium, any human or inanimate object that may cause the audience's perceptions to wander or be distracted, should be removed. You should do everything possible to focus attention where it belongs: on you and your presentation.
4. No doubt, the "best award" must go to audience participation, simply because it's the surest way to involve them in your presentation. Someone doing something, unless he's sleepwalking, presumably is paying attention.
5. There really aren't any limitations in terms of the creativity and ingenuity that you can exercise. The only real limitations would be tact, good manners, and not hurting another human being. We'd say never embarrass or insult anyone, but the truth is, there could very well be occasions when even these could serve as devices. The only other limitation might be that you wouldn't want to do something that would endanger your livelihood or career. But even here, too, there might come an occasion when the only honorable course could well be to lay your job on the line.

Answers to Scorable Quiz: (Each correct answer = 10%.) (1) look at, (2) presentation, (3) language, (4) smile, (5) people, (6) participation, (7) same-sense reinforcement, (8) personal motivation, (9) variety and relief, (10) curiosity.

LEARNING 31 SEGMENT

Analyzing Audience Feedback

PREMISE: That without awareness and analysis of what the audience is doing, the presentation becomes open-ended and one-sided. And since the concept of functionalism demands an attempt to measure, functionalism itself can be defeated.

SEGMENT OBJECTIVE: That you have the awareness necessary for perceiving and analyzing audience feedback and a base of knowledge of how to elicit it, what to look for, and how to evaluate it.

> *NOTE . . .*
> *How well do you think you've mastered the material we've been discussing in this course? Take the comprehensive test at the end of this Learning Segment and find out.*

Question A: Give some reasons why an audience member might ask you a question during your presentation.

_____

_____

_____

_____

Question B: List some specific things that you can do about an audience's questions.

_____

_____

_____

1 **A COMMUNICATION-TIGHT COMPARTMENT**
Many novice presenters make their presentations in a "communication-tight" compartment. There is an old saying that, "A person wrapped up in himself makes a pretty small package." We'll go a step farther and say that an idea presenter over-involved with himself, with his own emotions, trepidations, and subjective interaction, makes a pretty poor feedback analyzer. And if you can't analyze what your audience is doing and how they're reacting during your presentation, you're in serious trouble.

Your analysis of audience feedback ties directly to your functional approach. Remember, this approach dictates that you always seek to measure your progress toward objective accomplishment as well as the accomplishment itself. Feedback is your main tool for doing this.

2 **REMAIN OBJECTIVE**
Next to being free enough inside of yourself, to observe people in your audience is the most important key. Your evaluation of feedback must be objective and realistic. For example, if you permit an audience to anger or intimidate you or to make you feel that you are being indulged or patronized, you lose the ability to objectively analyze and control them. If you understand the mechanics of your own attitudinal reactions, you will not permit this to happen. A look of disbelief or disapproval from a member in the front row will be duly registered, but never taken to heart. If you ask a rhetorical question and get an unexpected reaction, you will contain it and continue. Having fully analyzed this audience, your chances of running up against such situations are reduced to a minimum.

Answers to Question A: Experienced presenters soon learn that audiences don't always ask questions just because they want information. No one to our knowledge has ever actually taken a survey, but it's a pretty good guess that simple, straightforward questions to obtain information actually represent a small minority in terms of reasons behind audience questions. Old hands in the audience-interaction business know this and have learned to see through audience questions. For example, an audience member is likely to ask a question because:
1. He needs attention.
2. He needs affirmation that he knows something, too.
3. He wants to tell you something he knows.
4. He wants approval from the group.
5. He wants to lead you in a certain direction.
6. He might consciously or unconsciously resent your knowing more than he does, perceive you as a threat, and have a need to define his ego.
7. He might be just "out for bear," bored, or "want a little action."
8. He could be fulfilling any one of the psychological needs we discussed in Segment 13, (and he more often than not doesn't even realize it).

Answer to Question B: When questions are asked of you, the first and most important rule is to never try to fool an audience. If the answer is not known, it should be admitted with an offer to follow up later. And again, the questioner himself should be analyzed. His real reason for asking the question might be to gain attention or recognition. He might be heckling, or he might

24

honestly need an answer in order to understand. Learn how to discern such reasons. For the novice, it is best to treat the question as sincere and to answer it as adequately and honestly as possible. You should also be reminded that every question asked of you need not be answered at the time it is asked—or at all.

Questions have a tendency to take the offensive, placing you on the defensive. A good presenter never stays in a defensive position too long, and avoids it altogether if he can. If you do not wish to engage in an interchange at that time, since you are in control, you have every right to state that the answer will be covered in a moment, or to offer to discuss the matter individually after the presentation. The point is that you are in control of the presentation. You have an objective, and you decide what is relevant to its accomplishment. You of course make such decisions with as much tact and empathy as possible, but you never relinquish control until you're ready. There are several tried and proven guidelines for handling the unsolicited question from the audience:

1. Prepare completely in advance. Survey possible questions which might arise and be equipped with the answers.
2. Listen carefully to the question and think while it is being asekd. Repeat the question to be sure all have heard it.
3. Observe the asker and attempt to determine how sure he is of himself, or if he knows the answer and is using the question for another purpose.
4. Pause before answering to give the impression of concentration.
5. Try to draw the questioner out further if necessary. Often the best answer to a question is another question.
6. Never argue.
7. Return to your main thought sequence pattern as soon as possible.

3 DON'T OVERRESPOND

Our emotions also tend to cause us to prejudge and emotionally evaluate an audience, often in direct contradiction to the facts. For example, in a recent presentation, as is our practice in establishing audience contact, we continually scanned the audience to detect the friendly faces, the hostile ones, the apathetic ones, and so on. One man in particular attracted attention. Throughout the presentation he stared directly at the presenter with a look of distinct hostility on his face to the degree that it actually became distracting. We felt certain that here was a skeptical individual who saw through the presentation devices and was in effect looking at the presenter's bare soul. Yet, at the end of the lecture this individual came forward with the statement, "I've always had a real problem in conveying my knowledge of my subject to an audience. It seems that no matter how well I know my subject, I just can't seem to establish a proper audience relationship. I was extremely interested in how you did it. Could you give me some additional advice on how to establish audience contact?" Needless to say, we were quite surprised. Actually, this individual turned out to be the most interested member of the entire audience. Complete misinterpretation of audience feedback!

What specific communication mistake did this illustrate? In the areas of emotions and feelings, it showed that no matter how practiced one is in making presentations, one must continually strive to counteract the natural human tendency to overrespond emotionally. It also showed that it is never really possible to completely understand people. Yet this in no way cancels out the value of practical, clinical, objective-as-possible audience awareness.

4 **OBSERVE AUDIENCE BEHAVIOR**

If you're really aware and alert, your audience's behavior, their faces, their bodies, their hands, their eyes, and their feet will literally transmit to you scores of "messages" about how you're being received, how much attention they're paying, and often how close you're coming to accomplishing your objective. For example, shuffling feet, yawns, general restlessness, glances at watches—or rapt attentiveness—all are things which should be consciously noted by the person at the podium. No person has a right to bore people in today's busy world. Yet some presenters ramble on despite the fact that every audience indicator tells them that as far as the audience is concerned the presentation is over. It is far better to call an unscheduled break and regroup forces than it is to continue without audience contact.

Question C: List here some obvious guidelines for a presenter who asks questions of individual audience members or of his audience in general, in order to get feedback or to progress his presentation toward his objective.

_____

_____

_____

_____

_____

Answers to Question C: When you have occasion to ask questions of an audience, you should follow these basic guidelines:

1. Ask "friendly" questions.
2. Put the "you" element into the question.
3. Limit the answer to the information wanted.
4. Give the answerer time to think and phrase his answer.
5. Be objective in evaluating the answer.
6. Give the answerer credit for his intelligence.
7. Avoid known "sore spots."
8. Be sure that the hearer can answer the question.
9. Always give the answerer an "out."

In your nervousness or desire to get the question answered and use the response to advance your thought pattern, you can easily gloss over the respondent's comments to the point of almost ignoring him. Such an offense can be avoided by developing the art of exaggerated attention, even leaning forward slightly or cocking the head to emphasize that you are interested and actually want to hear what the audience member has to say and are not just using him. This, although not used in normal conversation, is quite permissible at the podium. In conversing with individual members of the audience, always bear in mind that you owe them just as much attention and respect as you want from them.

If there is a single main guideline, it is to make the presentation a real-life situation for both presenter and audience. In the words of Cicero, the presenter ". . . must set forth with power and attractiveness the very same topic which others discuss in such tame and bloodless phraseology."

5 REACT TO THE ENVIRONMENT

Never pretend that things aren't happening. Since audience attention is directly affected by such factors as ventilation, temperature, lighting, acoustics, external disturbances, interruptions, visual aid equipment failure, late arrivals and early departures, the obvious answer to coping with most of these factors is to check in advance. How you handle an unforeseen environmental occurrence will be a direct result of how well you have prepared those aspects of your presentation which could be planned in advance. In a very real way, your thorough analysis and preparation do prepare you for handling the unexpected. Your confidence, ingenuity, alertness, and showmanship will enable you to take one of two courses of action.

First, you can do precisely what you would do if you were not in front of an audience giving a presentation. If a window or door needs opening or closing, you simply do it matter of factly, as a part of a real-life environment, without letting it interfere with the business at hand. If a microphone goes dead, you raise your own volume or move closer to your audience. There are few rooms in which a person cannot be heard if he tries. It is remote that well maintained visual-aid equipment will break down if checked and previewed just before a presentation, but if it does it need not be a catastrophe. In addition to the fact that a good presenter *knows* what his own visuals contain and should be able to improvise if necessary, your podium samples will save you.

The second alternative is to take the event and use it—build it into the presentation on the spot, if it contributes to your objective or a point you want to make when or closely after it happens. Such action adds a note of spontaneity and reality to the presentation, if it is done smoothly and appropriately. After all, it is a real-life situation, so why not treat it as such—if the occasion is appropriate. Most presentations are far too formal to begin with. Although they are really conversations among people, more often than not they sound like recitations or readings. You can do worse than behave spontaneously and naturally.

In interpreting and reacting to environmental factors during an actual presentation, then, the main key is awareness of the fact that it is a human process and that naturalness, common sense, tact, and consideration should be practiced. If an airplane roars overhead, it is natural to pause until the noise has passed. If a window blows open, it is natural to walk over and close it without fanfare or to ask the closest person to close it. If something funny happens, it is natural to laugh—but not at the expense or embarrassment of another human being.

6 RESPONSE POINTS PAY OFF

Spontaneous audience feedback provides some basis for measurement of how you're going. But you can also deliberately elicit feedback through the use of predetermined response points as we've already discussed. For example, an instructor might ask a test question at the conclusion of a major point. A salesman is more subtle because he usually asks his questions to lead his audience. An example is the "double-answer" technique, recognizable in many sales presentations, which essentially asks a question that gives a choice of two "yes's" but no "no." He asks, "Which do you like, sir, the red or yellow model?" "Do you like the office on the seventh floor or the fifth better, ma'am?" "Which of these systems best suits your needs, sir?" Later on he might ask, "Does your company usually purchase or lease?" Such questions can be subtly interwoven into a presentation to the extent that a hearer is not even aware that he is gradually weaving an affirmative net around himself, from which it will become increasingly difficult for him to extricate himself without "losing face," a form of ego involvement.

A similar type of response point is that of developing a kind of "cumulative affirmation" which goes something like this: "I'm certain you'll agree that solid-state technology is superior, isn't that right?" "Every efficient office needs good records, doesn't it?" The point here is to ask objective-oriented, generalized questions to which any normal person must answer with a yes and to reinforce the questions by actually giving the expected answers. The natural result is the creation of an affirmative atmosphere. After all, the hearer has agreed with the presenter throughout the conversation. True, many of the things to which he has agreed may have no direct bearing on the issue, but human nature is such that it will be difficult for him to do a complete public about face after he has aligned himself with the speaker all along. His pride usually will not let him. An audience must be conducted over such a course carefully and with a great deal of finesse, or they will see through the device.

Sometimes nothing is better than simply coming out and asking a direct question. This should be done only when the presenter is reasonably sure of what the answer will be. And he can be, on the basis of what has gone before.

Regardless of what response technique may be convenient in a given situation, one thing is certain for the presenter operating on an aware basis: every success or failure in the use of these techniques will drive him deeper and deeper into the realm of subtlety, which is precisely where the art of using response points belongs. You will frequently find the most sophisticated of people surprisingly naive when they are confronted with even an amateur use of questioning techniques. For the average presenter, direct test-type questions will undoubtedly be the best method for determining how well the idea presentation is progressing. Unskilled use of leading questions is insulting to the intelligent audience, as is inept employment of any communicative device. Yet if even the novice presenter *thinks* in terms of response points and objective measurement as he proceeds, he is far closer to making his presentation purposeful and functional than he would be if he simply dispensed his message in a one-sided fashion.

Question D: Indicate some types of response points we've used on you in this course.

_____

_____

_____

_____

_____

Answer to Question D: If you'll think about it for a moment, we're sure you'll agree that a course like this presents a number of interesting communicative challenges. When we set out to prepare it, one of our Wiley editor's most stringent admonitions was, "We want maximum teacher-student interaction—as close to a live classroom situation as you can create. Yet we don't want the learner left with any 'open-ended' questions. You, the course teacher, must give your student maximum feedback in anything that you have him or her do."

Well, you've seen our tests, our "make your own heading" devices, our flow charts, our questions and answers to you, our exercises, our scorable tests, and so forth. You've even given an actual presentation and drawn a chalkboard illustration. Among other things, we hope we've shown a little of what can be done in the area of response points and feedback.

7 PLANT A CRITIC IN THE AUDIENCE

If possible, have a friend or associate sit in on the presentation for the express purpose of serving as a critic. He should divorce himself as completely as possible from what would be the normal interaction of a regular audience member. His job is to evaluate the presentation in basically the same way as your rehearsal auditor did. In fact, it could be the same person. He should observe both you and your audience, and note your effectiveness and their attention and reactions. Your rehearsal can be used. In certain cases it might also be advisable to have prearranged signals similar to those used in broadcasting studios to tell speakers and performers to speed up, slow down, and how much time is left.

The main aim is to get an objective evaluation of yourself and your presentation for future reference and improvement. In line with this, it also often is wise to hold a post-presentation critique or de-briefing session among concerned intimates to evaluate the presentation's effectiveness and gain "input" for future presentations.

8 THE FINAL ANALYSIS

What is your final audience feedback? Of course, it's your action step as we discussed in Segment 21, and this is a good place to review that segment. Your action step will close the loop. It will help you to walk away from your presentation with a much greater chance of knowing not only how good a presentation it was, but often with a measurement of whether or not you've actually accomplished what your objective stated that you wanted to do.

Above all else, you should remember that you always must be just as much an audience analyst as a presenter of ideas.

Summary Exercise: As a summary exercise for this segment, let's see if we can put together some of the "pieces" we've been talking about. And let's also use your skill in putting together visual aids. Since this also is your last learning segment, although we've furnished a final scorable test on the whole course, let's also use this exercise as a kind of wrap-up of where we've come.

1. First, review the "cognitive map" we gave in Segment 2. This basically illustrates the presentation audience/situation as you first approach it, before you've done any planning, or delivered your presentation.
2. But now that you've planned your presentation:
   A. You understand the basic nature of any communicative interchange.
   B. You've analyzed the specific audience/situation.
   C. You've established a specific objective for each presentation and audience situation.
   D. You've sought to structure and control the three dimensions (rational, physical, psychological) as much as you possibly can.
   E. Hopefully, you've nullified, compensated for or used many random influences, such as unintended impressions and sensory and psychological distractions.
   F. You're analyzing live audience feedback as it occurs.
3. Let's see, now, if we can modify our original cognitive map to illustrate where you ought to be now and how the audience/situation ought to look. On page 31 you will find the "pieces" of the "puzzle." Your job: Put them together, in the space provided on page 30, into a new cognitive map that illustrates the controlled presentation audience/situation.

Paste the elements here.

30

You'll find it easier to cut out each element if you cut first along the dotted lines.

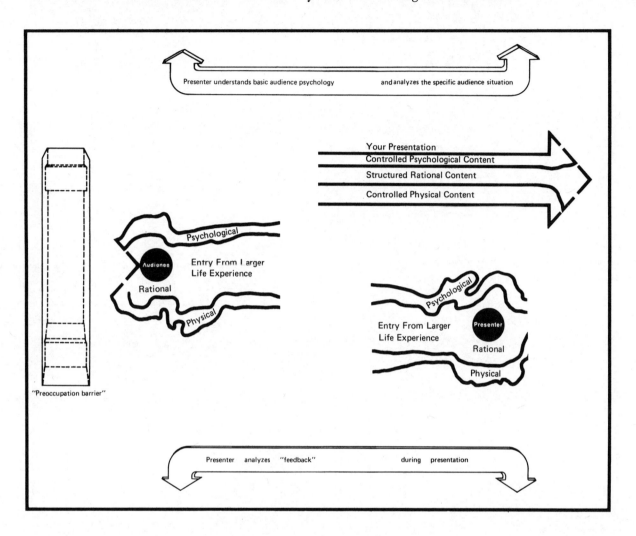

Scorable Quiz: Fill in the missing word or words.

1. When a presenter becomes too subjectively involved in his own presentation and personal reactions to observe and evaluate audience feedback, we call this a _____ compartment.

2. The first and most important rule in responding to audience questions is to never try to _____ your audience.

3. An audience member who asks a question might be seeking _____

from the group.

4. An audience member who asks a question could be trying to _____

you in a certain direction.

5. Spontaneous audience response provides you some feedback. But if there is none forthcoming, you can always evoke it by using a device we've mentioned several times throughout the study course. What is this device?_____

6. In the text, we list nine specific guidelines for when you have occasion to ask your audience questions. List any five of them.

a. _____

b. _____

c. _____

d. _____

e. _____

Answer to Summary Exercise:

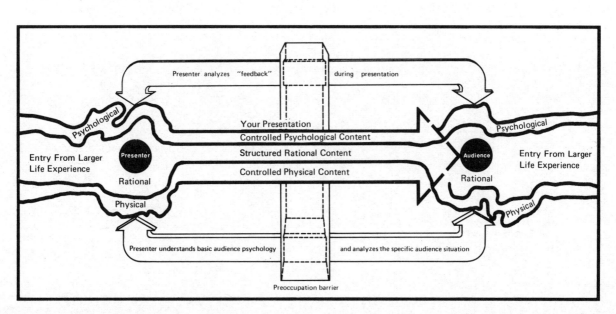

Answers to Scorable Quiz: (Each correct answer = 10%.)
1. communication-tight
2. fool
3. approval
4. lead
5. response points
6. Any five of the following:
   - Ask friendly questions.
   - Use the "you" element.
   - Limit answer to the information wanted.
   - Give the answerer time to think and phrase the answer.
   - Be objective in evaluating the answer.
   - Give the answerer credit for intelligence.
   - Avoid known "sore spots."
   - Be sure the hearer is capable of answering.
   - Always give the answerer an "out."

9 CONCLUSION

As we began without much ado, so will we end. It is our sincere hope that you now are a more effective presenter of ideas, and that you feel that you've gotten your money's worth out of this program.

Adieu and *bon chance*,

The author, your friend
and teacher

Comprehensive Examination

This test is designed to test your total comprehension of the course you have just completed. There are 100 objective-type questions. Each is worth one point, for a total possible score of 100%. As in a final examination that you might take in a classroom, some of the questions are taken directly from the text and others are designed to test your thinking ability based upon what you have learned.

It is suggested that you set aside a specific time and place (a maximum of two hours) in which you can take this test in its entirety without distraction or interruption. It also is suggested that you take this test without referring to the text.

After completing the test, turn to the answers furnished at the end, and score yourself one point or fraction of a point as indicated.

Fill in the missing word or words.

1. The main thesis of this course and the philosophy of communication represented therein can be summed up in the statement that all presentations should perform a _____ _____ .

2. All purposeful idea presentation should begin with a clearly phrased and written statement of the presentation's _____ .

3. The true beginning point in planning any purposeful idea presentation is at the _____ .

4. Any formal idea presentation is in reality only a momentary _____ of a larger, continuing process which actually began long before that formal presentation period and probably will continue for some time after it.

5. Although there may be other ways of describing this, we call the distortional influences in a presentation the _____ _____ (2 words).

6. We state in the text that the only sound first step in any form of personal improvement or development is _____ –confrontation.

35

7. We also state that there are in fact observable qualities or characteristics of personal

   _____ .

8. Egocentricity and ego–defensiveness are two of several things that we list

   as"_____" in the human communication situation.

9. There always are _____ dimensions in any human communications

   situation.

10. Even though a presentation audience may be quite large, from the point of view of a

    presenter thinking in terms of individual persons, there always are

    only_____ people in a communication situation.

11. The terms reasoning, thought sequence, pattern, order, logic and thought pattern are all

    synonyms for the vital presentation element that we refer to as

    _____ .

12. A fundamental principle of presentation outlining is that form follows

    _____ .

13. Every idea or group of ideas has some form or pattern as you perceive it, before you start

    to structure it for presentation to an audience. We call this the idea's

    _____ structure.

14. The two most fundamental categories of idea structure are (a) _____

    order and (b)_____ process.

15. The two main types of thought process are (a) _____ reasoning and

    (b)_____ reasoning.

16. The arranging of ideas in a sequence that builds up to a climax is a variation of

    _____ structure.

17. The main idea of your presentation is called its_____ .

18. Waiting until the end of a presentation before coming out and stating your thesis probably

    indicates that your presentation is of a _____ nature.

19. Beginning with a thesis, proposition, or main idea and then presenting details to support it is an example of the _____ process.

20. Leading to the statement of a main idea or conclusion by presenting details is an example of the _____ process.

21. Another term for the deductive process, used primarily in journalism, is _____ pyramid.

22. Giving information in the order in which it is most likely to be needed or used is known as the order of _____ .

23. The process of stating or establishing a certain condition, for example, a problem or a need, and then fulfilling or solving it, comes under the general heading of _____ structure.

24. By our definition, functional communication is a _____ in a human being.

25. Narrowness and specificity are characteristics of a good functional _____ .

26. We call the process of dividing large objectives into smaller, handleable objectives the _____ .

27. A good presentation objective, if at all possible, should be stated in terms of _____ behavior, rather than described in terms of the machinations of the presenter himself.

28. A _____ is a private objective converted for public consumption.

29. The main functions of _____ _____ are to identify, define, clarify, prove, or strengthen part of all of an idea (two words).

30. The three dimensions in which all communication takes place are the rational, the (a) _____ , and the (b) _____ .

31. We call the process of thinking in terms of alternatives to and combinations of the rational,

physical, and psychological dimensions the _____ approach.

32. When any physical need has reached a point where it interferes with communication, we say that it has reached the point of _____ .

33. The process of doing things to improve the efficiency of the senses is called _____ _____ (two words).

34. When one sense interferes with the use of another, for example, when something visual interferes with hearing efficiency, we call this _____ distraction.

35. We refer to the basic tendency of the human senses to perceive that which is easiest, most convenient, or comfortable to perceive as the "_____ of _____" (four words).

36. The principle of _____ means that any sensory experience must be perceived long enough for it to register and actually serve its communications purpose.

37. After you establish the basic physical possibility for communication, your main aim is to increase the _____ .

38. Supportively speaking, the (a) _____ dimension is parallel to both the emotional and the (b) _____ .

39. The basic grouping of human emotional drives that includes the need for belonging, acceptance, approval, and so on, is known as _____ .

40. The basic human needs to fight, to be competitive, to be aggressive or hostile come under the general heading of _____ .

41. Ambition, acquisitiveness, and the desire to possess things, space, or ideas are all forms of _____ extension.

42. One of the main reasons for giving ideas structure is not only for the purposes of comprehension but that most human beings actually also have a psychological and emotional need for _____ .

43. The frequent tendency of humans to think, feel, behave, or react in habituate or stereo-typed ways is called _____ .

44. Another way of viewing the human psyche (psychological makeup) is as a composite entity consisting of the (a) _____ and the (b) _____ .

45. Human experiences, impressions, and reactions that occur below the level of usual arousal are called _____ .

46. It not only is necessary to have a basic understanding of human nature and the "constants" in all communicative situations. One must also engage in a detailed analysis of the specific _____ / _____ .

47. A. Title

    B. _____ Description

48. C. Statement of _____ .

49. D. _____ Statement

    E. Introduction

50. F. Outline of Main _____ of Presentation

    G. Conclusion

Indicate true (T) or false (F).

51. If you have adequately given advance notice of the title of your presentation, most members of your audience will arrive with a very clear picture in their minds of exactly what they want to hear. _____

52. It is not necessary to affirm people in their preconceived ideas, so long as you accomplish your objective of reaching them. _____

53. It is not necessary to know anything about any larger program your presentation may be

a part of, because your presentation will have been constructed as a stand-alone entity and will speak for itself. ____

54. The conclusion of a presentation is strategically more important than the introduction. ____

55. The functions of the conclusion are quite different from the functions of the introduction. ____

56. The way to test the success of a presentation is to compare the stated objective with the audience response. If they match, you've succeeded; if they don't match, you've failed. ____

57. You can't have an action step when your objective deals with intangibles such as changes in attitudes, feelings, or beliefs. ____

58. Handout material should be passed out at the time it is mentioned in the presentation. ____

59. It is perfectly acceptable to use an assistant before or after, but not during, a presentation. ____

60. It is advisable never to make abrupt changes in visual mood or motif. ____

61. Audience size shouldn't have any real effect on the kinds of aids planned. ____

62. Stage fright is basically a form of ego defense. ____

63. One good way to overcome stage fright is to act as if you don't have it. ____

64. You can't rechannel the "energy" of stage fright because it is a basic human fear. ____

65. Your audience is very likely to stick with their first impression of you throughout your presentation. ____

Fill in the missing word or words.

66. _____ will function as a bridge between your audience's world and the world of your presentation.

67. Without audience _____ , there is no point in proceeding any further with the delivery of your presentation, because nothing will be perceived.

68. One of the functions of an introduction is to place your idea in the most _____ position possible.

69. Parallelism, consistency, reference, restatement, and repetition are all given as primarily methods of giving a presentation internal _____ .

70. An attempt to measure or precipitate the accomplishment of a presentation objective is known as an _____ or _____ (2 words).

71. Aids are simply another form of _____ _____ (2 words).

72. A good data-gathering and note-taking system will include a method of physically _____ material by outline point.

73. Professional designers usually prepare a _____ to quickly show the whole visual part of the presentation at a glance.

74. Speaking from a prepared outline but "filling in" the actual detail by reliving your thinking at the podium is known as _____ delivery.

75. When you ask an audience to respond or do something during a presentation in order to maintain attention or keep them with you, you are using _____ _____ (2 words).

Circle the correct answer.

76. The average audience member will react objectively to you and your presentation
    a. Most of the time
    b. If he is told to do so
    c. Pretty rarely

77. A company that mails free merchandise to you and requests you to do, buy, or send something to them is probably playing on your need for or sense of:
    a. Power
    b. Possession
    c. Guilt

78. The essential comparison that must be made for any presentation is
    a. Does the audience match the situation?
    b. Does the objective match what the audience wants?
    c. Does the audience response match the objective?

79. Arousing an audience's curiosity probably is an appeal to their
    a. Need for order
    b. Gregariousness
    c. Pugnacity

80. A teacher would be most likely to use
    a. The order of proximity
    b. The order of utility
    c. The order of agreeability

81. Presenters dealing with groups of people realize that they always are "working the percentages." Assuming an audience of twenty people, "objective accomplishment" would mean that you did what you intended to do to, for or with
    a. At least 30% of the audience
    b. Any audience member
    c. Over 50% of the audience

82. All humans
    a. Will exhibit most of the psychological needs and drives
    b. Will vary greatly in the kinds and intensity of the various needs and drives that they exhibit
    c. When grouped together, will tend to subvert their own needs and drives in favor of the common needs and drives of the group

83. Miniature reproductions of aids in delivery notes
    a. Prevent spontaneity
    b. Serve the same function as key words
    c. Make notes needlessly bulky

84. The three dimensions (rational, physical, and psychological)
    a. May be present in the situation but not the presenter
    b. May be present in the presentation and audience but not the situation
    c. Are always present in the situation, the presenter, the presentation and the audience.
    d. May be present in the presenter and the audience

85. The order of state, condition, quality, or degree is similar to the inductive process because
    a. It would be likely to present ideas in a basic specific-to-general process
    b. It would be likely to present ideas in a general-to-specific process
    c. Neither

86. Delivery notes should
    a. Be as concise as possible
    b. Not have stage directions in them
    c. Be memorized

87. Which of the following would lend itself best to presentation in the order of acceptability?
    a. A research report
    b. A political speech
    c. A floor plan description

88. A company that mails free merchandise to you and requests you to do, buy, or send something to them is probably playing on your need for or sense of
    a. Power
    b. Possession
    c. Guilt

89. Impromptu delivery is
    a. Being fully prepared but having no notes
    b. Presenting without notes or prior preparation
    c. Knowing your outline but having no notes

Complete the list.

The ten main learning units of this professional development course make an excellent check list of things you should always remember to do in planning, preparing, and delivering a presentation. List them here in the sequence in which they are presented in the text.

90. _____

91. _____

92. _____

93. _____

94. _____

95. _____

96. _____

97. _____

98. _____

99. _____

100. What color is an orange? _____

ANSWERS TO COMPREHENSIVE EXAMINATION

1. function
2. objective
3. end
4. intensification
5. preoccupation barrier
6. self
7. communicativeness
8. "constants"
9. three
10. two
11. structure
12. function
13. inherent
14. (a) natural (1/2 pt.)
    (b) thought (1/2 pt.)
15. (a) inductive (1/2 pt.)
    (b) deductive (1/2 pt.)
16. chronological
17. thesis
18. persuasive
19. deductive
20. inductive
21. inverted
22. utility
23. two-sided
24. change
25. objective
26. incremental
27. audience
28. thesis
29. idea support
30. (a) physical or sensory (1/2 pt.)
    (b) psychological or emotional (1/2 pt.)
31. multidimensional
32. intolerance
33. sensory reinforcement
34. other-sense
35. path of least resistance
36. duration
37. probability
38. (a) rational (1/2 pt.)
    (b) physical (1/2 pt.)
39. gregariousness
40. pugnacity
41. ego

42. order
43. conditioning
44. (a) conscious (1/2 pt.)
    (b) unconscious (1/2 pt.)
45. subliminal
46. audience situation
47. audience
48. objective
49. thesis
50. body
51. F
52. F
53. F
54. F
55. F
56. T
57. F
58. F
59. F
60. F
61. F
62. T
63. T
64. F
65. T
66. introduction
67. attention
68. advantageous
69. cohesiveness
70. action step
71. idea support
72. sorting
73. story board
74. extemporaneous
75. response points
76. c
77. c
78. c
79. c
80. b
81. b
82. b
83. b
84. c
85. a

86. b
87. b
88. c
89. b
90. personal communicativeness
91. Structure and thesis
92. The kinds of structure
93. The functional approach
94. Idea support and reinforcement
95. Outlining and data gathering
96. Idea integrity
97. Visual and other aids
98. Preparing to face the audience
99. At the podium
100. blue

ISBN 0-471-01636-5